Heroes of the Nations

EDITED BY
Evelyn Abbott, M.A.
FELLOW OF BALLIOL COLLEGE, OXFORD

> FACTA DUCIS VIVENT, OPEROSAQUE
> GLORIA RERUM —OVID, IN LIVIAM, 265.
> THE HERO'S DEEDS AND HARD-WON
> FAME SHALL LIVE.

JULIUS CÆSAR

AMS PRESS
NEW YORK

JULIUS CÆSAR.
FROM THE MARBLE BUST IN THE BRITISH MUSEUM.

JULIUS CÆSAR

AND THE FOUNDATION OF THE ROMAN IMPERIAL SYSTEM

"There may be many Cæsars
'Ere such another Julius."
Cymbeline

BY

W. WARDE FOWLER, M.A.

SUB-RECTOR OF LINCOLN COLLEGE
OXFORD

G. P. PUTNAM'S SONS
NEW YORK   LONDON
27 WEST TWENTY-THIRD STREET   24 BEDFORD STREET, STRAND
The Knickerbocker Press
1892

Library of Congress Cataloging in Publication Data

Fowler, William Warde, 1847-1921.
  Julius Caesar and the foundation of the Roman imperial system.

  Reprint of the 1892 ed. published by Putnam, New York, in series: Heroes of the nations.
  Includes index.
  1. Caesar, C. Julius. 2. Heads of state—Rome—Biography. 4. Generals—Rome—Biography. 4. Rome—History—Republic, 265-30 B.C. I. Title. II. Series: Heroes of the nations.
DG261.F7 1978   937'.05'0924 [B]   73-14443
ISBN 0-404-58261-3

Reprinted from an orginal in the collections
of the City College Library

From the edition of 1892, New York.
First AMS edition published in 1978.

Manufactured in the United States of America.

AMS PRESS, INC.
NEW YORK, N.Y.

PREFACE

In this volume I have tried to meet the wishes of the publishers, by explaining to those who are comparatively unfamiliar with classical antiquity the place which Cæsar occupies in the history of the world. He was not the founder, much less was he the organiser of the Roman Empire; yet his life marks a great change in European history. I have tried to show (and have done my best to express on the title-page) what this change means, how it was in part the result of pre-existing tendencies, and was due in part to Cæsar's extraordinary force of will and intellect. In a volume of this size, it has been impossible to keep this main object in view without sacrificing many details and avoiding criticism and controversy on innumerable disputed points, whether of Roman constitutional law, or of the geography of the Gallic and Civil wars. The tendencies of the age, and the growth of Cæsar's character, are the two leading themes of the book; and I have endeavoured to treat these as far as possible by the help of contemporary evidence, and chiefly of Cæsar's own writings and those of Cicero,

vi Preface.

omitting much that we are told by later writers, as matter for the detailed criticism of a complete biography.

A word is needed about the busts of Cæsar of which illustrations appear in this volume. One of these illustrations (p. 78) most probably does not represent Cæsar, but some other *pontifex maximus*; but it is included in this volume by the particular desire of Mr. G. H. Putnam. Another, the beautiful and striking basalt bust in the Berlin Museum, is somewhat doubtful; but I have the opinion of at least one excellent authority in favour of including it among the genuine busts. The two which are most generally recognised as genuine as well as good works of art, are the well-known busts in the British Museum (p. 18) and at Naples (p. 56), the latter representing a younger man than the former. These two at least present one or two peculiarities of feature visible also on the coin, which are the only certain contemporary representations of Cæsar's face. The very beautiful gem which we have attempted to reproduce (p. 92) may however also be of Cæsar's own time; this is in the British Museum, and I have to thank my friend Professor Gardner for drawing my attention to it.

I have also to thank the Editor of this series for his careful attention to my proofs, and Mr. P. E. Matheson of New College, for reading them all, and for many valuable suggestions. Other friends and pupils have given me occasional help, which I hope I have duly acknowledged at the time. I need hardly mention, in a book not primarily intended

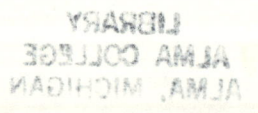

Preface. vii

for scholars, the many modern works, from that of Drumann downwards, which have been of use to me. But in any biography of Cæsar it is impossible not to allude with gratitude and reverence to the great genius and learning of Professor Mommsen; for even if they venture to dissent from some of his conclusions, all students of classical antiquity will allow that his life-long labours have wrought as great a change in the study of Roman history, as the work of his great hero brought about in the Roman state itself.

W. W. F.

Oxford, November 12, 1891.

CONTENTS.

CHAPTER I.

BIRTH, FAMILY, AND EDUCATION (102–89 B.C.) . . . 1

Great men of Italy—Sketch of rise and progress of Rome—Degeneracy of Roman oligarchy—Gracchi and Marius—Problems of statesmanship—Cæsar's birth and family—His mother—His tutor Gnipho—Defects of Roman education—Personal appearance of Cæsar.

CHAPTER II.

BOYHOOD DURING THE CIVIL WARS (89–82 B.C.) . . . 20

Victories of Marius—The social war and its results—Cæsar's connection with Marius and the Populares—Views of the two parties in the State—Civil wars—Sulpicius, Cinna, Sulla—Cæsar marries Cinna's daughter—Death of Cinna, and absolutism of Sulla—Cæsar under Sulla's rule.

CHAPTER III.

EARLY LIFE UNDER THE SULLAN GOVERNMENT (81–70 B.C.) 33

Cæsar's first military service—Lepidus' revolt—Cæsar as an orator—Captured by pirates—At Rhodes—Return to Rome—Paralysis of Sullan government—An imaginary traveller—Attacks on the Sullan constitution—Its overthrow by Pompeius and Crassus, B.C. 70.

Contents.

CHAPTER IV.

QUÆSTORSHIP ; AND SUPREMACY OF POMPEIUS (69–66 B.C.) 53

The political outlook—Cæsar quæstor in Spain—The Transpadani—Cæsar supports the Lex Gabinia—Nature of the power given to Pompeius by this law and the Lex Manilia—Indications of coming monarchy.

CHAPTER V.

ÆDILESHIP ; AND CONSPIRACY OF CATILINA (65–63 B.C.) 66

Pompeius' conquests—Their influence on home politics—Schemes of the democratic party—Cæsar curule ædile—Bill of Rullus—Its failure—Cicero consul—His policy of uniting Senate and equites—Trial of Rabirius—Cæsar's part in it—Cæsar elected pontifex maximus—Conspiracy of Catilina—Meeting of the Senate, December 5th—Speech of Cæsar—Conspirators put to death by Cicero's orders.

CHAPTER VI.

PRÆTORSHIP ; AND FORMATION OF TRIUMVIRATE (62–60 B.C.) 87

Attitude of parties towards Pompeius—His return from the East—Disbands his army—Effect on Cæsar's career—Affair of the Bona Dea—Trial of Clodius—Cæsar in Spain as proprætor—His government—Gades and Cornelius Balbus—Cæsar's return—Elected consul—Forms a coalition with Pompeius and Crassus—Negotiation with Cicero—Objects of the coalition.

CHAPTER VII.

CÆSAR'S FIRST CONSULSHIP (59 B.C.) . . . 104

Policy of conciliation—Publication of the Acta Senatus—Agrarian law—Its object—The bill obstructed—Cæsar defies the Senate—The bill passed—The Campanian land—Ratifi-

Contents.

cation of Pompeius' work in the East—Marriage of Pompeius and Julia—The law against extortion—Cæsar obtains the government of the Gallic provinces—Fresh negotiation with Cicero, and failure—Recapitulation.

CHAPTER VIII.

THE DEFENCE OF TRANSALPINE GAUL (58 B.C.) . 126

Cæsar's book on the Gallic war—Its value and style—Previous relations of the Gauls with Rome—Insecure state of the Transalpine province—Arverni, Ædui, Sequani—Ariovistus and the Germans—The Helvetii attempt to invade the province—The lines at Geneva—Battle near Bibracte—Cæsar master of southern Gaul.

CHAPTER IX.

THE DEFEAT OF THE GERMANS (58 B.C.) . . . 148

The Ædui ask help against Ariovistus—Cæsar negotiates with him and fails—Marches against him—Interview and treachery—Panic in Cæsar's army—Geography of the campaign—Battle near Mühlhausen—Cæsar master of eastern Gaul.

CHAPTER X.

CONQUEST OF NORTH-WESTERN GAUL (57 B.C.) . 161

Cæsar's position and views during the winter—The Belgæ combine against him—His march—Fighting at Berry-au-Bac—Cæsar advances to Amiens—Great battle on the Sambre—Treachery and punishment of the Aduatuci.

CHAPTER XI.

CONFERENCE AT LUCCA, AND CAMPAIGN IN BRITTANY (56 B.C.) 176

Cæsar in Illyria—News of rebellion in Brittany—Events at Rome since 59 B.C.—Cicero's exile and return—He attacks

xii   Contents.

the coalition—Conference of the triumvirs at Lucca—Its
results—Cæsar in Brittany—Naval defeat of the Veneti—
Severe treatment of the conquered.

CHAPTER XII.

INVASIONS OF GERMANY AND BRITAIN (55–54 B.C.) . 187

Cæsar's account of the Suebi—Migration of Usipetes and
Tencteri—Destroyed by Cæsar on the Meuse—He bridges
the Rhine—Advance into Germany, and retreat—Invasion
of Britain—The fleet broken by a storm—Cæsar returns to
Gaul—Second invasion—Criticism of his policy—Fleet again
damaged—Advance to the Thames—Forcing the ford—
Retreat—Results of the expeditions.

CHAPTER XIII.

THE GALLIC REBELLIONS (54–52 B.C.)   .   .   . 207

Fortune turns against Cæsar—He stays the winter in Gaul
—Disaster at Aduatuca—Q. Cicero in peril at Charleroi—
Relieved by Cæsar—Anxious winter—Second invasion of
Germany—Cæsar's sixth book—General rising in Gaul
under Vercingetorix—Cæsar forces his way to the legions—
Siege of Avaricum—Operations at Gergovia—Cæsar's defeat
and retreat on the Ædui—Vercingetorix at Alesia—Siege of
Alesia by Cæsar—Great battle, and rout of the Gauls—
Fate of Vercingetorix.

CHAPTER XIV.

PACIFICATION OF GAUL AND OUTBREAK OF CIVIL
    WAR (52–49 B.C.)   238

Sufferings of the Gauls—Cæsar's work of peace—Effect of
the Gallic war on Cæsar's character—Events at Rome since
56 B.C.—Strained relations between Cæsar and Pompeius—
Death of Clodius—Pompeius sole consul—The question
between Cæsar and the Senate—Schemes to ruin Cæsar—
His negotiations and concessions—No real hope of peace—
Outbreak of civil war.

CHAPTER XV.

CIVIL WAR IN ITALY AND SPAIN (49 B.C.) . 258

Cæsar unprepared for war—Crosses the Rubicon—Pompeius and Senate leave Rome—Cæsar takes Corfinium—His clemency—Siege of Brundisium—Pompeius escapes to Epirus—Cæsar in Rome—He undertakes the government—Leaves Rome for Spain—Campaign on the Segres—Operations at Ilerda—Surrender of Pompeian generals—Cæsar master of Spain—Siege of Massilia—Cæsar at Rome as Dictator.

CHAPTER XVI.

DYRRHACHIUM AND PHARSALUS (48 B.C.) . . 281

Cæsar's strategy—He lands in Epirus and takes Apollonia—Forced inaction till May—Antonius joins him—Pompeius cut off from Dyrrhachium—Cæsar attempts to invest Pompeius—Failure and defeat—Cæsar retreats to Thessaly, and draws Pompeius after him—Battle of Pharsalus—Flight of Pompeius to Egypt—His death and character.

CHAPTER XVII.

CÆSAR'S LAST WARS (48–45 B.C.) 308

Cæsar goes to Egypt—Cleopatra—Cæsar besieged in Alexandria—Extricated by Mithridates of Pergamum—Settlement of Egypt—Proceeds to Syria and Asia Minor—Defeat of Pharnaces—Return to Italy—Leaves again for Sicily and Africa—Campaign in Africa—Battle of Thapsus—Death of Cato—Cæsar in Rome—Triumph—Leaves for Spain—Last campaign and battle of Munda.

CHAPTER XVIII.

CÆSAR'S USE OF ABSOLUTE POWER (49–44 B.C.) . 326

The revolutionary tendencies to which Cæsar gave expression—Reconstruction of the machinery of government—Gradual increase of Cæsar's absolute power—His views for the future—Octavius—Cæsar's social legislation—Social and economic

xiv *Contents.*

state of the empire—His care for the provinces—Political re-organization—The empire in a state of chaos—Two principles of later imperial government initiated by Cæsar—His scientific method, and extraordinary intellectual power.

CHAPTER XIX.

THE END (44 B.C.) 360

Anxiety for Cæsar's return from Spain—His arrival—Outward signs of monarchy—His great projects—His visit to Cicero—Preparations for war with Parthia—Dictatorship for life and other honours—Ill-will against him—The conspirators—Character of Brutus—Assassination and funeral.

EPILOGUE 379

INDEX 385

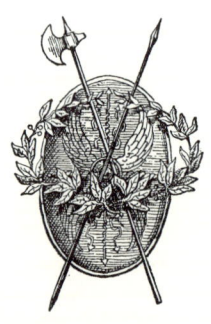

CHIEF EVENTS IN THE LIFE OF CÆSAR.

B.C.		PAGE
102 (or 100 ?).	Birth; July 12th	7
87.	Assumes the *toga virilis*	23
82.	Proscribed and pardoned by Sulla ; first journey to Asia Minor	29 *ff.*
78.	Returns to Rome on death of Sulla	34
76.	Accuses Dolabella ; second journey to East	36 *ff.*
74.	Return to Rome	39
70.	Aids in overthrow of Sulla's constitution,	51
68.	*Quæstor* in Further Spain	56 *ff.*
66.	Supports the Lex Manilia	62
65.	*Curule ædile ;* Pompeius in the East	68
63.	*Pontifex maximus ;* Cicero consul ; conspiracy of Catilina	77 *ff.*
62.	*Prætor ;* affair of Bona Dea	85 *ff.*
61.	*Proprætor* in Further Spain	94 *ff.*
59.	*Consul ;* coalition with Pompeius and Crassus	98 *ff.*
58.	*Proconsul* in Gaul ; campaign against Helvetii and Ariovistus	126 *ff.*
57.	Campaign against Belgæ	160 *ff.*
56.	Coalition reconstituted at Lucca	175 *ff.*
55.	Invasions of Germany and Britain	187 *ff.*
54.	Second invasion of Britain	200 *ff.*
53–51.	Gallic rebellions ; death of Crassus, and alienation of Pompeius	207 *ff.*

xv

B.C.		PAGE
49.	Civil war; campaign in Spain; *Dictator I.*,	238 *ff.*
48.	Battle of Pharsalus; *Dictator II.* . .	281 *ff.*
47.	Returns to Rome in Sept.; *Dictator III.*,	310 *ff.*
46.	Cæsar in Africa; returns to Rome in July; *Dictator IV.*	317 *ff.*
45.	Cæsar in Spain; battle of Munda . .	324 *ff.*
	Returns to Rome in September . .	325 *ff.*
44.	*Dictator for life;* assassinated March 15th,	362 *ff.*

ILLUSTRATIONS.

	PAGE
JULIUS CÆSAR. FROM A MARBLE BUST IN THE BRITISH MUSEUM . . . . *Frontispiece*	
JULIUS CÆSAR. FROM A MARBLE BUST IN THE BRITISH MUSEUM	18
THE FORUM. AS SEEN FROM THE CAPITOL. *Baumeister	26
BUST OF POMPEIUS. IN THE SPADA PALACE IN ROME . . . . . *Baumeister*	48
JULIUS CÆSAR. FROM THE FARNESE BUST IN THE MUSEUM AT NAPLES	56
CICERO. FROM A BUST NOW IN THE ROYAL GALLERY IN MADRID . . *Baumeister*	72
JULIUS CÆSAR (?) AS PONTIFEX MAXIMUS. FROM THE BUST IN THE MUSEO-CHIARAMONTI, IN THE VATICAN	78
HEAD OF JULIUS CÆSAR. ENLARGED FROM GEM IN BRITISH MUSEUM	92
HEAD OF JULIUS CÆSAR. FROM COIN IN BRITISH MUSEUM	92
THREE-HEADED TYRANNY	103

* Baumeister's "*Denkmäler des klassischen Altertums.*"

Illustrations.

	PAGE
JULIUS CÆSAR. FROM BUST NUMBERED 107 IN THE VATICAN MUSEUM, ROME.	106
MAP OF GAUL IN CÆSAR'S TIME	136
ROMAN SOLDIERS	140
ROMAN MILITARY AND CIVIL OFFICIALS	142
GALLIC SOLDIERS, AND CARNYX, OR TRUMPET. FROM THE TRIUMPHAL ARCH IN ORANGE (ARAUSIO). [21 A.D.]	144
THE CAMP OF A LEGION	146
CATAPULT. USED IN SIEGE OPERATIONS. *Baumeister*	152
TESTUDO, OR SHIELDS INTERLOCKED FOR THE STORMING OF A FORTRESS. FROM TRAJAN'S COLUMN. *Baumeister*	158
BALLISTA, OR STONE-THROWER. *Baumeister*	168
MAP OF BATTLE OF THE SAMBRE, 57 B.C.	170
BRIDGE BUILT BY CÆSAR ACROSS THE RHINE	194
SECTION OF THE BRIDGE, SHOWING METHOD OF CONSTRUCTION	196
A SIEGE FIGHT WITH ARCHERS, AND BATTERING-RAM. FROM TRAJAN'S COLUMN. *Baumeister*	212
SIEGE SCENE. FROM TRAJAN'S COLUMN. *Baumeister*	224
ALESIA, SKETCHED FROM MOUNT BASSY. Napoleon's *"César"*	230
ROMAN WORKS AT ALESIA. Napoleon's *"César"*	232
MAP OF OPERATIONS AT ALESIA. AFTER NAPOLEON III. "Jules César"	234
A ROMAN HEAD	237
MARCUS ANTONIUS. FROM THE BUST IN THE UFFIZI GALLERY IN FLORENCE (VISCONTI). *Baumeister*	256
ROMAN LICTOR	257

Illustrations. xix

	PAGE
A SEAPORT TOWN	264
THE YOUNG AUGUSTUS. FROM THE BUST IN THE VATICAN . . . . . *Baumeister*	268
A BESIEGED CITY	278
MAP OF OPERATIONS NEAR DYRRACHIUM, 48 B.C., (AFTER STOFFEL)	282
MAP OF MACEDONIA AND GREECE . . .	290
ROUGH MAP OF THE ENVIRONS OF PHARSALUS. (AFTER STOFFEL)	300
DEFENCES OF A CAMP	320
MARCUS BRUTUS. FROM THE BUST IN THE MUSEUM OF THE CAPITOL IN ROME (VISCONTI). *Baumeister*	362
ROMAN SWORDS	378
THE ROMAN EMPIRE AT THE TIME OF CÆSAR'S DEATH, 44 B.C.	378
AUGUSTUS AND IMPERIAL ROME. FROM A REPRODUCTION IN WIESELER'S "*Denkmäler der Alten Künst*" OF THE CAMEO IN VIENNA.	384

JULIUS CÆSAR,

AND THE FOUNDATION OF THE ROMAN IMPERIAL SYSTEM.

CHAPTER I.

BIRTH, FAMILY, AND EDUCATION.
102–89 B.C.

ITALY, the most beautiful of European lands, has also been the richest in men whom the world has acknowledged as great. Long indeed is the list of her men of letters, her artists, her men of action, and her great priests. Of the world's six greatest poets she has produced two, Virgil and Dante. And twice at least, in ages of general confusion and chaos, it has fallen to Italy to provide a leader strong enough to put an end to anarchy, and by virtue of a

powerful personality, to assert the force of a unifying principle.

In the Middle Ages, this principle was the spiritual supremacy of the Church, and the man who enforced it was Hildebrand, the greatest of the Popes. Eleven centuries earlier, Julius Cæsar, personifying the principle of intelligent government by a single man, had made it possible for the Roman dominion, then on the point of breaking up, to grow into a great political union, and so eventually to provide a material foundation for modern civilisation. It might seem indeed at first sight as if the work done by each of these men depended for its vitality on their own genius, and barely survived them. But the ideas they represented and enforced continued to govern the course of history for centuries after they had passed away ; and they affect us in some measure even now.

To understand adequately the position, the power, and the ideas of either of these Italians, and especially of the one whose life we are to trace, it is necessary to have at least some acquaintance with the history of the city of Rome for many generations before they came into the world. The influence of Italy on civilisation is in fact mainly due to the marvellous fortunes of the city on the Tiber. Not indeed that many of the greatest Italians have been natives of Rome : from Virgil downwards they have sprung from all parts of the peninsula, and from a variety of races. But to the fortunes of Rome, and to the discipline, the tenacity of purpose, and the political skill of her earliest rulers, the Italians owe their position as, in a sense, a chosen people.

In order to place Cæsar in his right position in the history of Rome and of the world, it is hard to dispense with a review of the growth of the Roman dominion, of the Roman constitution, and of Roman society, up to the date of his birth. But this volume must be occupied by Cæsar himself and his work, and we must be content with the very briefest outline of the evolution of the Roman power, down to that age of storm and peril, when the greatest of Romans—himself of the purest Roman descent—seized forcibly on the helm, and pointed out the state's true course.

The city of Rome was originally one of those little communities, consisting of a walled town with a small adjoining territory, the nature of which we learn best from Greek history, and from the writings of Greek philosophers. The Greeks lived entirely in such cities, which were for the most part quite independent of each other, self-subsisting, self-governing; federations and empires were violations of the spirit of independence which they cherished, and they never grew, or wished to grow, into a nation united by political ties. In Italy this passion for autonomy was less strong, though it was not absent. Leagues or federations, for the mutual support of a group of towns, were not unknown. When history dawns, we find the city on the Tiber in league with the other cities of the Latin race which lay around it, and in course of time it won a position as their leader and champion. When they rebelled against its increasing power, they were put down; and Rome began to be a mistress whose will other cities obeyed.

Some were absorbed into her own body politic, some were left to govern themselves in their own way; but all had to fight for her as she gradually increased her dominion. In course of time Rome, with the aid of the Latins, had overcome all the peoples of Italy up to the river Po. They were treated in different ways, as the Latins had been; but whatever their political status, they all had to supply soldiers to the Roman armies. Thus this wonderful city went forward, steadily storing up material strength; and wherever she went she took lands from the conquered, built fortified towns, establishing in them a Roman or Latin population, and connected these with herself by indestructible military roads. And after a long struggle with the Phœnician city of Carthage, in the course of which she learnt the art of naval warfare, she conquered also the islands of Sicily and Sardinia, the natural appendages of Italy.

At last it seemed that her downfall was at hand. In the sixth century of her existence (218 B.C.) the greatest military genius of antiquity, Hannibal the Carthaginian, invaded Italy from Spain, bent on her destruction. He annihilated one Roman army after another, and reduced her to the last gasp. But her vitality was marvellous; she kept him at bay for fourteen years, forced him to leave Italy, followed him to Africa, and broke the power of Carthage, taking from her all her possessions in Spain, which were added to the Roman dominion. Hannibal then tried to enlist the King of Macedonia in his life-long effort to war down Rome; but the Romans crossed the Adriatic, and in time both Macedonia and Greece acknowledged her sway. When in 146 B.C., she finally razed Carthage to the ground, she was the acknowledged arbiter of all the peoples living around the Mediterranean Sea. Twenty-five years later she was mistress not only of Italy, Spain, the Carthaginian territory in Africa, Macedonia, Greece, and Illyria, but also of a considerable portion of Asia Minor, and of a valuable territory in what is now the south of France.

This wonderful growth of a single city into a vast empire is without a parallel in the world's history; and it raised problems unparalleled for complexity and extent. It had been achieved partly by the stern and steady character of the conquering race, by their habits of self-denial and obedience, bred in them through their rigid family life and religion, and by their talent for political organisation; partly also by the nature of their constitution, which had grown in the last two centuries into a narrow and compact but shrewd and hard-working oligarchy. The outward expression of this oligarchy was the Senate or Council of Three Hundred, of which all or nearly all the members had seen state-service, and understood the work they had to do. In the course of the long wars this great council had shown extraordinary administrative ability and tenacity of purpose. The magistrates, who were elected for one year only, gradually lost their independence, and willingly obeyed the decisions of a body whose function was in theory only to advise them. When their year of office expired they became practically life members of the Senate; and thus it may be said that this wonderful council represented all the gathered wisdom and experience of the state. The people, theoretically sovereign, elected the magistrates from families of senatorial renown, and ratified laws which the Senate approved; but the Roman democracy was unrealised, and the senatorial oligarchy was supreme.

Such an oligarchy as this is better suited to rule in time of war than in time of peace. When the great wars were at last coming to an end, it was found that power, and the wealth which that power had brought with it, had corrupted the ancient virtue of the rulers of Rome. They owned half the soil of Italy; as magistrates, sent out to govern the conquered territories, they oppressed the conquered and enriched themselves. Their wealth made them luxurious and enfeebled them; they began to let the discipline of their armies go to ruin abroad, and at home their political efforts were all of a self-seeking kind. And now too the old Roman family life began to show signs of breaking up, and the old religion lost its hold. Greek rhetoric and Greek philosophy came in, and with them the love of art and literature; but these could not supply the place of the old faith and the old morality for men whose duty was to govern the world. Things began to grow worse and worse, and it was clear that some change in the government was at hand.

In 133 B.C., Tiberius Gracchus, by developing the latent power of the people, and of the Tribunate of the Plebs, an ancient and anomalous magistracy which the Senate had subordinated to its own ends, struck a severe blow at this oligarchy and its wealth ; but he was young and inexperienced, used violence, and was repaid with violence. Ten years after his death his brother Gaius succeeded for two years in displacing the Senate from supremacy ; but he was forced to rule himself, and his personal influence, unsupported by an army, was not enough to save him from his brother's fate. But Gaius sounded the note of revolution, and gave a practical example of better government, which was never forgotten.

Then followed a long reaction, in which the corruption of the oligarchy is seen at its highest pitch. Two great wars, grossly mismanaged by the Senate, produced at last a great general from among the people, who revolutionised the Roman army and was the first to make it a great factor in politics. For some months in the year 100 B.C., Rome was in the hands of Marius ; but the Senate was again too strong, and he was ignorant of politics. He yielded to senatorial prestige, and the oligarchy was established once more.

This man was a native of the Italian town of Arpinum ; but he had had the discretion to marry into one of the oldest and most famous Roman families. His wife was Julia, the sister of C. Julius Cæsar, and the aunt of the great man whose career we are about to trace. Her nephew, Gaius Julius Cæsar, was probably born on the 12th day of the month Quinctilis, which ever since his death has borne his gentile name, in the year 102 B.C.,* when his kinsman was drawing to a close that splendid military career, in which he saved Rome for the time from invasion and ruin, and began a new period of glory for the Roman armies.

Cæsar was thus born into a world full of doubt and insecurity, with problems confronting the statesman which few could understand, much less attempt to solve. The frontiers of this unwieldy empire had to be protected, and the generals to whom this task was committed had to be controlled. The conquered territories, or provinces as they were called, must be governed equitably, and gradually Romanised, if they were to be held together in any strong bond of union. Italy itself was disaffected, and demanding admission to the privileges of Roman citizenship. The capital was swarming with a mongrel, idle, and hungry population, who claimed to be the Roman people, and to legislate for the whole empire. The senatorial constitution was falling to pieces, and the only alternatives were mob rule or military rule. The distribution of wealth was fearfully unequal; capital and pauperism faced each other menacingly, and both were bred and maintained on a slave system unparalleled in its degradation. The slaves themselves constituted a permanent danger to the state. Piracy abounded on the seas, brigandage and murder in Italy. Lastly, the ideas

---

* The year is uncertain. Sùetonius says that Cæsar was fifty-six at his death in 44 B.C., and the date of his birth has been usually fixed at 100 B.C. But there are strong reasons for believing with Mommsen that the real date was two years earlier.

of loyalty, obedience, self-restraint, were growing steadily rarer among the rulers at the very time they were most called for. The outlook was a terrible one. Rome and her empire must surely come to an end, unless some statesman should arise, able enough to comprehend the problems, and strong enough to put his hand to their solution.

The family of the Cæsars descended from one of the oldest and purest of Roman stocks, and it was one of the many truly Roman characteristics of its greatest scion, that he set a high value on his noble descent, and knew how to turn it to advantage in pursuing his political aims. The Julii believed themselves to be descended from Ascanius or Julus, the founder of Alba Longa, the son of Æneas and grandson of Venus and Anchises, and thus carried back the legend of their origin to a period long before the foundation of Rome. Cæsar never lost an opportunity of bringing this splendid tradition before the minds of his contemporaries. When he delivered the funeral oration over his aunt, Julia, wife of Marius, he reminded his hearers of her divine ancestry. In the two pitched battles which decided his political fortunes, Pharsalus and Munda, he chose the name of Venus Genetrix as the watchword of the day. The image of his ancestral deity may still be seen stamped on many of his coins, and his own head, together with that of his ancestor Æneas, is found on those of the city of Ilium, which in the days of his supreme power he distinguished with special favour as the ancient legendary home of his race. The glory of a great ancestry passed on from

Cæsar himself, by the fiction of adoption, to the plebeian Augustus, and had its due influence in building up the prestige of the imperial system; and it still lives on, inseparably combined with the story of the fortunes of Rome, in the verses of Rome's greatest poet.

> Hanc adspice gentem
> Romanosque tuos. Hic Cæsar, et omnis Iuli
> Progenies, magnum cæli ventura sub axem.*

Of the various families belonging to the gens Julia, some were patrician, some probably plebeian; that one which, at least since the war with Hannibal, had borne the *cognomen* or surname of Cæsar, was undoubtedly patrician. The distinction implied by these terms had ceased to be of any real political significance long before the age with which this biography has to deal. The struggles between patricians and plebeians, or the originally privileged and unprivileged inhabitants of Rome, had ceased for over two centuries before Cæsar's birth, and the aristocracy of his day was composed chiefly of plebeian families, whose ancestors had won distinction by good service to the state either at home or in the field. When we speak therefore of Cæsar, Sulla, or Catilina, as patricians, we mean nothing more than that they traced their descent from one of those families which, in days of yore, had exercised the whole power of government in the state. Patrician descent was a proof of pure Roman birth, but in political life was of no more advantage in the last

---

* Virgil, Æn., vi., 756 foll.

century of the Republic than is at the present day in Swiss politics the patriciate of the ancient republic of Bern. In one respect at least it might be reckoned a disadvantage, for a patrician was disqualified from holding the powerful office of tribune of the plebs, through which so many young men of energy or ability entered public life ; nor could he vote in the plebeian legislative or judicial assemblies over which the tribune presided.

The family of the Cæsars, however, belonged not only to the old patriciate, but to the newer nobility, of which the test had been not so much either birth or wealth as honourable service rendered to the state. A Julius Cæsar had been consul in 157 B.C., another in 90 B.C., who was afterwards also censor; another had been prætor in the eventful year when G. Gracchus was for the first time tribune. Cæsar's uncle was consul in another critical year (91 B.C.), when another great tribune, Livius Drusus, failed in a noble attempt to remedy the evils of the time. His father and grandfather both held the prætorship; but nothing further is recorded of either than that the younger died suddenly at Pisa in the year 84 B.C., when his great son was just entering into manhood. Of these, as of the other Cæsars who attained to high office, we can only conjecture that they were ordinary Romans of industry and integrity ; nothing is recorded against them in an age of rapidly increasing corruption and degeneracy.

Cæsar's mother also probably belonged to an ancient family of high reputation, the Aurelii, who bore the surname of Cotta. Of this lady we are not wholly ignorant, for she survived her husband thirty years, and lived to hear the news of her son's great exploits in Gaul; and what little we know of her is such as to make us wish for more. Plutarch tells us that she was a discreet woman; and it is a pleasing guess, though no more than a guess, that some of those personal traits in Cæsar's character, which place him as a man so far above the majority of his contemporaries, were due to her example and precept. On her fell the task of completing his education, and throughout his life she seems to have remained his true friend. The story was told that in the year 63, when the son was a candidate for the office of Pontifex Maximus, he kissed his mother when he left his house on the morning of the election, and told her that he would return successful or not at all. When Clodius two years later crept into Cæsar's house at the women's festival of the Bona Dea, with the object, as it was said, of corrupting Cæsar's wife Pompeia, it was by Aurelia's vigilance that he was discovered and identified. We may imagine her as a Roman matron of the older type, strong, self-repressed, but yet womanly; devoted to her only son's best interests, and watching his career with anxiety and admiration.

In this, if it was indeed her aim, she was in the long run successful. Though Cæsar was the foremost man of what must be called a Græco-Roman age, there was very little of the Greek in him. As it was his special task in life to bring the western peoples into prominence in the world's history, and to start them on a career in which they were to leave behind them the effete and effeminate Hellenistic world, so it was also his lot to fight down in himself, with the help of ten years' sojourn in the West, the demoralising influences of a city steeped in pseudo-Greek ways of living and thinking. His character never became finally undermined; and if in this respect he rises far above the level of men like Catilina, Clodius, Cælius, and many other contemporaries who will be mentioned in these pages, it may not be going too far to attribute this in part at least to a mother's influence for good—the best chance for a youthful Roman of that unbridled age.

Of Cæsar's education in the ordinary modern sense of the word, we know hardly anything; and this is only what might be expected, for the bringing-up of the Roman noble was not a sufficiently important matter to invite a biographer's research. And indeed there was probably little to discover. Plutarch, whose aim in writing his "Lives" was an ethical one, and who was specially interested in education, has recorded little or nothing of Cæsar's early training. What we learn from other sources can be very briefly summarised. Suetonius in his work "On Grammarians" has given us some information about the man who was tutor to Cæsar when a boy. This man, Marcus Antonius Gnipho, was a Gaul by birth—*i. e.*, probably from the north of Italy. He was not a slave, as was usually the case with the tutors of the day; his ability and powers of memory were remarkable, and he was skilled both in the Latin and Greek languages; his manners were courteous and his disposition a happy one. At what time he began to teach Cæsar we do not know; but as Suetonius expressly tells us that he resided in the family, and only at a later time opened a school in a house of his own, it is at least probable that his pupil was then quite a young boy.

It is certainly remarkable that Cæsar, at that impressible age, should have been under the charge of a man of Gallic and not of Greek extraction. It is quite possible that his interest in the Gallic character and in Gauls, whether within or beyond the Alps, may have been first stimulated by Gnipho. The influence of an able and agreeable tutor living in the house with his pupil must far exceed that of a master to whose school the boy goes daily for lessons only; and when we reflect that Gnipho's tutorship must have extended over the very years of the Social and Civil wars and of the settlement of the great question of the extension of the citizenship to the Italians and the Gauls of northern Italy, we seem fairly entitled to assume that Cæsar's width of view in political matters was in part at least due to the nationality and character of his teacher. That he was fortunate in the society of a man of accomplishments and good breeding admits of no doubt.

This is practically all we know of his education in the strict sense of the word; for it was not until he was probably twenty-six years old that he studied rhetoric, as we shall see in the next chapter, under a famous Greek master of that indispensable art, in the island of Rhodes. We do not even know who were his boyish companions. It has indeed been conjectured that Cicero was one of them; for Cicero was a fellow-townsman of Marius, who had married Cæsar's aunt, and the younger Marius, Cæsar's first cousin, was probably intimate with both lads. In the year 56 B.C., when supporting the renewal of Cæsar's Gallic command, Cicero took occasion to allude to the early intimacy of himself and his brother with Cæsar; and though the passage must not be pressed too far (for it was the speaker's interest on that occasion to make the most of their friendship), it is beyond doubt that a personal good-will existed between the two men throughout their lives, with rare intervals, which may very well have originated in boyhood.*

The reader cannot fail to be struck, at this point, not only with the total want of interest in the training of the great men of that age shown by contemporary writers, but by the complete failure of the Romans to grasp the importance of education as a means of preparing their statesmen for their vast duties and responsibilities as rulers of the civilised world. It had not been so in the life of the old Greek republics. Though seldom approaching to a realisation of the ideal schemes of the philosophers, the education of youth in a Greek state was certainly intended to preserve the *true state-character*, to fit the rising generation to fulfil the civic duties which would devolve on it; and it is not to be doubted that human excellence and happiness, so far as it could be realised within the narrow limits of the city-state, could only be made durable by such means. Now even if Rome be regarded as no

* Cicero, De Provinciis Consularibus, 17.

more than a city in this sense, without taking into account the extraordinary duties that devolved on her, it must still be allowed that she made no proper provision for the education of her sons. There had indeed been once a strict traditional morality in the old Roman family, in which there was much that was worth keeping; there was "the power of conduct" in a high degree; there were the ideas of justice, obedience, self-sacrifice; and for many generations the influence of example and habit, and the healthy discipline of the *patria potestas*, were sufficient to maintain the reality of these virtues. They were also adequate to the needs of Rome until she became the arbiter of nations; and even then they might have been of infinite value, if they had not melted away in the strong heat of power and prosperity.

But in Cæsar's day some wider virtues were called for than those of a soldier-citizen; some more rational education than the *patria potestas*. To use the terms of Greek philosophy, the ἐθισμός had been tried, and had been useful in its day, but the λόγος was needed to make the rulers of the world into thinking beings. They dabbled, it is true, in Greek literature and philosophy, but only in idle hours, or because it was the fashion. Boys were given into the charge of slaves, who may have taught them something, but hardly their duties as Romans; and if these supplanted the Roman mothers, they did far more harm than good. And the "humaner letters," the more liberal education that makes men gentle and generous, and which is its own object and reward, was almost unknown at Rome. The Roman had indeed succeeded to his world-wide inheritance long before he was intellectually of age. He had not yet begun to think when he was called upon to think for the world; but his nature was not a thinking one, nor was his training of a kind to remedy his deficiency. The power of grasping great political problems, the power of self-command in dealing with them, the sense of justice and duty, the love of truth and right dealing,—these were not qualities easily to be developed in a Roman of the last century of the Republic.

Cæsar, then, though apparently fortunate in his early home-life, in the influence of mother and tutor, must for the most part have had to educate himself. That he did so, and intentionally, we may regard as certain; but the details of the process, which in the biography of a modern statesman would be full of interest, are entirely hidden from us. In one sense, however, his education was a life-long task. We can see him steadily growing, in self-restraint, in humanity, and in the sense of duty and in the love of work, as well as in political wisdom, in knowledge of human nature, and in the skilful adaptation of means to ends. Up to the time of his first consulship, when he was over forty years of age, we do not see much in him that places him apart from the ordinary Roman of his day, unless it be a certain tendency to reserve his strength, an apparent inclination to watch and wait; and the stories that are told of his conduct and morals by Suetonius, though utterly untrustworthy as evidence of fact, are at least sufficient to show what the popular belief ascribed to him. But from his first campaign in Gaul to the end of his life, during fifteen years of continual labour, whether military or administrative, he was always learning, noting, and advancing. No one can doubt this who reads his "Commentaries" carefully, with the object of discovering something of the nature of the man who wrote them. And he who in middle life, and in an age so giddy and exciting, could turn to the utmost advantage the opportunities offered by new duties and new experiences, who could gather in a harvest of knowledge from his sojourn among hitherto unknown peoples, and when absolute power was in his hands, could use it with consummate skill and moderation, must, in earlier life, however richly gifted by nature, have spent some time and thought on the education of his own mind.

It may be convenient at once to describe briefly the personal appearance of the man whose life we are to trace. All such descriptions must rest solely on the evidence of Suetonius, which probably represents the popular tradition, and on that of the busts and coins, which are numerous and not self-contradictory. He was tall for a Roman; but the Italian standard of height was probably then, as now, considerably below that of the northern races. His complexion was pale or fair; his eyes black and lively; his mouth somewhat large; the lips, as they are represented in the coins and busts, being firmly set together, with the corners slightly drawn downwards. His forehead was high, and appeared still higher in consequence of a premature baldness,

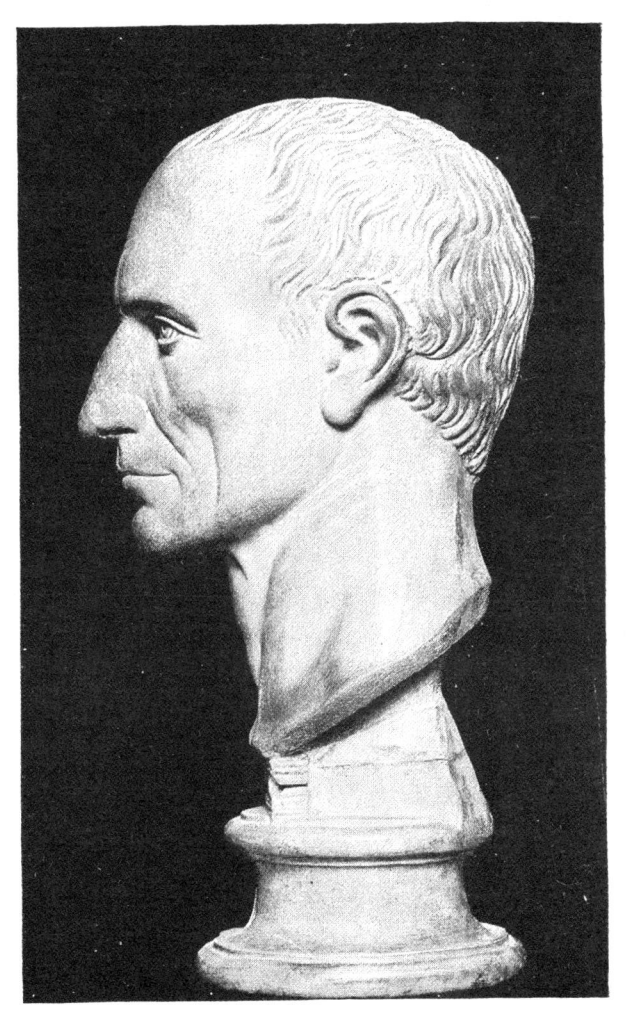

JULIUS CÆSAR.
FROM THE MARBLE BUST IN THE BRITISH MUSEUM.

which he is said to have tried to hide by combing his hair forwards. His nose was aquiline and rather large. The contour of his head, as represented in the well-known marble in the British Museum, is extremely massive and powerful; and the expression of the face is keen, thoughtful, and somewhat stern. It is the likeness of a severe schoolmaster of the world, whose tenderer side, with its capability of affection for friends and devotion towards women, is hardly traceable in the features.

His health was good, though late in life he was subject to some kind of seizure. He was capable of the most unremitting activity; his limbs were big and strongly made. Suetonius tells us that he was an extremely skilful swordsman and horseman, and a good swimmer. All his contemporaries agreed that he was very abstemious in regard to wine, though they would not allow him the virtues of which such moderation is usually the accompaniment. All were also agreed as to the steadiness and coolness of his temper and the courteousness of his manner and bearing, indicating the possession of that high breeding which the Romans aptly termed "humanitas." On the whole we may picture him to ourselves as a man the dignity of whose bodily presence was in due proportion to the greatness of his mental powers; and the words which Plutarch employed of Gaius Gracchus, "that he always maintained a certain seriousness of manner in combination with a good will towards his fellowmen," seem to be in the same degree applicable, among the many prominent figures of the Roman Revolution, to his great successor only.

CHAPTER II.

BOYHOOD DURING THE CIVIL WARS—EARLIEST POLITICAL EXPERIENCES.
89–82 B.C.

WE saw that in the year of Cæsar's birth, Marius, his aunt's husband, was at the height of his military glory. It was in that summer that he utterly destroyed a vast host of wandering Germans, who for several years had been imperilling the very existence of the Roman Empire in the West. The battle was fought at Aquæ Sextiæ (Aix in southern France), in the same Gallic province which Cæsar himself was destined to rule so long, and to protect, like his uncle, from barbarian inroads. Next year (101 B.C.), in conjunction with the aristocrat Catulus, Marius destroyed another army of invaders, who had penetrated by the Brenner Pass into northern Italy, and were actually within a few days' march of Rome. Italy was saved, and the conqueror was elected consul for the sixth successive year.

It is hard for us to appreciate the full value of these victories. We are apt to think of the Roman Empire as a system of marvellous stability, and of Rome as the Eternal City. We do not easily grasp the fact that, at this time and for many years afterwards, the Empire was often in a condition of the utmost peril. As we shall see, the northern barbarians were not the only enemies of Rome who seemed likely to change the course of history. Mithridates, the great King of Pontus, was soon to overrun her territory in the East. Internal discord and civil war were to sap her material strength and destroy what little moral force was left in her. He who would judge truly of Cæsar's place in the history of the world must understand that the Empire, during all the earlier part of his life, was terribly deficient both in stability and unity.

But at the time of his birth the immediate danger was passing away. Two years later (100 B.C.) the wars were over, and Marius was supreme in Rome. It turned out, however, that this great master of armies was helpless as a statesman. He was a man of the people, and the re-assertion of democracy seemed inevitable; but he bungled, hesitated, and finally subordinated himself to the Senate. After his year of office he left Rome, and disappeared from politics for many years. A senatorial reaction followed; and ten years later there broke out a terrible struggle between Rome and her Italian subjects, who united to obtain by force of arms that Roman citizenship which they had so long coveted and sought for in vain. Once more Rome was in the direst extremity. Face to face with the Italians, she was as weak materially as her position was morally unjust. By their help she had been adding for more than a century to her dominion and her wealth, yet she made no sign of renewing for their benefit the old policy of absorption which had raised her to her supremacy in Italy. Now that her citizenship had far outstripped in value that of all other states, and was indeed the only one worth having in the world for men of business, of pleasure, or of ambition, she would not share it even with those who had done so much to make her what she was. Real statesmen like Gaius Gracchus had urged it on her, but both senate and people had turned a deaf ear. Selfish motives, which this is not the place to examine, had prevailed over a large-minded and liberal policy.

It was soon shown how weak she was without her Italian supports. Everywhere her armies were beaten by their old comrades; one disgrace followed another. At the first gleam of returning fortune, the Senate seized the opportunity to yield the whole point at issue; bills were passed which, in conjunction with other measures taken later, had the effect of enrolling the whole Italian population south of the Po on the register of Roman citizens.

We may not pause here to consider the immense importance of those measures in the history of Rome and of the world. But in a sketch of Cæsar's life, it is necessary to point out that they were very far from removing all difficulty in the relations between Rome and her new citizens. Though the question of citizenship had been settled, other questions of adjustment and organisation at once arose. How was the local government of these Italian communities to be co-ordinated with the imperial government in the city of Rome? How were the Italians to find time and means to come and vote in the elections of the Roman magistrates who were now to govern them? How were these city magistrates to discharge the business of all Italy? A complete re-organisation was called for; a task of great difficulty, for the position was an entirely novel one, and no such problem had ever yet confronted either Greek or Roman statesman. Nor was it really grappled with until Cæsar himself put his hand to it more than forty years later.

The storm of civil war broke out in Cæsar's thirteenth year; he was therefore too young to take any part in the struggle. He probably only assumed the *toga virilis*, or mark of Roman manhood, in 87 B.C., when his older contemporaries, Pompeius and Cicero, had already seen their first military service. But if his youth prevented his bearing arms in these wars, whose mercilessness must have vitiated many noble natures and hardened many generous hearts, his political instincts were now assuredly generated and growing rapidly into definite opinions resting on principles never to be abandoned while he lived. Boys were doubtless apt, then as now, to take the colour of their political ideas from family tradition, and from relations and teachers who could win their admiration and worship. Both these influences were at work on the youthful Cæsar, and secured him once and for ever for the cause of popular government as against the Senate, for the Many as against the Few. Though his relations were not uniformly " Populares," the marriage of his aunt with Marius, which must have taken place long before the outbreak of civil war, makes it probable that in his own family circle the views held were not of the narrow oligarchic type. And when this Marius, who was the greatest soldier Rome had yet produced, and the saviour of his country from barbarian enemies, now became the victim of exile, persecution, and degradation, in the cause of Italian liberty, he must at once have become a hero in Cæsar's boyish mind.

It is not to be supposed that Cæsar then fully understood the principle of the policy for which the Marian party were struggling; it is indeed unlikely enough that Marius understood it himself. But as Cæsar's later life shows plainly not only that he eventually came to understand it, but that he understood it more effectually than any of his contemporaries, it will be as well once for all to place it succinctly before the reader, as the solidly laid foundation-stone of all Cæsar's political training.

Just as in a modern state there can be found, underlying the varying phases of action of a political party, some deeply rooted principle which permanently but secretly governs them, so at Rome, even in that unreasoning age, both sides in the political battle had a basis of reasoned conviction, on which, in the minds of the better men at least, their immediate aims were supported and steadied. Among those who were called " Optimates," this might almost be described as a definite rule of faith, inherited from the fathers of their constitution. They believed that the Senate, as embodying all the gathered wisdom and experience of the State, and as exercising supervision over the magistrates elected by the people, was alone capable of administering the business of the city and her dependents in Italy; to this axiom, which had in former times been proved sound, they had naturally enough added the conviction that the vast territories which had been acquired since the war with Carthage could likewise only be governed by the same machinery. This political creed, coinciding with and confirming their own material interests, floated them on a course of dogmatic selfishness which has rarely been equalled in history; but that creed was a perfectly natural and intelligible one, and was rooted not only in the accumulated experience of their own countrymen, but also in the whole history and philosophy of the ancient city-state.

The views of the Populares, on the other hand, which were newer and less definitely shaped, were based on the conviction that in the task of government which had fallen to the lot of Rome the material interests and well-being of the governed must be taken into account, as well as the convenience and glory of the governors. This party in fact, or the leaders of it, was dimly aware that Rome had vast responsibilities; that the whole condition of the civilised world had changed, and that it lay with her to accept the position, and accustom herself to the ideas—new then in the political world—of progress and development. Such views, unpractical and unreasoned as they must have been, and often obscured by the selfish aims and personal bitterness of the leaders who held them, can nevertheless be traced in almost every great measure of reform proposed by this party, from the tribunate of Tiberius Gracchus onwards. Whether the question of the moment were the better distribution of land, the reform of corrupt law-courts, or the extension of the citizenship to the Italians, the true interests of the mass of the governed were in the minds of the more thoughtful of the leaders of this party, and guided their policy steadily in one direction, in spite of checks and back-currents.

When Cæsar was growing towards manhood, and beginning to understand politics, under the influence, as we may suppose, of his hero Marius, a new question arose in which the convictions of both parties, not unadulterated by personal aims, came into such violent collision that civil war at once broke out afresh.

The two parties, forced into a temporary union by the death-struggle of the Social war, had, as we saw, combined to bestow the full citizenship upon all Italians who chose to claim it within sixty days of the passing of the bill. But the Senate had been strong enough to introduce a provision which greatly modified the practical effect of this resolution. All new citizens were to be enrolled, not in the thirty-five " tribes " into which the whole Roman population

THE FORUM.

AS SEEN FROM THE CAPITOL.

The Temple of Saturn in the Foreground, in the Background a Portion of the Arch of Titus and the Ruins of the Colosseum.

(*Baumeister.*)

was divided, but in eight new tribes; and as all questions were decided, not by a majority of the whole citizens, but by a majority of tribe-votes, their influence both in legislation and in elections would be comparatively small. It was an insult to men who had fought so splendidly for the coveted privilege, and who had been for generations serving bravely in the Roman armies, to deal with them in this niggardly spirit; and in 88 B.C. the Marian party put up Sulpicius, a tribune of extraordinary eloquence, to propose the abolition of the new eight tribes, and the distribution of the new citizens in the old thirty-five. The result of this, and of a simultaneous proposal to give Marius the command against Mithridates, was that the aristocratic consul Sulla marched on Rome with his army and broke the power of the Populares at a single blow. Sulpicius was murdered, Marius fled into exile, the laws were abrogated, and the senatorial constitution was set on a firm basis by Sulla. But when Sulla left Italy early in the following year for the East, the Marians returned, and re-enacted the law of Sulpicius, which was never again called in question. The person who brought it forward on this second occasion was the consul of that year, L. Cornelius Cinna, who on the death of Marius in January, 86 B.C., became the leader of the party, and established himself for the next three years, not only as self-elected consul, but as absolute master of Rome.

This crucial question, whether the new Italian citizens should or should not be placed fairly and frankly on a level with the rest, was thus the first in which Cæsar's youthful mind must have been actively interested. It was he who, long afterwards, was to put the finishing touch to Cinna's work by extending the full citizenship to the Gauls living north of the river Po. That he at once became a hot partisan is hardly to be doubted. He had already been noticed by Marius, who had caused him to be nominated Flamen Dialis (priest of Jupiter); and after Marius' death he entered into the most intimate relations with Cinna himself. Discarding the project of a wealthy marriage which had been arranged for him, he boldly and successfully sought the hand of Cornelia, Cinna's daughter, who lived with him, happily as far as we know, until her death some sixteen years later.

Under the absolutism of his father-in-law, and no doubt in the closest intimacy with him, Cæsar lived during the three years of comparative quiet in which the Marian policy was supreme, and the Senate bowed to its yoke. But unfortunately we know as little of him at this time as we know of Cinna and his rule. Cinna is one of the lost characters of history; these years are hidden from us in deeper shadow than any others in the history of the Revolution. But we can at least be sure that these three years familiarised the young Cæsar with the sight of power wielded by a single man, and with the spectacle of a senate feeble and cowardly enough to submit to a self-appointed consul. And from this time forward he was bound with the closest ties, personal and political, to the party and principles of the Populares.

These ties were strengthened by the misfortunes that befell him when in the year 82 B.C., on the triumphant return of Sulla, the power of the Marian party melted rapidly away, and their enemies chastised the people with scorpions. His father-in-law was killed by his own soldiers; Sertorius, the only other capable leader of the party, fled in despair to Spain, to keep the Marian watch-fires smouldering in the far West for many a year, till Cæsar himself had grown to mature manhood. In the course of a year Sulla had crushed all opposition in Italy, shut up the younger Marius in Præneste, fought his way into Rome, and as dictator, with absolute power so long as he chose to keep it, and with a vast army of veterans at his beck and call, had begun the grim task of reprisals by killing off every prominent Marian.

Cæsar was then barely twenty, too young to be a victim. Sulla contented himself with ordering him to put away Cinna's daughter, as he had made his lieutenant Pompeius put away his wife Antistia. Pompeius obeyed him; so did M. Piso, who had just married Cinna's widow. Cæsar would not obey; but he suffered for his disobedience. He lost his wife's dowry and his own property, and was deprived of the priesthood of Jupiter, to which Marius had had him appointed. Then he fled in disguise into the mountains of Samnium. Here he was pursued and captured by the Sullan bloodhounds, who were everywhere; and the story ran that he bribed his captor to set him free with a gift of two talents. He ventured back to Rome, where his friends were bringing influence to bear on Sulla on his behalf; his uncle, Aurelius Cotta, and, as we are told, the college of Vestal Virgins, who probably had had relations with him in his priesthood, succeeded in obtaining his pardon. Sulla was unwilling and ungracious, but he yielded. "I grant you this boon," he is reported to have said to the petitioners, "but I charge you look after this youth who wears his belt so loosely."

By Sulla's advent to power, Cæsar's opening career was suddenly cut short. Sulla was absolute, and used his absolutism to prevent all future possibility of another democratic reaction. He had put to death all the prominent members of the democratic party on whom he could lay his hands; he now sought to make it impossible for youthful aspirants like Cæsar to set on foot a fresh democratic agitation. He saw that the old constitution, which had never been defined by statute, but rested almost entirely on custom and tradition, held both oligarchic and democratic elements in solution. He saw that so long as this was the case, it might be worked in an oligarchic or a democratic sense, as each party happened to be uppermost. He knew that the history of the last half century had been a history of repeated oscillations, from oligarchy to democracy, and back again; that in the course of these struggles, democracy had shown a strong tendency to generate monarchy, and that oligarchy had degenerated into weak and corrupt government, while both sides had lost all sense of law and order, of duty and self-restraint, as the bitterness of the strife increased. He saw clearly that the constitution must be fixed once for all, and secured by legislative enactment.

Sulla rejected monarchy, though he was himself for the time monarch; democracy he detested. By birth and feeling an aristocrat, he set about recasting the constitution in an oligarchic form, and securing it by definite legislation. The Senate was made once more supreme by a series of arrangements which subordinated to it the ordinary magistrates, the tribunes of the plebs, the popular assemblies, the administration of the law, and, so far as was possible, the provincial governors and their armies. It was not indeed the old Senate, for it was increased in numbers, and was henceforth to be recruited from ex-magistrates only, *i. e.*, indirectly by popular election. But as a working power in the constitution, it was now placed in a far stronger position than it had ever occupied since its moral ascendancy began to wane. That position was now fenced all round by a series of legal enactments, which would have to be removed by legislation if the constitution was to be once more changed; and Sulla so contrived that neither popular agitator nor statesman of genius could pass laws in a democratic sense without encountering obstacles almost insurmountable.

This is not the place to explain these arrangements, or to enter on a description of this singular man's work and character. This much, however, must be grasped by everyone who would follow Cæsar's career intelligently: that Sulla thus gave the oligarchy one more chance, and that an excellent one, to show what mettle they still had in them.

He gave the reins into their hands, and invited them to govern adequately. He placed them in an almost impregnable stronghold, and bade them make good use of their defences. Then he laid down his absolute power, retired into private life, and left the machine he had so elaborately constructed to work by itself. How it did work, and how the oligarchy acquitted itself, we shall see in the next chapter. As our story proceeds we shall also have occasion to note that Sulla's work was in many respects incomplete. Wonderful as it was, and however lasting its contribution to the progress of Roman law and to the conduct of the business of the Empire, it hardly touched some of the greatest problems that were now urgently calling for solution. It needed a greater than Sulla to see that the problem of constitutional re-organisation was only one among many, and that even that needed to be dealt with in a more humane and intelligent spirit.

CHAPTER III.

EARLY LIFE UNDER THE SULLAN GOVERNMENT.
81–70 B.C.

CÆSAR did not stay long in Rome to risk the Dictator's wrath a second time; and he was indeed now old enough to serve his first campaign, a duty still obligatory on all young men of his age. He sailed for Asia Minor in the year 81 B.C., and remained in the East until Sulla's death. The war with Mithridates, the formidable enemy whom Sulla had driven to a doubtful peace, had broken out afresh the year before, and was still smouldering; and there was always plenty to do on the Asiatic coasts, for the pirates of Cilicia were hovering round every port, and as yet entirely unbridled.

It was an important part of the military education of a young Roman of high birth, that he should serve his first campaign under the immediate eye of a commander-in-chief, living with him in his tent as a kind of page or youthful aide-de-camp, and learning from him the traditions of the arts of warfare and provincial government. If the general were a man of character and ability, much might be learnt by the youth thus pleasantly associated with him, besides the details of business and the military art. But of the character of Cæsar's first military master we unfortunately know nothing. As Sulla's legatus it is not likely that Minucius Thermus was a congenial companion to the young Marian. But we know that at the siege of Mytilene, the last town that held out for Mithridates, he bestowed on his pupil the "civic crown" for saving the life of a fellow-soldier; and thus Cæsar began his military career under no imputation of effeminacy, such as was invented for him in later times.

This exploit was in 80 B.C.; how he was employed in the following year we are not told. In 78 B.C., apparently in search of active service, he joined the fleet of an able commander, Servilius Isauricus, who was operating against the pirates on the Cilician coast; but he had not been long at sea when the news arrived of Sulla's death, and he felt himself at liberty to return at once to Rome. There he found agitation and mutiny already beginning to threaten the constitution which Sulla had set up; and the question which confronted him at once, and continued to confront him during the next eight years, was whether he should openly join the agitators and mutineers.

The reader has already been made acquainted with the leading features of Sulla's reconstruction of the senatorial government. The plan of his work was elaborate and in itself admirable, but the new constitution was insecure from the outset, because it had no foundation in the good-will or moral force of the people either in the city or in Italy. The constitution was like an ingenious and complicated machine, whose inventor has died without training a successor to work it. The true Sullan partisans were not numerous, and they had no men of real political ability among them. And nothing but the strength and cohesion of the machinery itself could have saved it from the repeated efforts to pull it to pieces, which were made by the popular party during the eight years succeeding Sulla's death.

Almost before Sulla was in his grave, Lepidus, the Sullan consul, began to play his master false. Cæsar and his advisers did not yield to the temptation to join him. They probably knew the man well: he had changed sides once before, and was a mere weathercock. His proposals, calculated to please the mob for the moment, had no reference to the constitution, and would not unlock the fetters that Sulla had placed on all popular action. They could not impose on Cæsar, who, as Suetonius tells us, "withheld himself from Lepidus' company, though invited with the most favourable promises, for he distrusted the man's disposition and talents." He saw Lepidus decline to free the tribunate from its bondage—the one essential preliminary to the undoing of Sulla's work,—and he probably guessed that the consul's real object was only to turn himself into a monarch.

This danger passed away, for Lepidus, who through the folly of the Senate had been able to raise an army in Etruria, was defeated outside the walls of Rome, and crossed over to Sardinia, where he died. No further attempt was made to break down Sulla's machinery by force. There remained the ordinary method of legislation, with its accompaniment of popular oratory; and though the Sullan restrictions on the tribunate had made it difficult either to get any law promulgated, or to obtain a hearing for any would-be orator without the sanction of the all-powerful senate, it was none the less to these expedients that the opposition now looked with confidence for ultimate success. Young Cicero had already made his mark, and had even ventured to beard Sulla himself in the admirable speech for Roscius of Ameria. Cæsar, too, now began to turn his attention seriously to oratory. Perhaps he was urged to this by the example, possibly even by the precept, of his talented and versatile friend, who was a few years older than himself; but in any case it was the only course open to a young man who had determined to work his way to the front rank.

He appears for the first time this same year (77 B.C.) as counsel in a criminal trial, and in the most important of the standing law-courts which Sulla had organised. He took charge of the prosecution of Dolabella, lately proconsul of Macedonia, for illegal extortion during his government; and though he lost his case, he is said to have been applauded, and to have left an impression on the public mind that the senatorial judges were corrupt. The next year he tried his hand again, and in the same court, by prosecuting C. Antonius, who during the Mithridatic war had enriched himself in Greece by plunder. That this man was guilty is certain, for he was ejected from the senate by the censors six years later on the same grounds; but again Cæsar's oratory failed to move the consciences of interested judges. Whether bribed or not, they had at least to defend the prestige of their order, and to secure for it an advantageous immunity from the ordinary consequences of thieving.

After the second failure Cæsar seems to have determined to learn the art of rhetoric from its best living master; and though this would compel him to leave Rome for some time, he was probably not unwilling to leave the political situation to develop itself without his aid. He started for Rhodes, where the great rhetorician Molo was then teaching. On his way he was caught by some of the pirates who were then swarming on the seas and laughing at the clumsiness and venality of the Roman naval commanders; and Plutarch has given us a picturesque account of his adventures as their prisoner, which was certainly not his own invention, and probably represents something like the truth. Suetonius, who wrote somewhat later than Plutarch, has the same story with less detail. Both tell us that Cæsar had with him at the time three companions; either of whom may have preserved the recollection of what happened. The rest of his suite had been despatched to obtain the necessary ransom; and meanwhile, during thirty-eight days of captivity, " he behaved to them as if they were his body-guard, rather than his captors, and joined in their games and exercises with perfect unconcern." He amused himself by writing poems and speeches, and by reading them to his pirate audience; and when they were slow in applauding, he called them illiterate barbarians, and threatened laughingly to hang them all. The story runs that he afterwards carried out his threat literally. For when the ransom came and he was set free, he manned some ships at Miletus, and surprised and captured most of them; and failing to get the immediate sanction of the governor of the province, he took the law into his own hands, and crucified all the prisoners.

After this adventure he reached Rhodes in safety, and enrolled himself as a pupil of Molo. Cicero, whose admiration for the great teacher was unlimited, had also been lately studying under him, not for the first time: it is even possible that it was by his advice that Cæsar took the same step. Cicero threw himself into the work with characteristic ardour, and turned out about this time a rhetorical treatise (the " De Inventione ") which we still possess. Cæsar, from what we know of his tastes and character, could hardly have found the same delight in his studies at Rhodes; his mind was too practical and scientific to enjoy the tropes and figures of the most artificial of all arts, and he did not stay long under Molo's tuition. But he nevertheless became one of the greatest orators of his day, and according to some accounts, second only to Cicero. The purity and force of his style, the lucidity of his diction, and the good taste and courteousness of his manner are praised not only by later writers like Quinctilian, Suetonius, and Plutarch, but by the best of all witnesses, Cicero himself. It is characteristic of the man, but unfortunate for us, that Cæsar never took any pains to collect and preserve his speeches; even in the lifetime of Augustus there was considerable doubt about the correctness and authenticity of some of them. They served their purpose, and were thought no more of.

Though we can only guess that Molo's lecture-room was not entirely congenial to him, we know that he left it on the first chance of more active occupation. The Roman dominion in Asia was at this moment in very serious peril. A great storm was gathering. Mithridates, whom Sulla had but half crushed, had long been in correspondence with Tigranes, the powerful King of Armenia, with Sertorius in Spain, and even with the pirates of Cilicia. The Romans had but a small army in their Asiatic province, and hardly any ships, and the king swooped down on them before they were ready to resist him. The position was critical; and Cæsar, though he had no official position, at once left Rhodes, collected a few volunteers, and if Suetonius' account is correct, secured the loyalty of the provincials, and expelled Mithridates' general. But meanwhile a senatorial proconsul of ability had been sent out from Rome, and Cæsar, who had found himself for the moment fighting against an alliance of which his own partisan

Sertorius was an important member, dismissed his levies and left Asia. He probably reached Rome in the winter of 74–73 B.C.

He was now nearly thirty, and was of standing and experience enough to be listened to. He had just been elected in his absence to a place in the college of the pontifices, vacant by the death of his uncle, C. Aurelius Cotta, and on his return he was placed, as we should say, at the head of the poll, in the yearly election of military tribunes. Of his service in this capacity our authorities tell us nothing, though at this very time Italy itself was the field of one of the most dangerous wars Rome had ever had to face. The honour of the Roman arms was once more at its lowest ebb; the legions were being disgracefully beaten by insurgent slave-bands under their brilliant leader Spartacus. It is hard to believe that Cæsar remained in the capital while such events were passing; still harder to believe that if he had any share in the struggle it was not of a kind to be worth recording. But the historians are silent, and conjecture is useless. They only tell us that he now began to join eagerly in the political agitation for the overthrow of the Sullan constitution. "He supported with the utmost vigour," says Suetonius, "those who were agitating for the restoration of the tribunician power, which Sulla had diminished." As this is his first appearance in the arena of politics, it is as well to take a brief survey of the circumstances which already were bringing about the destruction of Sulla's constitution and opening out new resources, new possibilities of action, for men who were only just beginning to set foot on the ricketty ladder of political life at Rome.

What more than anything else destroys the credit of a modern government, whether in the hands of a despot or a cabinet, is weakness in dealing with foreign affairs, and want of readiness and resource in coping with an enemy. Actual disaster is not necessarily fatal to a government, if anything like heroism has been shown in the effort to avert it; but the popular mind rarely forgives slackness or cowardice in its rulers. It was the same at Rome; and the "people," such as they were, or at least their more intelligent leaders, had good reason to complain, not only that the Sullan Senate was incompetent to take charge of the interests of the Empire and to conduct foreign wars, but that they themselves had no means of bringing their rulers to book.

If it had chanced about the time when Cæsar returned from Asia (*i. e.*, at the end of 74 B.C.), that curiosity had prompted an intelligent Jew or Parthian to travel through the Roman Empire from east to west, and to record his observations, his book must have been singularly depressing to the patriotic Roman reader. The undertaking would have been a bold one; the traveller in constant personal insecurity. In Asia Minor he would find a gigantic war just breaking out. He would learn as he passed through the interior that the great King of Pontus had blockaded Chalcedon, and that a beaten Roman general was with difficulty holding out within its walls. He would wonder that Tigranes of Armenia did not lend a hand to his natural ally of Pontus, and help to sweep the vanquished Romans once and for ever out of Asia. He might well marvel, as Plutarch did long afterwards, at the extraordinary fortune of these Romans, who lived down constant disaster by the constant disunion of their enemies. Taking ship at some port in the Asiatic province, and witnessing perhaps the arrival of troops and stores for the newly appointed general, Lucullus, he would wonder at their apparent inadequacy, and mark the total inability of the harassed and impoverished provincials to make up the deficiency of preparation. In his voyage to Italy he would be told thrilling sailors' tales of the pirates; of capture and slavery, of ransom and ruin. Even off the port of Brundisium he would be still in danger; he would hear of Roman fleets unable to leave the port except under cover of night, and of attacks made in broad day on the rich cities of the western coast.

He might reasonably prefer a journey through Italy to further risk of capture by the masters of the sea, and would be warned against visiting Sicily by stories of the insecurity of all life and property under the government of the infamous Verres. Nor would such stories be needed to convince him that the Romans were their own worst enemies; for in Italy itself he would see signs enough of cruelty and misgovernment. He would find the roads occupied by bands of armed slaves of powerful physique and formidable mien, fresh from victories over Roman legions, and expecting the speedy downfall of the tyrant city. If he fell into their hands, and were lucky enough himself to escape the ignominious fate of their Roman captives, he might witness the astounding sight of the conquerors of the world being forced to fight as gladiators at the bidding of men who a year ago had been working in chains on their own vast estates. And arriving with difficulty at Rome, he would see no sign of prosperity, vigour, or unanimity; he would find an idle population starving for want of grain, and a government without a single member whose character seemed to command respect and confidence. He would be told of news arriving from the East and West at once, from Spain and from Asia Minor, of serious defeat or at the best of doubtful success ; of demands for reinforcements, stores, and money, which could ill be provided when Spartacus was master of Italy and the revenue at the mercy of the pirates. And last, not least, he would be amazed to find that every other Roman with whom he talked was not only against the senatorial government, but really in sympathy with its enemies ; that in Further Spain there was a great Roman organising a new Rome, for whose victories over his own countrymen one whole party in the city was thanking the gods ; and that this man in the far West was about to join hands with Rome's great enemy in the East, and was hoping by his means to crush the paralysed republic, and revolutionise the Græco-Roman world.

Such a traveller would have seen quite enough, without going farther westward, to assure himself that the time was at hand when the Roman Empire must either break up altogether or find some one strong enough to command universal confidence;

some one in whom political ability, united with military skill, would be able to bring the state and its government into harmonious relation with its dependencies and their needs. He would seek in vain for the signs of such a genius. Three generals were in command of Roman armies: Pompeius in Spain, Crassus in Italy, Lucullus in Asia. But none of these had as yet achieved signal success in the field; even Pompeius, the youngest and most brilliant, had been no match for his able enemy in Spain, though he was now wearing him out by superior resources and by treachery. All three were men of ability, but so far had shown no conspicuous political skill; all belonged to the Sullan party, and were reckoned as loyal officers of the Sullan constitution. Yet to each of them the chance was open of saving Rome and relieving a distressed world. He whom good fortune might bring to the crest of the wave, if the needful insight also were his, the width of view, and the command over himself, might satisfy a boundless ambition and win the gratitude of posterity.

If our imaginary traveller had inquired, during his stay at Rome, into the aims and tactics of the political leaders of the day, he would have learnt that the senatorial government, to whose maladministration the evils he had noticed were chiefly due, was confronted by an opposition with a distinct policy of its own. This policy was nothing less than the alteration of the constitution set up by Sulla in its two most characteristic and vital points.

Sulla's object had been, as we saw, to make the Senate once more supreme in every department of government; and in order to effect this, he had to fence it from attack at those points where attack had before his time been most successful. It had always been theoretically possible—and since the days of the Gracchi the thing had often been done—to override the Senate by direct popular legislation. If a tribune of the plebs chose to introduce a measure to the assembly of the plebs in their tribes, and if he succeeded in passing it without a veto from a fellow-tribune, it became law in spite of senatorial opposition. It was in this way that the popular feeling had made itself felt in the years of the Jugurthine War, when the venality and misgovernment of the Senate had been at least as bad as at the time we are writing of; corrupt generals had been punished and superseded, and Marius sent to Africa, through the instrumentality of vigorous and indignant tribunes. Doubtless it was not Sulla's wish to shield bad rulers from either criticism or punishment. But the powers of the tribunate had so frequently been abused, to the destruction not only of bad government but of any government whatever, that he boldly determined to reduce that anomalous office to a nullity, and to trust to his newly constituted Senate to control and punish magisterial shortcomings. He let the tribunate survive; but the tribune was no longer to legislate independently, and his veto was hedged about so as to be no longer a fatal obstacle to the wishes of the Senate. Without leave from the Senate, no tribune could even address the people in the forum; and the office was deprived of much of its old attraction by the regulation that when once a man had been a tribune, he must aspire to no other magistracy, and end his political career for good and all on the day he laid down that now insignificant office. So far as the tribunate had been the mouth-piece of genuine public opinion and the means of legislating in accordance with it, its use and effectiveness had been entirely destroyed ; it was there still, but gagged and bound.

Sulla had fortified the senatorial position at another point where it was weak. He enacted that the body of judges selected to hear any criminal case should be taken exclusively from the members of the Senate, as had been the rule before the tribunate of G. Gracchus. His elaborate re-organisation of criminal law and procedure, though in itself admirable, was thus rendered futile as a means of checking misgovernment either at home or in the provinces; for such was the condition of morals in high places, that senatorial judges were unwilling to convict men of their own order even on the clearest evidence. We have seen this exemplified already in Cæsar's failure to procure the conviction of Antonius and Dolabella. The corruption and partiality of these judges had been sufficiently proved in other notable cases; it was the common scandal of the time, as we may see from Cicero's language in the Verrine orations. It was as plain as possible that Sulla, who could not himself have wished for such a state of things, had entirely miscalculated the character of the new Senate ; he had provided it with an excellent machinery for controlling its own unworthy members, but had entirely failed to see that independence and unselfishness were not to be looked for from it. No constitution, no judicial system, can ever be worked successfully, unless men can be found to work it in a right spirit. And though there may have been such men in Italy at that time, they were not the majority among those who came to the front in politics, and won seats in the all-powerful Senate.

At these two points then, the fortress of the Sullan constitution was most obviously open to attack in spite of Sulla's fortifications; and when Cæsar returned to Rome in 74–73 B.C. he found the battle going on, and joined in it at once vigorously. In each of the three preceding years (76 to 74 B.C.) some attempt had been made to free the tribunate from its bonds; but the only success gained had been the passing of a bill in 75 B.C., through the agency of Cæsar's uncle Cotta (a moderate senatorial), allowing tribunes to proceed in due course to the higher magistracies. This removed a serious disqualification, and opened the tribunate again to men of vigour and ambition; but, as Cicero says, it restored to the office not its power, but only a little of its old dignity. In 73 B.C. a vigorous attempt was made by the tribune C. Licinius Macer, to restore the tribunate to all its ancient freedom; and it was this effort to which Cæsar gave the whole weight of his support, such as it then was.

It was not, however, by democratic agitation that the Sullan fortress was after all to be captured. The events of the two years following Cæsar's return to Rome entirely changed the position of affairs. The Slave war, which for a time placed the very existence of the state in peril, not only diverted men's minds from the orators of the forum,—to whom they probably listened in these years without much enthusiasm,—but eventually brought to the gates of Rome two victorious generals and their armies. Pompeius, after a long series of campaigns against Sertorius and the democratic state in Spain, had at last returned in triumph to Italy, and was called in to assist Crassus in putting an end to the war. This was done in the year 71 B.C.; the slave-hero Spartacus was killed, and Pompeius arrived in time to help in extinguishing the embers of rebellion. The two generals, who might claim the credit of having saved Italy from anarchy and the Sullan government from disgrace, arrived at Rome with their veterans; and the question on the lips of every citizen was whether they would be content with that credit, and continue the obedient servants of the Senate, or seize the tempting prize of supreme military dominion.

It was an extremely critical moment. The destinies of Rome hung on the action and character of these two men, and Cæsar must have been well aware that his own future was no less in their hands. Pompeius was but six years older than himself, and had no ancestry, no accomplishments, no civic education, to secure him influence. But he had what was then far more important, the reputation of a tried general, and the support of a victorious army. Though he had never yet filled even the lowest magisterial office, these would make him secure of absolutism if he chose to demand it, and if he could dispose of

BUST OF POMPEIUS.
IN THE SPADA PALACE IN ROME.
(*Baumeister's "Denkmäler des Klassischen Altertums."*)

Crassus, who was on bad terms with him. Crassus himself was older and more experienced ; his boundless wealth gave him an immense secret influence, and he too had an army, which had borne the brunt of the struggle against the slaves. But he was never at any moment of his life capable of being made into a hero. He was not a man to be trusted ; and to repose trust in some one was just what the wearied Roman world was beginning ardently to desire. If the two came into collision, and fought for the possession of Rome, the best chance lay with Pompeius, as the better soldier and the more honourable man. He might be vain and inexperienced in politics; but of all the men then living of assured reputation and power, he was the only one whose character was really respected, and whom all parties could by any possibility agree in trusting. And indeed this confidence, though not whole-hearted, was not entirely a mistaken one ; for in the course of a long and varied career, Pompeius never wholly lost the reputation he had won.

But neither Pompeius nor Crassus was anxious for a bloody civil war: the day of military despotism was to be postponed for a while, and Cæsar might feel that he was not yet to be shouldered out of the race for power, or to submit himself to the will of a soldier-king. The two rivals made up their quarrel, and agreed upon a policy. They could not combine to govern by force, and they would not combine to serve a senate which they both despised ; but in spite of the fact that both had been bred in the school of Sulla, they could unite as leaders of the democratic party. They were to be elected consuls for the year 70 B.C., though Pompeius was below the required age, and had never held any magistracy. The Sullan Senate humbly sanctioned the illegality, and then had to see its fortifications quietly demolished. The tribunate was freed from its bonds, and the law-courts were taken from the absolute control of the Senate; two-thirds of the number of every panel of judges were henceforward to be men of equestrian and even lower census, one third only being composed of senators. Even the Senate itself was not left unpunished; the censorship which Sulla had let drop was revived, and the censors who were elected had to deprive more than sixty corrupt senators of their seats, among them the Antonius who had escaped from Cæsar's prosecution. The work was complete; the Sullan constitution was destroyed. What the democratic party had been for years struggling for in vain, was carried out at one stroke by men whose armies were outside the walls of Rome.

We can, of course, only conjecture the motives of these men in performing this singular *volte-face*, which makes the year 70 B.C. a landmark in the history of the period. Nor do we know who were their advisers, if they had any. These questions have been often discussed, and do not specially concern us here. But those who would follow the political life of Cæsar must pause here for a moment and consider how exactly the new policy must have coincided with his feelings and his aims. One is almost tempted to think that he must have had a hand in it. Cicero undoubtedly supported it, and Cicero was intimate with Cæsar, and as yet politically at one with him. The man who, with the approval of the consuls, proposed and carried the bill for reconstructing the tribunals, was one of Cæsar's uncles, L. Aurelius Cotta. Cæsar had most likely already come to know Crassus through the medium of money transactions, and as the ablest of the rising democrats may have been called by him into consultation. But whether or not Cæsar was behind the scenes, the actors certainly played their parts in a way which he must have approved. They pulled down the Sullan constitution, and gave the shattered Marian party another chance. They declined the absolutism that was open to them, and preferred to let the old constitution have a new lease of life. They even disbanded their forces before the year was out, and at the close of it retired into private life without securing to themselves fresh provinces and armies. Thus they seemed to be leaving free space for younger aspirants to power, whether at home or in the provinces; for they subjected the Senate and the magistrates once more to public opinion in the forum or the law-courts, and by letting the military supremacy slip out of their hands they left at least a chance to any young genius in whose way the next great war might come. Had they done otherwise than they did, Cæsar might never have risen to power; the task of solving the great problems of the age might have fallen to men of hardly more than average ability, and wanting in the breadth and generosity of view that was altogether indispensable. As we now see it, these two men seem to have been already marked out by destiny to act as pioneers to make Cæsar's path easier for him; and though one of them was to have his chance of monarchy once more offered him, he was once more to refuse it, and to own his inability to rule the Republic and the army at the same time.

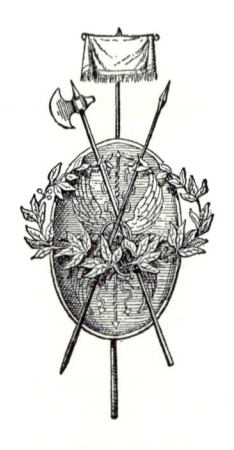

CHAPTER IV.

QUÆSTORSHIP; AND SUPREMACY OF POMPEIUS.

69–66 B.C.

TO a superficial observer, at the close of the year 70 B.C., it might possibly have seemed that the Republic had been given a new lease of life. The constitution was again almost in the same condition as before the Social and Civil wars, and a sense of past errors and dangers might suggest to the leaders of all parties the desirability of trying to work it in harmony for the good of the Empire. No serious danger was imminent at the moment; the Slave war was at an end, and the democratic power in Spain had been crushed. Lucullus seemed on the point of finishing the Mithridatic War. This eminent member of the senatorial party had shown great vigour and military ability, had penetrated victoriously into the heart of Armenia, and yet might be counted on as a loyal servant of the Republic.

And, indeed, for two or three years this promising condition of things continued. The years 69 and 68 B.C. must have been tolerably quiet ones, for our authorities have very little to tell us of them. The Mithridatic War was not, indeed, brought to a close, as might have been expected, and Lucullus began to have difficulties with his own soldiers. The pirates had not been effectually checked, though a senatorial general, the father of the famous Marcus Antonius, had been invested with an extraordinary command with that object. The economic condition of Italy was also alarming; for the long series of wars, ending with the Slave war, and the violent displacement of landholders by Sulla to make room for his own veterans, had destroyed all sense of the security of property, and the material of revolution was to be found everywhere. Still, had a single real statesman appeared on the scene at this moment, or even if the average senator or citizen had been possessed of some honesty and insight, it was not impossible that the government might have been carried on fairly well even under republican forms. But there was no leading statesman of a character suited to raise the whole tone of politics; and there was no general disposition on the part of either Senate or people to make the best of the lull in the storm, to repair damages, or to set the ship on her only true course. So the next few years show her fast drifting in the direction of revolution; and the current that bore her was not a local one, or visible to the eye of the ordinary Roman, but one of world-wide force, whose origin and direction could only be perceived by the highest political intelligence.

It was during these years that Cæsar was quietly learning the business of government, both at home and in the provinces. In the year 70 B.C. he had been still a young and inexperienced man, without even a seat in the Senate, and, as we saw, any part he took in politics had been entirely unofficial. Under Sulla's regulations, the Senate could be entered only through the quæstorship, the lowest step in the ladder of official life; and Cæsar was in 69 B.C. of age to become a candidate for this office. Sulla, whose talent for organisation was great, had raised the number of quæstors to twenty, and had spread their activity over the whole of the minor business of the state; so that whether it fell to a young man's lot to preside over the details of finance, or of the water-supply, or of the city government, or of provincial administration, he had, in spite of obvious temptations to which he might only too easily give way, the best of opportunities for learning the duties of a magistrate. This was a point by which the old Romans had set great store. As in their religion, so in their government, they insisted that things should be done in the traditional and therefore the only right way, and that the aspiring youth should go through a regular course of training in minor offices before he could be a qualified candidate for the highest of all.

It was fortunate for Cæsar that, as a patrician, he was not eligible for the Tribunate of the Plebs. In every way the quæstorship was a better training. The young tribune, when Sulla's restrictions on the office were removed, was again the possessor of a great power; but it was a power which brought with it no regular duties, and entailed no knowledge of the conduct of business. But a quæstor, if he chose to attend to his duties,—and it was hardly possible that he should shirk them entirely,—must at the close of his year have learnt something, from his experience of business, of the elementary grammar of politics. He would have been brought face to face with some one at least of the many difficulties which went to make up the greater problems of the age, and would not be carried at once into the whirlpool of pseudo-legislation and passionate partisanship. The management of the corn-supply and water-supply, *i. e.*, the satisfying of the actual needs of a vast city, or the details of finance at home and in the provinces, would force him to understand how things were actually done, and would invite him to reflect on the discomfort and danger which even a moderate amount of maladministration may cause.

Cæsar was elected quæstor in 69 B.C., and served the office in the following year. It fell to him to begin his acquaintance with government in the province of Further Spain, and thus began his lifelong connection with the peoples of the West. It must have been just before his departure that he lost his wife, the daughter of Cinna, and also his aunt, Julia the

JULIUS CÆSAR.
FROM FARNESE BUST IN THE MUSEUM AT NAPLES.

widow of Marius ; and he seized the opportunity to make an honourable demonstration in favour of the memory of Marius and the almost extinct Marian party. He caused the bust of Marius to be carried in the funeral procession of Julia; a sign that the Sullan *régime* was actually at an end. He delivered funeral orations over both these ladies, which may have been inspired by a genuine glow of affection. But their main object was undoubtedly a political one. The languid and fickle population of the forum was forgetting the names of Marius and Cinna, and needed to be reminded that there had been such men, and that there was still some one who was ready to carry on the tradition of the party they had led.

These funerals over, he proceeded to his province with the proprætor, Antistius Vetus, a man of whose character we know nothing. The province was one which must have been specially interesting to him, for it was there that Sertorius and the remnant of the Marian party had held out so long and triumphantly against a succession of Sullan generals. It is lamentable that we are left almost entirely in the dark as to Cæsar's thoughts and occupations this year. He is said to have been sent, as quæstors sometimes were, on a special judicial circuit, and to have discharged his duties with tact and industry.[*] Both in business of this kind, and in the management of the provincial finance, which was the quæstor's special duty, he must have learnt much of the actual condition of the governed people, and of

---

[*] Vell. ii., 43. Suet., 7.

the nature of the huge task of government which had fallen to the Roman people. But what we should chiefly wish to know, is the impression made on him by what he heard and noticed of the extraordinary work of Sertorius. It must have been this that made him, as he told the Spaniards more than twenty years later,* choose out this province as his own peculiar charge, and work it all the good in his power both now and afterwards in his prætorship. Sertorius is, in fact, the real connecting link between the Gracchi and Cæsar in the history of the democratic party. It was he who first actually put in execution the idea, vaguely conceived perhaps by G. Gracchus, of Romanising and educating the provincials; of treating them as members of an empire, and not merely as tax-paying property. He was probably the first who showed in his dealings with them not only an honest or a generous mind, but a really intelligent humanity. His work—his schools, for example, where the children wore the toga and learnt Greek and Latin—may have been destroyed after his murder and the defeat of his generals, but the memory of them must have long survived, and Cæsar must have talked with many who, like himself, had known the man and felt his generous influence.

Instead of inquiring into the really interesting aspect of this sojourn of Cæsar in the far West, our biographers are content to tell us a story, of which the date is as uncertain as the fact. He is said to have visited the temple of Hercules at Gades, and

---
* Bell. Hisp., 42.

there, while gazing at a statue of Alexander the Great, to have lamented his own indolence, which had brought him to an age at which Alexander had conquered the world, without having achieved a single memorable action. Urged by this reflection, says Suetonius, he repeatedly asked for his "*missio*," or release from provincial duties, and hurried home to Italy.*

On his way home by land, he made his first acquaintance with another people in whom he ever afterwards took a lively interest, and whose provincial governor he was destined to be for no less than ten years. These were the Transpadani, or Gauls living north of the river Po; a lively and vigorous population, living in a land of great beauty and fertility, and beginning already to produce men of eminence, especially in literature. Sulla had fixed the boundary of Italy proper at the Rubicon, a little river flowing from the Apennines into the Adriatic, and had made the whole of the Gallic country watered by the Po into a province; the dwellers on the south side of the river were, however, made full Roman citizens, while to their brethren on the north side was given only the inferior status called the Latin citizenship. This was an anomalous and irrational arrangement, and the Transpadani had ever since been claiming to be reckoned full citizens. Cæsar now went from city to city, exhorting them to further efforts, and promising aid; and is even

---

* The story seems to be brought in by Suetonius to account for Cæsar's premature departure from his province. Plutarch tells it in a different context.

said—with what amount of truth we cannot tell—to have been on the point of urging them to back their demands by forcible means. The consuls, however, so the story runs, delayed the departure of the legions which had been raised for Cilicia, and with the prospect of a military occupation of the country before them, the Transpadani abandoned the project of an uprising. It was not till after twenty years of fruitless effort to get this piece of justice done, that Cæsar himself was able to carry it out, in the first year of his supreme power.

On his return to Rome, which must have taken place about the beginning of 67 B.C.,* Cæsar was drawn at once into closer connection with the man who during the next twenty years was to be his friend, his rival, and his enemy. Pompeius was by this time tired of a quiet life. He had been living in dignified retirement, rarely showing himself in the forum, and when he did so, surrounded with a train of friends, who screened him from the eye and touch of the vulgar. By this means, says Plutarch, he contrived to keep up his reputation, which was purely military. At last, both to him and his friends, it seemed impossible to be idle any longer. There was real and abundant reason for the employment of the ablest soldier of the day. The audacity of the pirates was greater than ever. Lucullus, too, in Asia, had begun to meet with disasters, and was unable, with his troops in a mutinous temper, to cope with the combined forces of the kings of Armenia and Pontus. To make arrangements for a campaign was con-

* Plut., Pomp., 23.

stitutionally the business of the Senate; but the Senate was not likely to recall its faithful and able general, Lucullus, nor to give any single individual the exclusive powers necessary to enable him to act with success against the pirates. But this *laissez-faire* policy, as in the Jugurthine War, was to work the ruin of the senatorial oligarchy.

In this year, 67 B.C., a bill was proposed by a tribune, Gabinius, in the assembly of the plebs, in spite of opposition in the Senate, giving Pompeius exactly that extensive power against the pirates which he himself desired, and which was really necessary if the work was to be done swiftly and completely. He was to have exclusive command for three years over the whole Mediterranean, and over the resources of the provinces and dependent states. For fifty miles inland in every province bordering on these seas—*i. e.*, in the whole Empire— he was to exercise an authority equal to that of the existing provincial governor. He was to have almost unlimited means of raising both fleets and armies, and was to nominate his own staff of twenty-five "legati" (lieutenant-generals), who were all to have the rank of prætor. Nor was this all; for it was quite understood that this was only part of a plan which was to place him at the head of the armies in Asia Minor, superseding the able but now discredited Lucullus. In fact, by another law of Gabinius, Lucullus was recalled, and his command given to one of the consuls of the year, neither of whom, as was well known, was likely to wield it with the requisite ability. Whichever consul it might be, he would only be recognised as keeping the place warm for Pompeius. And when, after a brief and brilliant campaign, showing how much might be done by an able organiser of unlimited resources, Pompeius had rooted out the pirates in every quarter, it was proposed and carried in the next year by another tribune that he should have the Asiatic command in addition to his previous one. Without delay he set about his new work, and started on that wonderful career of conquest and organisation in the East, which not only made him the greatest military figure of that day, but promised to secure for him at last the position of master of the whole civilised world.

We need not enter here into the details of his power and his work. But he who would understand the nature of the power which Cæsar and his successors were eventually to exercise, and the way in which it came into their hands, must needs reflect for a moment on this story of the startling growth of Pompeius; for it was only the political weakness of the man himself that prevented his seizing the opportunity and putting an end to the Senate's incapable rule, as Cæsar did later on.

Let us then notice, in the first place, that it was the paralysis of constitutional government that produced this unconstitutional, or at least unprecedented, supremacy of a single man. What ought to have been done long ago by or through the Senate, the Senate would not do. Perhaps it may be said that they could not do it; for they had no member of their own political views who was likely to carry out these great undertakings with success. But it was quite as obvious that they did not care to do it. The majority were too far gone in indolence and self-seeking to trouble themselves about the pirates or Mithridates; with the former it is said that some of them actually did business. There was, of course, a minority of more vigorous men, including members of the popular party, like Cæsar himself, and Cicero, both of whom supported the appointment of Pompeius; but from the Senate as a body no energetic initiative or real administrative skill was any longer to be looked for.

Secondly, it should be observed that the agents in this legislation were tribunes of the people, and that they laid their bills—or at least the second of them—directly before the sovereign assembly of the plebs. There was the more apparent reason for this, because the vast population of the capital was dependent for its food supply on sea transport, and was even now in some distress owing to the depredations of the pirates. But the point is, that the Senate and its conservative majority were now simply disregarded by Pompeius and his tribunes. It was as if the opposition in the British House of Commons were to succeed in passing a bill in the teeth of the existing government, to recall one Viceroy of India and appoint another with extraordinary powers. Not indeed that the Senate itself refrained from employing a tribune to oppose Pompeius' plans, as they were constitutionally entitled to do. But this man, one Trebellius, was frightened into withdrawing his veto by a threat of deprivation; and when the second bill was produced, in 66 B.C., no tribune ventured to oppose it. No facts could be more significant of the direction in which the tide was running. The tribunate was passing out of the hands both of the Senate and people, and was destined henceforward to be associated with the power of the preponderant military leader of the day; for the next twenty years as his instrument in dealing with affairs at Rome, and afterwards as an essential part of the new military monarchy.

Thirdly, we must notice that the prize aimed at, though in appearance only a great military command, was in reality much more. It was not so much an office, responsible and subordinate to the state, that was created by these bills, but a power independent of the state, and quite incapable of being controlled from Rome save by the erection of another power like it. The hold that the government had on its provincial governors was at no time a strong one; and if any of them had had the will and ability to develop the resources of his province, he might easily have erected his dominion into an independent kingdom. This was, in fact, exactly what Sertorius had done; and the efforts of the Senate to crush Sertorius had only resulted in the development of a new military candidate for power. Now if Sertorius could do so much with a single province and scanty resources, what might not be done by the man who now had at his disposal the military and financial means of at least half the Empire? It was perfectly plain that these two tribunician bills were meant to place in the hands of

Pompeius the destinies of the whole Roman world; and that if he chose to accept the position, nothing could save Rome from another military despotism but a general and an army which should be stronger than he.

Thus in whichever direction an intelligent Roman might look in these eventful years (67, 66 B.C.), the signs of coming autocracy were too plain to be mistaken. The indolence of the Senate; the rehabilitation of the tribunate and of its direct legislative power; the ever-increasing importance of provincial commands, and the enormous preponderance of the military element in the state;—all pointed in the same direction, warning the observer that in some form or other absolutism was a necessity. It may even be said, not without much appearance of truth, that the Republic practically ceased to exist when Pompeius received the Asiatic command. But the Roman was essentially conservative, and clung tenaciously to the old forms. The prestige of the Senate was as great as its action was weak; senatorial government was, in fact, almost a necessary law of the Roman mind. No formal revolution was effected for another twenty years; and even for centuries afterwards the Senate, as the last survivor of republican forms, continued to live and to work side by side with the combined and concentrated powers of the tribune and the provincial governor.

CHAPTER V.

ÆDILESHIP;   CONSPIRACY OF CATILINA.

65–63 B.C.

POMPEIUS left Rome in the spring of 67 B.C., rapidly cleared the seas of piracy, and in the following year superseded Lucullus in the command of the war against Mithridates. He did not return till the beginning of 61 B.C.

At first sight it might seem as though his absence should have cleared the air, and left the political leaders at Rome a freer hand. But the power and the resources voted him, and the unprecedented success with which he used them, made him in reality as formidable to the parties at home as he was to the peoples of the East. He put an end at last to the power of Mithridates, received the submission of Tigranes of Armenia, and added to the

Roman dominion the greater part of the possessions of both these kings. The sphere of Roman influence now for the first time reached the river Euphrates, and the Empire was brought into contact with the great Parthian kingdom beyond it. Asia Minor became wholly Roman, with the exception of some part of the interior, which obedient kinglets were allowed to retain. Syria was made a Roman province. Pompeius took Jerusalem, and added Judæa to Syria. Such a career of conquest had not been known for many generations; the credit of the Roman name seemed everywhere to be restored, and her imperial destiny more amply confirmed than ever.

The man to whom all this was due became at once the leading figure in the world. It became clear that when his career of conquest was over yet another task would devolve on him, if he chose to accept it—the re-organisation of the central government at Rome. It was also obvious that he might perform this task without allying himself with any political party; simply by seizing on the supreme power, and holding it by means of his army. Yet no one could guess what course he would actually take, and no political leader could strike out a path for himself while this remained uncertain. His gathered power overhung the state like an avalanche ready to fall; and in the possible path of an avalanche it is waste of time and labour to build any solid work.

So these years, for Cæsar as for the rest, are years of plotting and intrigue on one side, and of halfhearted government on the other; a false light distorting every object in the political world, and a heavy lowering atmosphere making the actors in it either languid or hysterical. For a young statesman no worse education can be imagined. In these five years many men were ruined for ever as statesmen; both Cicero and Cæsar, now on opposite sides and the two most promising leaders, received serious damage; and Cæsar was only able to repair it because he still had the consulship before him, and because the thunder-cloud in the East suddenly passed away.

He was elected to the curule ædileship—the next above the quæstorship in the series of magistracies—and entered on his office on January 1, 65 B.C. On this very day a plot was to come into action of which there is hardly a doubt that he had at least some knowledge. What the conspirators wanted is tolerably clear; they meant to provide the democracy with an executive power, and with the means of arming itself against Pompeius on his return. But how they intended to do it no one knew for certain then, and no one can ever know. It was said that the consuls were to be assassinated, Crassus to be made Dictator, and Cæsar his Master of the Horse, or chief lieutenant. The plot is not represented as being in the hands of either Cæsar or Crassus, even by the senatorial writers from whom the information comes; the leading figures in it were reckless and ruined men of whom we shall hear more in this chapter, such as Catilina, Autronius, P. Cornelius Sulla, who had belonged to the Sullan party and now led the left wing of the democracy. Such a left wing will always attach itself to a party of advance in revolutionary times; and for its blunders and misdeeds the finer spirits must necessarily be to some extent held responsible. It was fortunate for Cæsar that the plot missed fire; it would have certainly resulted in a bloody struggle, and probably in pure anarchy, neither Senate nor democracy being strong enough to crush its enemy completely. The field would have been open to Pompeius, and he could not have refused the chance.

Cæsar's political connection with Crassus at this time is by no means clear. The two were sailing the same course, and watching Pompeius with the same anxiety; but there could not have been much in common between them, and they were in fact rapidly getting in each other's way. The great moneylender, however, must have been in the main responsible for the enormous expenditure which Cæsar risked in this ædileship and the next three years; and in fact he eventually covered it by satisfying the actual creditors with a sum of eight hundred talents. A large proportion of this sum was spent in this year 65 B.C. in performing the usual functions of an ædile with a lavish profusion such as had never been known before. Cæsar was not content, says Suetonius, with building open temporary porticos in the forum, the comitium, and the basilicas, but extended them even to the Capitol. These acted as booths in a grand fair, as we should say, and the lazy people of Rome had a time of thorough enjoyment and cheap prices. On the 4th of April and following days, being in charge of the games in honour of the Great Mother

(Cybele), he gave this entertainment, and again, apparently, in September at the Roman games. He brought on one occasion—we are not told when—no less than 320 pairs of gladiators into the arena; and it is said that the number would have been even greater had not the Senate interfered in alarm at the introduction into the city of such a formidable force. Amusement was, however, to be combined with instruction; and great were the astonishment and joy of the people when they discovered one morning that the statue of Marius and the trophies of his victories over Jugurtha and the Cimbri, which had been taken down by Sulla's order, were once more in their old position on the Capitol.

All this was meant to secure the favour of the democracy, and gain the position of its leader, which was in fact vacant; for Crassus was never popular, Pompeius was away and fast becoming an object of alarm, and there was no other candidate sufficiently qualified either by his wealth or by connection with the memory of the Marians. But it seems that Cæsar had other and more substantial objects in view. As Mommsen has pointed out, there are signs that he was now entertaining designs of a much more far-reaching character than the attraction of the city populace. It is Suetonius again * who tells us that he put up tribunes to propose for himself an extraordinary military command in Egypt. Pretext was not wanting, for Egypt had been bequeathed to the Romans by its late king, Alexander; and the existing king, Ptolemy Auletes, had been expelled from

* Suet., 11.

his capital by a rebellion in defiance of the Roman government, under whose protection he certainly was. The Senate had taken no steps to make Egypt a Roman province; and it might be reasonably argued that something should now be done. An ex-ædile, with hardly any military experience, was certainly not the right person to hold such a command, and the attempt to obtain it was a failure. But the real meaning of the design cannot be mistaken. Pompeius was at this time in Syria, if not himself at least in the persons of his lieutenants Gabinius and Scaurus; and in the winter of 64 B.C. he followed them, to make the country a Roman province and regulate the affairs of Judæa. Only one territory in the Levant was as yet unoccupied by his forces—viz., the basin of the Nile; but that was strategically the strongest of all, and of inexhaustible fertility; and if it could be seized in advance by the rivals of Pompeius, he would not only be taken in flank, but if he returned to Italy, he would be leaving an enemy strongly intrenched in his rear with a magnificent base of operations to work from. It is tempting to speculate on what would have been the result had this audacious design been carried out; but we must be content to treat it as an indication, and an almost certain one, if the story told by Suetonius be true, that Cæsar was ready to play the part of Sertorius again, and to organise a province as a shelter for the democratic party in case the thunder-cloud in the East should break and Pompeius become a second Sulla.

At the close of the year 64 B.C., on the accession to

office of a new board of tribunes, another attempt was made, but this time by means of legislation instead of by violence, to set up a power at home that should be competent to counteract that of Pompeius, and should place the resources of the state in the hands of the democracy or its leaders. An agrarian bill on a vast scale was promulgated by the tribune Servilius Rullus. The two most startling features of this were: first, the creation of a board of ten to carry out its provisions, each member of which was to be invested with military and judicial powers like those of the consuls and prætors; and secondly, the clauses which entrusted this board with enormous financial resources, to be raised by the public sale of all the territories and property acquired since the year 88 B.C., together with the booty and revenues now in the hands of Pompeius. The bill included, as its immediate object, a huge scheme of colonisation for Italy, on the lines of the Gracchan agrarian bills; in which it is not here necessary to distinguish the good and bad points. But it was really an attack on the weak fortress of senatorial government, in order to turn out its garrison, and occupy and fortify it in the name of the democratic or Marian party against the return of the new Sulla, which was now thought to be imminent.

The bill may also have had another and secondary object—namely, to force the hand of the able and ambitious consul who would come into office on January 1, 63; at any rate it succeeded in doing this, though it succeeded in nothing else. Cicero's great talents, and the courage and skill with which

CICERO.
FROM A BUST NOW IN THE ROYAL GALLERY IN MADRID.
(*Baumeister.*)

he had so far for the most part used them, had made him already a considerable power in Rome; but no one knew for certain to which party he would finally attach himself, or in whose interest he would use his power as consul and his growing influence with the Senate. He had spared no pains of late to gain the good-will of all parties. By connection and tradition he belonged to the Marian party, and had joined it in supporting Pompeius in 67 and 66 B.C.; but the conspiracies in which that party had engaged since then were revolting to his political temperament, and he seems to have believed that Pompeius himself might be kept true to the Republic, and might become the defender of the constitution, if the senatorial position could be held firmly until his return. This position Cicero determined to hold at all cost. On the very first day of his office, he attacked the bill in the Senate and exposed its real intention, and showed plainly that his policy was to convert Pompeius into a pillar of the constitution, and to counteract all democratic plots directed against him. He claimed for himself in this speech that he was the true leader of the people (consul popularis), and declared that this bill was really against their interests.

That Cicero had the people of the capital with him at this moment can hardly be doubted; and he also had a strong following among the voters of the Italian towns. Whether it was his eloquence, or the people's indifference, that caused the bill to be dropped, can only be matter of conjecture; but it was withdrawn at once by its proposer, and the whole scheme fell through. This was Cicero's first and only real victory over Cæsar. His position was greatly strengthened for the moment, and the democrats for some time abstained from further attack. His resources were not to be despised, for he now effected a combination of which the materials were ready to his hand, between the weak senatorial party on the one side, and the powerful body of equites on the other, to which he himself by birth belonged; *i. e.*, between the members of the Senate, their families, clients, etc., and the wealthy men, who, without being in the Senate, had great influence both in Rome and the provinces by reason of their mercantile importance and their position as judges in the law courts. This alliance Cicero always calls " the agreement of the two orders," and for the next few years he relied on it as the only safeguard of the constitution. It was thus the watchword of his policy—a policy purely defensive, destitute of any active regenerative force—to make the whole mass of the respectable and comfortable elements of society into a strong bulwark, with the aid of Pompeius and his own eloquence, against the encroachments of the popular party with its reckless and dangerous left wing.

As it had now become plain that the Senate, backed by Cicero and the equites, would be strong enough to have things their own way this year, Cæsar resorted, probably as a kind of forlorn hope, to a curious device for bringing the memory of Gracchus and Marius once more before the eyes of the people, and for asserting the principles of popular liberty in opposition to the theory of senatorial prerogative.

This was clearly his own contrivance, and not merely a design entrusted to the left wing, to be repudiated if necessary. Wherever he himself is seen in open action at this period, he is always at work on the strict lines of the constitutional theory of the older democratic leaders; in all unconstitutional projects, he is in the background, and his connection with them is uncertain.

At his instance, the tribune Labienus, who had served with him under Servilius against the pirates, and was afterwards to be his ablest general of division in the long Gallic war, now brought an impeachment against a certain obscure old man named Rabirius. The victim was of no importance, but the questions involved in his trial were vital to the constitution. He was popularly believed to be the man who had shed the blood of the tribune Saturninus thirty-seven years before, in violation of the "sacrosanctitas" of the tribunate, and of the first maxim of the Roman constitution that no citizen could be put to death without trial. But this murder had been committed under orders from the consul Marius, and the consul was himself carrying out a decree of the Senate, by which the ordinary constitutional laws and guaranties were suspended, and what was practically a state of war was proclaimed. The Senate had from time to time, in moments of extreme peril, assumed the power to issue such a decree, and until the era of civil disturbance began with Tiberius Gracchus, no one had thought of disputing it. But it is obvious that when once the Senate's authority had come into serious collision with the popular will, such a power might justly be regarded as a weapon of faction, and could no longer be used, as such a resource always should be used, for the protection of the majority of citizens, and with their own tacit sanction. G. Gracchus had therefore reasserted by legislation the fundamental principle of the constitution that no citizen could be put to death without trial; but the senate, trusting to the immense prestige it had inherited from earlier generations, still continued to assert its right, and to exercise it on occasion; as it did in the case of Saturninus. And there was every probability that the Senate of 63 B.C., under the influence of its vigorous consul Cicero, would not hesitate to act as the Senate of 100 B.C. had acted, and to put down democratic violence (if need were) by means of this tremendous engine of government. The consular elections were approaching; it was known that there would be a fierce struggle on the part of the democratic left wing to possess itself of the consulship, and it might be that a crisis would soon arise in which the government would have to use every weapon in their armoury.

It was either in view of such a crisis, or simply for the purpose of asserting the sanctity of the person of the tribune and the leading axiom of Roman constitutional liberty, that Cæsar put up Labienus to indict Saturninus' supposed murderer. By an ancient and obsolete form of procedure, the adoption of which only illustrates the utter absence of straightforward dealing in this most miserable time, Labienus had to nominate two judges to try the accused; and the two he named were Cæsar himself and his relative L. Julius Cæsar, who had been consul in 64 B.C. These two judges convicted Rabirius, and sentenced him to death. This sentence was, however, a mere matter of form; Rabirius could, and of course did, appeal to the people in their centuriate assembly, and with them the ultimate decision constitutionally rested. They would have certainly confirmed the sentence, but that Cicero, using a device as antique and absurd as that of Labienus himself, unfurled the red flag on the Janiculan Hill, which had formerly been the signal that an enemy was at hand and that the assembly must be dissolved. Thus this grotesque trial came to an end without any immediate result. But Cæsar must have felt that it had in some degree answered his purpose. The people had been reminded of the sacred rights and liberties of themselves and their tribunes, and the Senate had been reminded that they and their executive could no longer violate those rights and liberties, even under the pretext of removing an imminent danger to the state, without running a serious risk and exposing themselves to popular vengeance.

It was about this time, in the spring of 63 B.C., that the office of Pontifex Maximus became vacant by the death of old Metellus Pius, and Cæsar at once took steps to secure it for himself. The chances in his favour were small, but the prize was a tempting one. Success would place him at the head of the whole Roman religious system. He would have the Vestal Virgins and the Flamens under his immediate control; he would be the referee in all matters of religious law, public and private; he would have the superintendence of the calendar, then a matter of the utmost weight in Roman politics. It is difficult to realise the great importance of this high priesthood, for we are rarely able to detect it actually at work, and have to be content with what we learn of it in the abstract. We may roughly describe it as uniting for the term of the holder's life, the powers of a magistracy and a priesthood, in a state where religion and politics had always been inextricably intertwined. In an age when the cultivated sceptic adhered no less closely to religious forms than the ignorant masses to their own superstition, its prestige was as great as it had ever been, and the man who held it must be of necessity always before the eyes of the people. This was doubtless exactly what Cæsar wished for. He probably little thought at this time that he would live to make his pontificate the most famous and fruitful in Roman history, by reforming the calendar, and laying a new and solid basis for chronological calculations.

He was eligible, for he had already been for several years one of the college of pontifices, but as the law of election stood, a man so young and so democratic would have no chance against candidates like the venerable conservative leader Catulus, and Cæsar's own old commander in the east, Servilius Isauricus, both of whom were standing. Sulla's law, which placed the election in the hands of the college itself—a law framed expressly to exclude persons of Cæsar's stamp—must be repealed, and

JULIUS CÆSAR (?) AS PONTIFEX MAXIMUS.
FROM THE BUST IN THE MUSEO CHIARAMONTI, IN THE VATICAN.
Engraved by W. B. Closson after a Photograph from the Original.

the choice vested once more in the people. The useful tribune Labienus was again set to work, the law was passed, and on March 6th Cæsar was elected by a large majority. The disgust of Catulus and his friends must have been real and bitter; it had very seldom happened that a man who had not yet reached the prætorship had been raised to the place of highest permanent honor in the state. Cæsar himself seems to have staked everything on it. He is said to have refused a bribe from Catulus, and to have added to his already enormous debts for the purpose of canvass, and it was on the morning of this election that he told his mother that he should return that night successful or leave Rome for ever. Soon after this the people also elected him prætor for the following year.

The latter part of this memorable year was occupied with a last and desperate attempt of the democratic party to possess themselves of the state power while there was yet time to forestall Pompeius. This is the famous conspiracy of Catilina; it was an attack of the left wing on the senatorial position, and the real leaders of the democracy took no open or active part in it. It always has been, and always will be, a debatable question how far Cæsar and Crassus were concerned in it; we incline here to the conclusion that they had some knowledge of it, as of the earlier plot, but inwardly reserved the right to betray it, if it should seem good to them. They might use it, if it were successful, for their own ends; when it promised to be a failure, they probably gave information about it to the government.

The story of this conspiracy more properly belongs to the life of Cicero, who was the chief agent in detecting it, and it shall be told here as briefly as possible. Catilina, who had already been twice defeated, was to stand once more for the consulship, in the interest of all the discontented classes in Italy; of all who had nothing to gain and everything to lose by the advent of another Sulla. Among these were the Sullan veterans, who had a precarious tenure of their allotments, and had never taken kindly to agriculture; the landless folk who had been dispossessed for their benefit; the sons of exiled Marians; the ruined young nobles of the capital, as well as in part its idle proletariate. Then there were the Transpadani, urged, as we have seen, by Cæsar to assert their claim to the full citizenship; and some at least of the Transalpine Gauls, driven by Roman misgovernment into sympathy with any movement of this kind. And as even the vast slave population seems to have been prepared to rise, we may look on the scheme as, in some sense, what we should now call a great uprising of labour against capital; an attempt at social revolution, an attack of the uncomfortable against the wealthy classes, as well as a precautionary movement in view of the alarming power of Pompeius. If Catilina were not elected, then armed violence was to be resorted to; an army was to be formed in Italy, the city, unprotected by police, was to be set on fire, and, in the midst of a general upheaval, all debts were to be cancelled and the most radical programme of democratic speculation to be realised.

Catilina failed; the senatorial party postponed

the election, strained every nerve, and secured the success of their own weak candidates, Silanus and Murena. The conspirators at once began to put their further plans in execution, but they were already known to too many. Information came to Cicero in plenty. He knew that a rebel force was being concentrated at Fæsulæ, in Etruria, under a vigorous soldier, Manlius, and that there was to be a rising in the city itself, which (so it was alleged) was to be burnt down, while his own assassination was contemplated, with that of the other leading optimates. Early in November the Senate unsheathed that dangerous weapon of which Cæsar had tried to rob it by the prosecution of Rabirius, and proclaimed a state of war, giving the consuls unlimited power "for the protection of the state against all harm." Catilina left Rome to join the army at Fæsulæ, leaving the plot in the city in the hands of the other chief conspirators—Lentulus, Cethegus, Gabinius, and Statilius. On December 4th, upon information given by the envoys of the Allobroges, these four men, with one Cæparius, who was believed to have been planning a slave-rising in Apulia, were arrested under the powers conferred on the consuls by the Senate's decree, and given into the custody of eminent senators; Gabinius and Statilius were allotted to Crassus and Cæsar, without doubt in order to compel them either to act with the government or openly to proclaim themselves rebels.

The next morning Cicero summoned the Senate to advise him as to what should be done with the prisoners. He presided as consul and, according to practice, called on the senators in a certain due order to give him their advice. The first who spoke was Silanus, the consul-elect, who proposed that the prisoners should be put to death. Next came the members who had already been consuls, and these all followed the lead of Silanus. Tiberius Nero, the grandfather of the Emperor, suggested that the prisoners should be detained and the question adjourned. Cæsar then rose and delivered a speech which was long remembered, and which fully attained its object of vindicating the democratic view of the constitution, while at the same time it extricated himself from a dilemma. He was in a difficult position; he could not vote for the punishment of death without stultifying his whole career, yet by actually defending the conspirators, or even by asking for lenient treatment, he would be all but acknowledging himself an accomplice.

He began by deprecating the indulgence at such a crisis of any passionate feeling, whether hatred, affection, anger, or pity; previous speakers had tried to rouse such feelings by rhetorical pictures of the horrors of war and rebellion, but their eloquence was quite alien to the matter in hand. The anger so excited would be inevitably interpreted some day as cruelty. " Not that Silanus has proposed death in a cruel spirit ; he is himself a moderate and humane man. And, indeed, for the crimes we have to deal with, no penalty is in itself too cruel ; death at least cannot be so, for it puts an end to the misery of this life and brings no fresh torment in another. But the penalty will be looked on as cruel, simply because it is unconstitutional. It has been over and over again forbidden by express legislation to scourge or kill a citizen without trial. You do not propose to scourge these men, presumably because the law forbids it; why, then, do you propose to put them to death? Both penalties are equally illegal. I must remind you also of the precedent your action will create. Once place such a power as you claim in the hands of a government, and you cannot put a limit on its use ; it may and will be used against good and bad alike, as it was by the Thirty at Athens, and in our own recollection by Sulla. I do not fear this now, or with Cicero as consul ; but I will not answer for the power of the sword in the hands of future consuls. Let us abide by the law, and not seek in a panic to overrule it. My advice is, not, indeed, that we let these men go, and thus increase the resources of Catilina; but that we commit them for life to close custody in the largest Italian towns, securing them by holding over each town the heaviest possible penalty in case they should escape. And I further propose that we pass a decree embodying our opinion that no proposal touching them shall be made henceforward either in senate or assembly ; and that disregard of this decree be treated by the Senate as high treason against the state." *

This is the speech of a statesman, though of a statesman in some embarrassment. The calm cour-

---

* I have given the substance of the speech put into Cæsar's mouth by Sallust in his "Catilina." Plutarch tells us (Cato, 24) that shorthand was used in this debate ; and there is no reason to doubt that in outline Cæsar's speech was much as Sallust has represented it.

tesy and moderate tone of it are quite in keeping with what we know from other sources of Cæsar's style of oratory. In its thorough grasp of the situation, and its adhesion to the issue, it falls in with all we have to learn of the character and intellect of the speaker. He fully accepts the proofs of the conspiracy, and fully acknowledges the guilt of the conspirators, but he declines to vote for a punishment that would be simply remedying one evil by another. As always in this period of his life, it is the memory of the long struggle for constitutional freedom that is uppermost in his mind ; and he applies the principles of his party with force and point to the present issue. The Senate cannot override the laws, without risking the recoil of their lawlessness on their own heads. " We have confidence in the laws," he might have added, had he been speaking in the forum ; " but in these days we have no longer the old confidence in the Senate." There is a covert threat implied, but it is expressed with tact and delicacy. " The more violent your measures," he seems to hint, " the more you tempt the democracy and its leaders to act with violence, in the day, which will surely come, when they will be again in power."

The weak point in the speech is the practical course suggested, as Cicero did not fail to point out. So powerful, however, was Cæsar's appeal to constitutional law, that several leading members of the Senatorial party were strongly affected by it. Cicero's brother Quintus, who, as a prætor-elect, must have followed close on Cæsar, signified his agreement with it. Silanus rose a second time to explain away his former speech, and to state his intention to vote with Tiberius Nero for delay. Cicero thought it time to intervene; he could do this, as consul, at any stage of the debate. He criticised Cæsar's proposal with caution, claiming him cleverly as a loyal supporter of the constitution; and he let it be seen, though without the eloquence of conviction, that he preferred the penalty of death. Such a speech could not efface the impression Cæsar had made, and the minor penalty seemed likely to be carried. Then Cato, in a speech taken down accurately at the time by Cicero's order, and given in abstract by Sallust, warmly urged the Senate not to be weak, but to realise their danger, and save the state, as their fathers had so often saved it. "The prisoners have confessed their guilt," he concluded. "Our law allows the criminal taken in the act to be punished without trial. These men are in the same position, and we have a right to put them to death."

This legal quibble, and the appeal to act like men, decided the wavering Senate, and a majority voted for immediate execution. Cicero and other magistrates escorted the five prisoners through the forum, to the state dungeon under the Capitol, where they were at once strangled. The consul was for the moment the idol of the frightened populace, who had no wish to see fire and sword at work in their city. Cæsar was so unpopular that he barely escaped with his life in returning from the Senate to his own house. This is not the place to argue out the much debated question as to which of the two

was right in the abstract. It is obvious that Cicero
held one view of the constitution, and Cæsar another.
Cicero believed in constitutional practice, and in the
senatorial prerogative which that practice had
created. Cæsar believed in constitutional law, and,
looking at the facts of the case and the history of
the last sixty years, refused to repose confidence in
the use of the senatorial prerogative. The difference
of opinion was not unlike that between Royalist and
Roundhead at the outset of the English Civil War;
prerogative and the necessities of government were
on one side, law and distrust of rulers on the other.
In each case, though much might be said for both
views in an abstract argument, no one who read the
signs of the times intelligently could doubt that
victory would eventually declare for that side which
most accurately represented the feelings and tendencies of the age. In the Italy of that day, as in the
England of Charles I., peace, order, and comfort
were earnestly desired by the great mass of the
people; but neither Senate nor King could harmonise
society under such a strong government as would
secure these blessings. When such a government
did at last arise, it was in each case the government
of a single man, resting on military force, but ex-
pressing in some degree the will and the needs of a
weary and distracted people.

CHAPTER VI.

PRÆTORSHIP, AND FORMATION OF TRIUMVIRATE.
62–60 B.C.

THE conspiracy, quelled in the city by the execution of the ringleaders, was soon brought to an end by the defeat and death of Catilina in Etruria, after a struggle which showed the finer qualities of the man of whom Cicero afterwards allowed that he had "the outlines of virtue without the details."* The two parties were now compelled to turn their attention again more closely to Pompeius, who was expected in Italy at any moment. To resist him was hopeless, if he chose to come as conqueror. All the democratic attempts to set up a military power against him had failed, as we have seen; the senatorial party was equally helpless, for they had

---

* When defending Cælius in 56 B.C. See Pro Cælio, ch. v., 11.

only the one small army in the field which had defeated Catilina. Rome and Italy were entirely at his mercy; this year was the zenith of his greatness, and his cognomen of Magnus, which had been given him half in jest, must have seemed as fully justified as Sulla's surname, " the Fortunate."

When a conqueror approaches whom it is impossible to resist, the natural course is to negotiate with him; where force is wanting, flattery and humility may do something. To this policy both parties now applied themselves in opposition to each other, and to a cynical looker-on the game must have been sufficiently amusing. Cicero wrote more than once to the great man in flattering terms, telling him that his old friends the democrats were now his enemies, and that a great career lay open to him as the champion of the Senate and the constitution; but Cicero mixed up his own praises too much with those of Pompeius, and he had nothing solid to offer him but the "agreement of the orders" (see p. 74). Cæsar and the democrats went about the work with better resources and more substantial diplomacy. On the first day of his prætorship Cæsar proposed to the people that the rebuilding of the great temple on the Capitol (burnt down in 83 B.C.), should be taken from the hands of Catulus, who had been dallying with it for many years, and entrusted to Pompeius. The proposal was not carried, but it served excellently as a declaration of policy. Now, too, Cæsar allied himself with Pompeius' own agent, Metellus Nepos (tribune this year), in an attempt to pass a bill appointing the great general to a military command in Italy, under the pretext of putting out the embers of Catilina's rebellion. This bill was stopped by Cato's veto, and by an outbreak of rioting, which called forth a fresh declaration of martial law from the Senate. Cæsar and Nepos were deprived of their offices under this decree; they refused to obey, and more violence followed. Cæsar, thus finding himself in the position of a riot-leader, to him utterly distasteful, used his influence with the mob to quiet it, and shut himself up in his house; the Senate then cancelled the deprivation, and peace was restored. The affair was not creditable to either party; but Cæsar's main object was gained of letting Pompeius see that their interests were now again the same. A really free-handed policy was as impossible as ever, with a military despotism impending; the only thing to do was to make the best possible terms with Pompeius, and to wait and see what he would do.

When in December Pompeius actually landed at Brundisium, the tension must have been extreme; a very few days might see all political parties annihilated, and Rome at the mercy of a dictator. But the cloud suddenly cleared away. No sooner had he landed than Pompeius dismissed the veteran legions, renounced all idea of a military monarchy, and proceeded slowly to Rome only to claim his triumph, and the natural influence of a mighty conqueror still loyal to the Republic. This act of renunciation, which in these days would excite no wonder, was to the Romans of 62 B.C. a marvel rather of stupidity than of self-denial. There could not have been many, who, looking at the events of the last sixty or seventy years, really believed that the Republic could continue to exist without supporting itself on the strength of one man; and the majority undoubtedly expected something more than a Periclean presidency. Great must have been their amazement when the man to whom the greater prize was offered passed it by, and announced himself content with the lesser.

This lesser prize—the position of leader and guardian without military power—was one which Pompeius might honourably claim; and he now found a warm and flattering supporter in Cicero. But from the first the notion was a hopeless one. Pompeius was far too ignorant and unskilful to exercise a moral influence strong enough to enable him to dispense with an army; Cicero was far too egotistic and clever to keep a lasting hold on a man like Pompeius. And indeed the times were utterly unsuited to any such fanciful combination of empty prestige and versatile talent. The alliance lasted but a few months, and failed because neither Pompeius nor Cicero could see facts as they were. Within a year from Pompeius' return, both he and Cicero were helpless and alone, and the prize was still open to the next man who should claim it.

There was but one man strong and bold enough to do so. From the moment of Pompeius' renunciation, Cæsar saw his way clearly. Ambition entered into his soul; not merely the old ambition of making the best of untoward circumstances, or of resuscitating an almost extinct political party; nor yet the mean ambition of a narrow mind, which seeks power for its own sake; but an irresistible desire to get his hand on the true springs of power, in order to work them for the salvation of the state, on the principles he had inherited from his family and his party. So far he had been groping blindly for them, baffled at all points, and misled by the false light thrown on all objects while Pompeius' intentions were doubtful; now all was clear, the levers were within his reach, consulship and proconsulship were certain, and if all went well, the power would be in his hands to carry out the ideas which the Gracchan democracy had initiated. Power was to him, as to Cromwell, never more than a means to an end; it had to be gained and used only because nothing could be done without it. From this time forward it was the work to be done that wholly filled his mind; and till his death, seventeen years later, he never once slackened in a life of constant and unflagging activity. The month of December, 62 B.C., is indeed the real turning-point in his career, and all the work that has made his name so mighty was done in the years that followed.

Of Cæsar's duties as prætor, which would consist chiefly in the discharge of judicial business, we have no information. But every prætor, when his year of office was over, became a proprætor, and the governor of a province. The province which had fallen to Cæsar was the same in which he had served as quæstor, viz., Further Spain; it had, as we have seen, a special attraction for a man who revered the memory and the great ideas of Sertorius, and he had probably used his influence in the Senate to secure it for himself. There were more tempting provinces to be had, and nearer home; but we may conjecture that so long as Pompeius' intentions were doubtful, the idea in Cæsar's mind was to follow in Sertorius' footsteps, and make once more of this distant territory a civilised Roman home for the oppressed democracy. When the impending absolutism was renounced, such a plan was no longer necessary; it was, in fact, rather inconvenient than otherwise to have to go so far from home at a time when the utmost vigilance was necessary to prevent Pompeius from falling under the influence of the senatorial party and Cicero. So we find Cæsar postponing his departure for some time in the spring of 61 B.C.; and this delay was caused not only by his desire to keep his eye on Pompeius, or by difficulties with his creditors,* but by a startling event in which he was himself involved, and which eventually proved to be a piece of good fortune for himself and his party.

On the night of December 5, 62 B.C., there had been, as usual, a meeting of matrons in the house of the Pontifex Maximus, to celebrate the mysteries of an ancient Roman agricultural deity, usually called the Good Goddess. Only women were admitted, and Cæsar himself was of course absent. His mother Aurelia, and his wife Pompeia, were to receive the worshippers; the elder lady, if Plutarch is right, being at this time in some anxiety as to the conduct of the younger. Her fears were justified; for in the dead of night a suspected lover, a young quæstor-elect named Publius Clodius, was detected by a servant-maid disguised in woman's dress, and was

---

* Suet., 19.

JULIUS CÆSAR.
ENLARGED FROM GEM IN BRITISH MUSEUM.

JULIUS CÆSAR.
FROM COIN IN BRITISH MUSEUM.

identified and detained by Aurelia. Such sacrilege was a serious crime, even in the eyes of educated sceptics; it was committed in the house of the head of the State-system of religion, and his wife was now an object of grave suspicion. A people who believed so profoundly in good and bad omens as the Romans did, could not but be greatly disturbed ; and Cæsar at once divorced Pompeia, saying that Cæsar's wife ought not to be even so much as suspected.

The trial of Clodius, a few weeks later, raised a commotion which well illustrates the petty nature of party spirit at the time, but does not specially concern us here. After much squabbling as to the method of empanelling the special jury (for there was no standing court for cases of sacrilege), Clodius was finally acquitted, in spite of the clearest evidence, by the usual method of bribing the judges. Cicero appeared as a witness for the prosecution, and gained the lasting enmity of the accused. Cæsar was also called, and is said to have denied any certain knowledge of the truth of the matter, but to have pointed to his divorce of Pompeia as an indication of his suspicions. The result, according to Cicero, was a complete defeat for the senatorial party, arising from their own weakness and want of union, and a severe blow to the "agreement of the orders," since they could not act together honestly even as judges without betraying the best public interests for gold. Pompeius, too, had arrived in Rome during the excitement, and was a witness, himself helpless, of the helplessness of Cicero and the Senate.

Cæsar might now depart for Spain without any serious anxiety as to an alliance between Pompeius and his own political opponents. The two men must have met frequently in the early months of this year, and the younger had probably taken a more accurate measure of his future rival's calibre than had been possible before. Pompeius, for those who knew him well, was an amiable and engaging man, honest and simple even to awkwardness ; and Cæsar, with his courteous and conciliating manner, his genuine admiration for the other's great career, and his own splendid gifts and high birth, was surely a much more welcome ally than Cicero, who was always tutoring Pompeius to his face, and laughing at him behind his back. Before Cæsar left Rome, the two had no doubt already made some way in the direction of friendship, or at least of mutual regard. With Crassus, whose mind, unlike his own, was small enough to harbour jealousy of Pompeius, he was also on good terms ; and it was now that he borrowed from him the enormous sum of eight hundred talents, in order to satisfy his creditors before leaving Italy.

Of his work in Spain we only have a meagre account, contained in two short chapters of Dio Cassius' history. Here certainly he first seriously addressed himself to the art of war. War, we are told, was not forced on him in the province ; but he undertook two campaigns against the hill tribes of the far West, which may have been making raids on the civilised Romans and their subjects in the valleys of the Tagus and Guadalquiver. The first field of operations was the south of what is now

Portugal ; the second was the mountain tract of Galicia, where his army seems to have penetrated to the Atlantic. In each case the land force was assisted by a fleet. He was everywhere successful, and he must have learnt many lessons in the art of dealing with barbarian enemies, and of coping with the difficulties of warfare in a country as yet almost entirely unknown.

Of his civil government we get one or two valuable glimpses. The provincials were, as was usual, deep in debt ; they had had to support large Roman armies for several years in the Sertorian wars, as well as to pay their usual tribute. Cæsar ordered each debtor to pay two thirds of his income to the creditors, and forbade the latter to seize on the land or capital of the debtors ; thus fairly satisfying the one, and saving for the other such little property as he possessed. We do not know how the expedient answered ; but it would seem to have been suggested by the same rare combination of practical justice and good-will which was brought to bear, many years later, on the economical troubles of Italy.

In the case of one particular city we incidentally get a glimpse of Cæsar's work from a later speech of Cicero's. The ancient Phœnician city of Gades (now Cadiz) had been, ever since the destruction of Carthage, the most flourishing port of the western seas. It was one of those towns, like Massilia, which were nominally free, and had entered into alliance with Rome. It had its own local government, and Cæsar could not legally interfere with it except within the terms of its treaty, and by express invitation. It happened that a wealthy inhabitant of Gades, who had served with distinction in the Roman armies in the Sertorian war, had been made a Roman citizen by Pompeius; this man had taken up his residence in Rome when the war came to an end, and had there made the acquaintance of Cæsar, and of most of the leading men of the time. Lucius Cornelius Balbus, as he had been called since his admission to the Roman citizenship, had now returned to his native country as Cæsar's *præfectus fabrum* (chief of engineers), and it was through his influence with the people of Gades that his chief was called in to reform their laws and settle their internal disputes. We are unluckily in the dark as to the details of his reforms. Cicero, when defending Balbus in 55 B.C., in an attack brought against the validity of his enfranchisement, had no need to refer to them except in general terms. But from the language he uses, and from what we know of the extraordinary prosperity of the city under Augustus, we may safely conclude that Cæsar and Balbus did their work at once thoroughly and judiciously. The laws, Cicero says, were revised, quarrels were settled, certain barbarian practices were abolished, and honours and privileges conferred on the citizens. Twelve years later they received the full Roman franchise at the hands of Cæsar; a singular token not only of his regard for themselves and Balbus, but of the breadth of his policy towards provincials, and of his faithfulness to the principles of the democratic party.

The man who was thus so loyal to the best interests of his native city remained no less loyal to his friend and commander. From this time to the day of Cæsar's death, he acted as his confidential secretary and agent, and, so far as we know, there never was a moment's break in their friendship. Balbus must have been a man of singularly happy temperament. He knew every one, and he quarrelled with no one. He was ready to do any amount of work, to travel any distance, for the man to whom he had so closely attached himself, and who reposed in him such unlimited confidence. He inherited an excellent faculty for business from his Phœnician ancestors, and he probably understood the art of war thoroughly, especially in the department of mechanics and engineering. How much Cæsar owed to him in military matters we cannot conjecture; but we have certain evidence of his invaluable services in delicate negotiations, and in the management of property; and it is likely enough that to his cool head and supple disposition Cæsar was indebted for something at least of that singular facility for surmounting difficulties which was due no doubt in the first place to his own firm will. Such a man as Balbus was of course the object of much envy and ill-will, and doubtless he looked after his own interests as well as those of Cæsar; but he gained and deserved his reward for faithful service, for he eventually rose, though not in Cæsar's lifetime, to be prætor and consul, and was the first enfranchised foreigner who attained to the highest magistracy.

Cæsar must have been hard at work in the spring of 60 B.C., to carry out a campaign in Galicia, wind up the affairs of his government, and travel back to

Rome before the consular election, which took place usually in the summer. He was, however, in time; but not in time to combine the triumph which the Senate had voted him with the personal canvass in the city which was at this time necessary for a candidate. He could not legally pass within the walls without giving up his *imperium* or military command, with his lictors and insignia ; and without these no triumph was possible. He was placed in a dilemma, and one which was evidently carefully prepared for him by his opponents ; either he must submit to be disqualified as a candidate, or he must give up the triumph. Unhesitatingly he chose the latter alternative, and showed his enemies at once what stuff he was made of. There were two other candidates: Bibulus, his old colleague and opponent as ædile and prætor, now the representative of the ultra-senatorial party ; and Lucceius, a man of wealth and ability, with whom, though he was a moderate optimate, Cæsar had formed an agreement for common action and common expenditure before he left Italy for Spain. Cæsar was himself elected, but the Senate was strong enough to bring in Bibulus, who is said to have spent as much money on the election as the other two together.

There had never been any real doubt about this result. The ultra-senatorial party, by a suicidal policy of spitefulness, had made Cæsar's election more certain than that of their own candidate. They had checked and worried Pompeius by refusing to ratify his arrangements in the East, by discouraging his expectation of a second consulship, by criticising and opposing his plans for rewarding his veterans by allotments of lands in Italy; and thus they deliberately drove him once more into the arms of Cæsar and the democracy. Bitterly must he have rued the day when he gave up his army in loyalty to such a set of meddling ingrates; and in sore vexation of spirit, he brought all his influence to bear in Cæsar's favour. And another powerful interest was exerted unexpectedly on his behalf— that of the equites, including the whole of the *publicani*, or farmers of the taxes. The agreement of the orders had lately gone quite to pieces, and with it all Cicero's hopes of a really strong conservative party. We have already seen that in his opinion the acquittal of Clodius had done much to damage this highly valued alliance; since then war had openly broken out between the two orders. The *publicani* had demanded a reduction of their contract for the revenue due from the province of Asia; the Senate, urged by Cato, refused it. " The equites have declared war against the Senate," wrote Cicero, sadly. They were disgracefully wrong, he tells us, and Cato unquestionably right; but in this case rectitude should be sacrificed to keep alive the indispensable alliance. Cato destroyed it in the cause of rectitude; and the equites transferred their support to the Senate's political enemies.

So Cæsar was elected without difficulty, and now had only to secure his position and strengthen his influence by what was to him the thoroughly congenial task of conciliation. The springs of action were now under his hands, and the democracy had at last a consul who would not hesitate to use them. But every statesman who pursues a daring policy in a weak and selfish age must expect to be hampered and opposed at every step; and he must prepare not only for vexatious opposition, but for hatred and treachery. Cæsar knew indeed that he could not altogether escape either opposition or hatred; but he set himself to defeat the one and neutralise the other by recruiting his own political forces with every possible interest and influence that could be brought into any kind of an alliance with him. And he did succeed in bringing together a combination of forces which for the time constituted a really strong government; a combination which left its mark for ever on the history of Rome and of the world.

First, it was absolutely essential that he should have on his side the immense reputation and the dormant military strength of Pompeius. It was not so difficult to achieve this end; for, as we have seen, Pompeius had been slighted and irritated by the senatorial party, and was at this moment in sore need of help to carry out his promises to his veterans and to get the sanction of the Senate for his arrangements in the East. Under the circumstances, then, his best course was clearly to swallow all jealous feeling, and to ally himself with the only man who was likely to help him out of his difficulties; whether he looked further ahead, or realised in any sense what this coalition might result in, we cannot even conjecture. But we may be sure that he needed delicate management in such a negotiation ; and it was fortunate for both parties in it that they had a common friend and a faithful servant in the patient and astute Balbus.

A much harder task lay before Cæsar in his dealings with the other personage who was indispensable to him. He must still have been deep in debt to Crassus, and might yet need both his purse and his goodwill. He had been for many years in close political alliance with him, but it was unlucky that one chief object of that alliance had been to defeat the supposed ends of Pompeius. For Cæsar it was easy enough to combine with the old enemy ; here his interest and his generous temper were entirely at one. But Crassus had never really been on cordial terms with Pompeius, and his disposition seems to have been a narrow if not a mean one. Still, he too was looking for a second consulship, and dreaming of military commands which should enable him to outdo even the mighty deeds of his rival; and rather than fall out of the race altogether, he would consent to a second reconciliation. It was possible that he and Pompeius might act in some sort of harmony, with the courteous Cæsar at hand to charm away their rising irritation.

There was one other person whom it was most desirable not to have as an antagonist, and whose adhesion to the new power would give it the aid of a brilliant intellect and an influence not to be despised. That Cicero, even in a minority, was a real power in the Senate, is beyond all question. He was no less powerful in the law-courts ; and then his circle of acquaintance was large and influential, and his fame widely spread in the country towns of Italy. His policy of the agreement of the orders had indeed broken down of late, but he was clever enough to repair the damage on the first chance that offered. Their old friendship, and Cicero's former connection with the anti-Sullan party, made it quite natural for Cæsar to ask for his support ; and the invaluable Balbus was entrusted with the message. Cicero tells Atticus * that Balbus had been with him, and had promised that Cæsar in his consulship would consult him equally with Pompeius, and would undertake that Crassus should not be a difficulty in the way of either. But Cicero had his suspicions that these men would not abide by those traditions of the constitution which had become sacred to him since his consulship ; he would not compromise himself, and this attempt at negotiation failed.

There was no other man of mark strong enough to be an object of solicitude, for Cato was of course hopeless. So the coalition was composed of the three, Cæsar, Pompeius, and Crassus. There is nothing, except the evidence of much later writers, to show that it was a conspiracy to override the constitution. It was at first in fact no more than the attempt of a strong man, just succeeding to the highest magistracy, to turn that magistracy to thoroughly good account by uniting with his own interests those of the most influential persons in the state. It was an expedient to prevent useless squabbling, waste of time, and obstruction, when

* Ad Att., ii., 2.

matters of vital importance had to be settled; to secure, as we should say, a working majority for a vigorous democratic policy. Naturally enough, when that policy took a definite shape in the following year, it suffered from the very nature of a coalition, as well as from the bitter opposition brought against it; and the bitterness of its enemies transformed the coalition itself from an honourable union into the semblance of a three-headed tyranny. There were of course personal ambitions in the minds of each of the three; there were provinces to be ruled, and armies to be commanded. But such prospects were equally before every Roman who was mounting the ladder of political fame; and it cannot be proved that either Cæsar, Pompeius, or Crassus, any more than the rest, seriously thought as yet of using such power to destroy an ancient constitution.

THREE-HEADED TYRRANY

CHAPTER VII.

CÆSAR'S FIRST CONSULSHIP.

59 B.C.

WE have now to see how Cæsar used the opportunity for which he had been looking so long. So far he has had no fair chance of showing his real character as a statesman; but in this year, 59 B.C., we watch his every act with the utmost interest, and with the feeling that our judgment of the rest of his great career must inevitably be influenced by the result of our examination. We have to determine whether he was true to his own political principles, as well as to his political allies; whether he did his best to overcome difficulties wisely; whether he yielded to the obvious temptation of imitating Marius and Cinna, the last democratic holders of power, and of making himself and his party secure by measures of violence.

Appian and Dio Cassius are agreed that he began his work with studied moderation. He treated the Senate with marked respect; he appealed in its presence to his colleague Bibulus to act in harmony with him for the public interest; and he revived an old practice which gave to Bibulus, as the senior consul, the advantage of being preceded by his lictors during the first month of the year, while he himself had only a single servant to go before him, his lictors following behind. All this we may interpret, with Appian, if we please, as a piece of fine acting; but it is more reasonable to suppose that Cæsar was quite in earnest, though probably without much hope of success. The history of his party supplied him with an admirable model for such a policy. Gaius Gracchus was by far the ablest leader that party had as yet produced; and there is such a striking resemblance between his use of power and Cæsar's that we are strongly tempted to believe that it was not wholly accidental. Gracchus worked by using his unrivalled personal charm, by his eloquence, by his indefatigable industry; these were qualities which Cæsar too possessed, and it is only natural to suppose that he was ready to make the most of them.

His first act was democratic in its tendency, but in itself reasonable and suited to the needs of the age. Hitherto the proceedings of the Senate had been strictly private; more so by far than those of the English Houses of Parliament before the authorised publication of debates. Any one who chose might publish his own speeches, and a record of debate was kept in the Senate's archives; but all that the outside world knew of the proceedings of the assembly which had so long ruled their destinies was derived from informal harangues of the senators in the forum, or from the publication of the senatorial decrees which had been passed. Through Cæsar's influence, a summary of each debate, containing a list of the various proposals made, was now exposed to view in the forum, and could be copied by any one who wished to do so. This must have been a great convenience to absentees in the provinces, who could now get accurate information as to what was doing at home; but it had more important results. It was part of a deliberate attempt to make the Senate feel itself at once more representative and more responsible. Neither Cæsar nor any other Roman statesman ever thought of doing without the Senate; but the Senate, if it were really to do good work in an imperial state, must be felt, understood, and criticised. It must be in touch with the worldwide interests over which it ought to watch. It must cease to be the mere council of a city-state, and must begin to recognise the fact that the eyes of the whole civilised world are fixed upon it.

But this was only a preliminary step. The first piece of real work to be done was to fulfil the engagement entered into with Pompeius, and to make some settlement for his veterans, who had now been hanging about the capital for quite two years, and increasing the number of those who lived on the public distribution of cheap corn. It is not easy for us to realise the economical difficulties which had arisen since these great armies of professional soldiers

JULIUS CÆSAR.
FROM BUST NUMBERED 107 IN THE VATICAN MUSEUM, ROME.

had taken the place of the simple citizen soldiery of the older Roman system. That system had been proved quite unequal to the needs of an imperial state. The Roman and Italian citizen could not endure prolonged service in the provinces. Discipline had broken down, defeat and even surrender were becoming ominously frequent, when Marius revolutionised the whole recruiting system, and began to pick up soldiers wherever he could lay hands on them, disdaining neither the very poorest Italians, nor even freedmen and slaves, and welcoming the natives of the provinces, who had already for some time been serving in certain special capacities. The result was a vast improvement both in discipline and organisation, and these again produced a marked rise in the standard of generalship and in the whole art of war. But every reform creates some new difficulty of adjustment; and long before Cæsar's consulship the formidable question had arisen, what was to be done with the disbanded warriors from the long wars, who had little or nothing to live upon but the booty they rapidly squandered, and who had lost the taste for any occupation they might ever have had? These were not men like Cromwell's Ironsides, stout yeomen or labourers, whom a strong sense of duty to God and man could compel to lay down their arms and return to their fields when the word was given them that their work was done. The difficulty was indeed a most serious one, and would in a healthy state have received most earnest attention from the government. But the Roman state was no longer a healthy one, and the fact that each great general had been left to shift for himself and his veterans as he best could, is one of the most striking proofs of the utter incapacity of the Senate to administer the business of a vast empire. Marius had tried to combine with a tribune for the passing of an agrarian law which should settle his soldiers on the land. Sulla had imitated the principle, but with his usual high-handedness had turned a peaceful population out of their homesteads in order to make room for his own veterans, thus remedying one evil by another. Already the bad effects of such expedients had been felt in the appearance of an idle and discontented population, ready to serve under a Lepidus or a Catilina, or to find its way back to the overcrowded city, and swell the numbers of dangerous banditti who thronged its unprotected streets. And yet here was another army to be disposed of somehow, and there seemed to be no other way of dealing with it than by trying once more to find sufficient land to be distributed to the men in allotments.

Here was really the difficulty. There was no longer any land available in Italy without disturbing private rights, except one valuable public estate in Campania, and one or two other smaller properties These public lands were leased to tenants, and unless these tenants were to be ejected no use could be made of the land for distribution. It had already been proposed to eject them in the bill of Rullus, four years before this; and Cicero then argued with force that such a course would be only to get rid of good cultivators in order to put in men who were quite unused to agriculture. It had again been in part proposed in 60 B.C., in the bill drawn up for Pompeius by a tribune Flavius; and again Cicero had opposed himself to the policy of using the little remaining public land for allotments. If this, however, were not done, the only way in which the state could procure land was by buying it from private owners.

This was what Cæsar now proposed to do. The purchase-money was not difficult to find, for the incomings from Pompeius' conquests in the East had greatly enriched the treasury. Dio Cassius states distinctly that the Campanian estate was excluded from the action of the bill, and Cicero's letters show no anxiety about this property until the end of April. The general object of the measure, as it was first introduced early in the year, must have been to invite private owners to sell their lands in good time, and for the sum at which they were valued in the registers of the censors. The bill was to be carried out by a commission of twenty, including Pompeius and Crassus, who were also to be members of an inner executive of five, charged with general supervision. From this commission Cæsar expressly excluded himself.

But the irreconcilables in the Senate would simply have nothing to say to the bill. It was to be resisted simply because it was an agrarian bill, and the work of a democratic consul. Cato himself said that he had no objection to the bill in itself; but he obstructed it by speaking for hour after hour, until Cæsar, using a method which has been found necessary of late years in coping with such tactics, ordered him into arrest, releasing him, however, in deference to a demonstration on the part of the Senate. It became at once obvious that it would be hopeless to get the bill through the Senate in the ordinary course; either it must be abandoned altogether, or Cæsar must fall back on the democratic method of presenting it to the people without the senatorial authorisation which was constitutionally proper in practice.

This was a course which was perfectly legal, and it had often been resorted to since Tiberius Gracchus first found it impossible for a reformer to work with the Senate. But it was an ominous act to dispense with the sanction of the collective wisdom of the Roman world, and nothing could have justified it but the absolute impossibility of getting anything done without it. To put complicated bills before a vast assembly of voters, without any discussion of details except from the orator's platform in the forum, was a deplorable method of legislation, and had already had most mischievous results. But if the council, whose constitutional business is to discuss these details, entirely refuses to play its part, it simply drives the legislator to dispense with it. Cæsar now learnt, if he had not learnt it before, that the Senate was not willing to deliberate, nor the sovereign people fit to legislate. Some new way must eventually be found to get the work of the Empire done; but for the present he had no choice but to face the facts as they were and make the best of them. If the people refused the bill, there was an end of the matter; but to the people it must certainly go.

In the form in which it was presented to the people, it contained a clause compelling the senators and the candidates for office in the ensuing elections to swear to observe its provisions. This clause is most significant of the political temper of the age. It was well known that in one way or other the bill would be repealed next year; probably by means of a senatorial prerogative, by which obnoxious measures had from time to time been declared invalid. Cæsar was only attempting by this provision to secure his law from such treatment; and if the method seems to us in these days a harsh one, we must remember that he had to deal with men who, representing only themselves, had no intention of abiding by a law to which they had not consented. They had declared open war against it, and for the consequences they alone were responsible.

The bill was now brought before the assembly of the people after preliminary informal meetings, in one of which Cæsar appealed to Pompeius to support it against violence, if necessary, by the arms of his veterans; showing that his anger was roused, his will firm, and his mind made up not to be defeated by any methods but legitimate rejection. There was reason both for the anger and obstinacy of a resolute and masterful spirit; and the Senate now learnt that they had to do with a man who would no longer bear with constitutional trifling and unreasoning obstruction. They used every rusty weapon in their armoury. A tribune was as usual found to exercise his veto; it was simply disregarded. Bibulus used the power of summary interference which each consul could bring to bear on the actions of the other; but Pompeius' old soldiers drove him from the forum. He then announced his intention to "watch the heavens" on every day of assembly for the rest of the year, and thus stop all legislation; but he might as well have tried to stop the tide. Finally, on the day after the passing of the bill, he summoned the Senate and proposed to declare it null and void; but the senators were by this time fairly frightened and would give him no support. He then shut himself up in his house and sulked there for the remaining eight months of the year like an angry infant, showing us beyond all doubt the manner of man he was.

Cæsar troubled himself no more about the Senate and its irrational use of constitutional methods of obstruction; the rest of his laws were taken directly to the people. We may here follow his example and leave Bibulus and his friends for the rest of the year, in the assurance that, however much a constitutional lawyer might be hurt by Cæsar's conduct, every man whose mental vision could take in the necessities of the Empire, as well as the history of the city, must have felt that some such rigorous dealing was necessary. We will simply note that those who in this year so obstinately stood in Cæsar's way are the very men of whose narrowness and selfishness even Cicero so often and bitterly complains in his letters of the next few years. They were the men whose jealousy eventually drove the most brilliant advocate of constitutionalism to ally himself with their enemies, thus bringing on him a charge of time-serving, which has done much to damage an honourable name. As they did their best in 56 B.C. to annoy their best friend, so in 59 B.C. they did all they could to destroy their most rational opponent; and the result was only to make Cæsar absolute master of the situation, so that the joke-loving Roman mob used to speak of the consuls of the year as Julius and Cæsar, instead of Cæsar and Bibulus.

At one of the later stages in the progress of the bill, when the Senate's inexorable hostility had been declared, or more probably by a new bill altogether, the Campanian land, which had been originally left untouched, was now finally dealt with. Combined with the distribution of this rich territory was another scheme which had for years been a part of the policy of the Marian party, and was in every way just and reasonable. The famous town of Capua, the centre of this fertile land, had been punished for its disloyalty in the war with Hannibal by the loss of its territory, and of its privilege of local self-government, and had ever since been ruled by an officer appointed yearly by the Roman Senate. Every attempt to make it a "colonia," *i. e.*, to people it with Roman citizens, and to give it municipal rights, had been a failure. Cæsar now took up the plan, and carried it through successfully.

Though this bill was quite of a piece with Cæsar's political views, the fierce battle he had fought for it had been undertaken immediately in the interest of Pompeius. He still had engagements to fulfil of the same kind, and he set about them now with his hands free. We find it hard to believe in these days that the Senate, to whom by wise constitutional practice all such business had been for centuries entrusted, had for two years refused to ratify or even to modify the long list of regulations by which Pompeius had sought to place the results of his vast conquests in the East on a permanent and satisfactory basis. Frontiers had been laid down, kings received into vassalage, towns punished or privileged, new cities founded, tributes imposed ; but not one of these arrangements had any legal force until the Senate should have taken them in hand. The person chiefly to blame seems to have been Lucullus, who was jealous of his rival's successes. Cicero was also to blame for not using his senatorial influence to help his friend and hero ; but Cicero was never greatly interested in foreign or provincial affairs. Pompeius was himself to blame ; for the immense prestige he enjoyed at the moment of his return should have enabled him to insist on the great work of his life being completed. And it was a just and wholesome retribution, when Cæsar, strong just where Pompeius was weak, again passed the Senate by, and brought the necessary measures before the people. Thus, though it is with the West that Cæsar's name will be always indissolubly linked, it needed his force of will to put the coping stone on his great rival's work in the East.

He had now fulfilled his promises to Pompeius, who was doubtless duly grateful. The friendship which had begun two years before was now cemented by the marriage of the elder man with the daughter of the younger, at this time about twenty-two years old, and gifted with every charm. Julia is said to have been a faithful wife, and to have won the passionate affection of her husband. Her father, too, was devoted to her; and there can be no doubt that for the few remaining years of her short life she found a noble vocation in harmonising, whether consciously or not, the views and interests of the two most powerful men then living. Few women in history have had a weightier part to play; few have in their death been so bitterly and universally lamented.

Cæsar had next to undertake a task, which, if we understand him rightly, could hardly have been a grateful one. It seems likely that in order to secure the adhesion of Crassus to the triple league, he had been obliged to make a promise which was not, so far as we know, in itself an honourable one, though it is characteristic enough of the political morals of the age. The tax-farmers of the province of Asia had in 61 B.C. (see p. 99) applied for a reduction of their contract, at Crassus' instigation; the great capitalist probably had some personal reason for this step, and continued to urge their demand. Cicero himself had warmly supported it in the Senate, though he privately told Atticus that it was a shameful one.* Cato, the financier of the day, and

---

* We have no positive knowledge of the justice or injustice of this demand; Cicero was often hasty and inaccurate in his conclusions. But in this case, as he was the representative of the equestrian order, and was writing in confidence to one of its most important members, his opinion may be regarded as free from bias, and it falls in with what else we know of the public morality of the *publicani*. See Cic., Ad Att., i., 19, and ii., 1.

the enemy of all injustice, had opposed it with all his vehemence. It was not carried, and the failure, as we saw, had produced a breach between the Senate and equites,—a fatal blow to Cicero's " agreement of the orders." Cæsar now laid a bill before the people, by which the contract was reduced by one third ; a masterly piece of policy, for it not only put the final touch to the discord which Cato's severity had begun, but it brought the whole mercantile class with one stroke over to the side of the triumvirs. Here, however, we may prefer to side with Cato and his ideal standard of right and wrong, rather than with either Cicero or Cæsar, who yielded to political exigencies. Every practical statesman has indeed occasionally to consent to that which he cannot approve ; his life is spent rather in choosing between evils, than in pursuing the ideal good. But actively to advocate what you know to be wrong, even though it seem necessary to a policy which you believe to be the true one, is not to be defended by any appeal to expediency ; and this is exactly what the two ablest men of the time were each of them ready to do, though for different objects.

This blot in Cæsar's work was in some degree made up for by another law of far wider scope, which remained on the statute-book for centuries. This was the famous law against official extortion in the provinces.

It was by no means the first of its kind. At least five others had been passed during the preceding ninety years ; and since 149 B.C., a standing commission had been at work on the trial of offences under these laws. But extortion had become a habit and almost a necessity with the governors of provinces; they spent so much on bribery in their efforts to rise to high office, that they looked on their propraetorship or proconsulship as a perfectly fair chance of recouping themselves. The two great evils of the day worked together—corruption at home, and cruelty in the provinces; and there was a continual drain on the exhausted provincials to supply the exorbitant demands of the greedy Roman voter. And it was not only the governor himself who was guilty; with him went a numerous staff, all eager to be let loose on the province. No legislation seemed capable of putting a check on an evil which the legislators themselves did their best to encourage; there was hardly a Roman who was not interested in keeping it up, hardly a public man who had not profited by it, or who did not expect one day to do so. The whole spirit of government was bad, as well as the system; not only were there no adequate checks on the governors, but there was no real desire to impose any. Nothing but a wholly new system, which should make it the *interest* of rulers to rule justly, could have the least permanent effect in saving from ruin either the resources of the provinces, or the morality of the Roman people.

At a later time Cæsar was able to carry into execution the dimly conceived projects of the democratic party, by inventing such a system and working it in a new spirit; as yet his contribution could only be another law, though it was one the excellence of which won strong praise even from Cicero himself.* It extended the action of previous laws, or in other words the jurisdiction of the existing court for cases of provincial extortion, in respect not only of the definition of crime, but of the persons liable, and of the penalties that could be imposed. The resources of the bad provincial governor in the way of extortion were boundless, as we know from Cicero's Verrine orations. This law seems to have covered all that had so far been in use; illegal taxes and tolls, the selling of privileges, the acceptance of presents except within narrow limits, and the use of Roman soldiery (for a " consideration ") to help in the recovery of debts. The whole of the retinue, as well as the governor, were made liable, the equites alone being for the present excepted, as had always been the case. The penalties, which originally had been of the nature rather of damages than punishment, were now made very serious: restitution to four times the amount of the value extorted, which Sulla had imposed, was now the mildest of them. *Intestabilitas*, or deprivation of power to bequeath property by will, together with expulsion from the Senate, followed on conviction as a matter of course; exile was reserved for very serious cases.

The legislation that has been thus briefly sketched was a fair allowance for one year, great part of which had been occupied by overcoming obstinate and irrational obstruction; and it would probably have been impossible to accomplish even so much as this, if agrarian laws and laws against extortion had not

---

* Pro Sest., 64.

frequently been framed before, making the work of the later legislator and draughtsman a comparatively easy one. As the year wore on, however, there was still much to be done. The three leaders knew well, and Cæsar knew better than his allies, that all this work would be thrown away, unless they took further steps to secure their own position for at least the next year or two. If the senatorial party came again into power, these laws would be at once declared null and void; Cæsar himself would be attacked in the law-courts; the legions and the provinces would be given to senatorial incapables; and by abundant bribery, the city populace itself might be persuaded to restore the Sullan constitution. In fact the battle was by no means at an end, though for the moment the Senate was beaten all along the line.

It was necessary in the first place to put Cæsar not only out of danger, but in a position whence he might continue to watch over Italy and Rome, and to give his weaker allies both moral and material support. In the previous year, the Senate, using a constitutional right secured to them by Gaius Gracchus himself, had set apart for both consuls of 59 B.C., as soon as their year of office should expire, the duty of attending to the internal condition of Italy; and if this arrangement held good, Cæsar's " province " as proconsul would have meant no more than the supervision of roads, forests, and public works, without legions, without freedom, and without adventure. Doubtless there was plenty of good work to be done in Italy; in such work Gaius Gracchus had voluntarily busied himself. But that was before the military arm had become the mainspring of action in the political world; and Cæsar could no more dispense with that arm, if he wished himself and his work to survive, than Cromwell could dispense with his Ironsides. It was of course known to every one that the Senate had made this arrangement with the express object of destroying him.

There was, however, a part of what we now call Italy, the most fertile, populous, and flourishing district south of the Alps, the possession of which would give him at least three legions, the necessary proximity to the capital, and a magnificent base of operations, if he should be attacked, or should find himself driven to become himself the aggressor. And apart from its resources and its strategical strength, Cisalpine Gaul had long been peculiarly attached to Cæsar himself and the democratic party. The eager and intellectual Celtic population north of the Padus were still without the full Roman citizenship; and we have seen how Cæsar on his return from his quæstorship in Spain had visited them and encouraged them to agitate for it (see p. 59). How justly founded were their desires, we may see at a glance when we reflect that Catullus, Virgil, Livy, and the elder and younger Pliny, among many others, were all natives of this district, which long continued to present in its purity and simplicity of manners, as well as in the health and vigour of its culture, a marked contrast to the selfish and worn-out population of the capital.

This basin of the Padus was not politically a part of Italy at this time, and had been governed by an ex-magistrate, like any other province, since the time of Sulla. It was now proposed to set aside the Senate's arrangements for the consular provinces, and to give Cisalpine Gaul to Cæsar, together with the adjoining less important province of Illyria, for five years by a vote of the people. The tribune Vatinius, who was the proposer, had several important precedents to go upon; but there was wanting a sufficient pretext for the unusual procedure. No immediate danger threatened Cisalpine Gaul, and Cæsar was not to be called on to crush an inveterate enemy like Mithridates or Jugurtha. But at this juncture the Senate itself came to the rescue, and relieved Cæsar and his agents of all responsibility for their action. On the motion of Pompeius, they added to Cæsar's government the Gallic province beyond the Alps, together with an army and an ample staff, and directed him to take measures for the defence of that province against invasion from the north and east. No one at the moment could have been aware—not even Cæsar himself—that this was to open up for him a career of conquest more lasting in its results than the uncompleted projects of Alexander. But it was known that there was work to be done there; the Alpine peoples to the eastwards, and on the north the Germans beyond the Rhine, were alike threatening the fair province on the lower Rhone; the Senate had as usual let the danger approach without due provision, and were even now quite unaware that no one but a consummate commander could save them from grievous damage and disgrace.

When Cæsar laid down his office at the end of the year, and left the city as proconsul to prepare for the campaign that was impending, he offered Cicero the chance of accompanying him in the honourable position of staff officer. There was nothing unusual in this, though Cicero was entirely ignorant of warfare. Every public man was still expected to be able to discharge military duties, and, as we have just seen, such an offer held out prospects of material advantage. But Cæsar's immediate object was to get Cicero away from the capital, and to keep him under his own eye. Though Cicero had not actively opposed the triumvirate, it was perfectly well known that he would seize the first chance of undoing their work; and Cæsar was aware that his first efforts would be to renew his old attempt to flatter Pompeius into an alliance with him (see p. 102), to re-establish the agreement of the orders, and to patch up the old republican forms in which he so profoundly believed. It was indispensable, from Cæsar's point of view, that he should be induced to leave Rome, and the prospect of the companionship of an old friend so congenial and so gifted must have influenced Cæsar in his offer hardly less than political necessity.

Cicero hesitated for a moment, but then decidedly rejected the proposal. "I prefer to *fight*," he wrote to his friend Atticus,—to fight, that is, with an enemy who would shortly be let loose on him if he remained. Cæsar was not content with his first offer; he made others; he left no stone unturned to get that dangerous genius out of the way of doing mischief to himself and others. He asked him to become a member of the commission under the agrarian bill. Cicero laughed at the idea. He suggested a " *legatio libera*," which would have enabled him to travel in his favourite Greece and elsewhere, with dignity and leisure. But it was all in vain ; and Cicero had reason to regret most bitterly, but two or three months later, that he had recklessly determined to run every risk, rather than take the smallest favour at the hands of political adversaries.

The melancholy story of Cicero's exile, and of the violence of his personal enemy Clodius, does not fall within the scope of this volume. Cæsar's part in it was simply a negative one ; he might probably have saved Cicero even then if he had chosen, and he did not do so. He had tried to give him the means of securing his own safety, but without success ; and he was hardly to be expected to go further out of his way to save a man who, if rescued, would do him all the damage in his power.

In whatever way we may judge the conduct of either of these men, at this moment so critical for both (and we shall always form different judgments according to our views of the political condition of Rome at the time), we may perhaps all agree in regretting that Cicero did not see his way to accepting Cæsar's first offer. It would have taken him out of danger, without seriously compromising his political position ; and it might have had a result far more important, in introducing a brilliant mind, narrowed by continued city life, to fresh scenes and peoples, to new responsibilities and new aspirations, to a new sense of what the Roman dominion was, and of its vast possibilities and inherent weaknesses. From such a man, too, Cæsar himself could not but have learnt much ; and if the two finest intellects of that day,—the man of action and the man of letters, the man who saw facts and the man who saw visions, —could have grown to a mutual understanding as well as a mutual respect, it is possible that, even though the march of events towards absolutism could probably not have been stayed, the lives of each might at least have been smoothed, and each might have been spared at the last the fatal blow of the assassin.

Let us return for a moment to the questions suggested at the beginning of this chapter. How did Cæsar use power when it was first placed in his hands? Was he true to his political faith? Can we trace the hand of a real statesman in the work he did this year?

The history of affairs in the city during the next two years would seem to show that Cæsar, departing for Gaul, had left nothing but confusion behind him. We have now to follow his military career, and cannot dwell on this period of anarchy. But it is true that such influence as the Senate possessed had been undermined during Cæsar's consulship ; that Pompeius and Crassus were helpless without Cæsar ; that Clodius' attempts to legislate for the democratic party were ill-judged and violent, and that it was a mistake of Cæsar's to allow him to slip into the position of a legislator. If some strong authority were needed before 59 B.C., it was still more needed when the year was over.

Yet all this is in itself evidence that Cæsar, during his term of power, had done what no one else could do. The Senate had failed to perform the most pressing duties of government; he carried them through successfully, without violence, and without more hurt to a constitution which could not work than might be expected sooner or later to befall it. He did his best to avoid any violence, and by a union of political leaders and interests to make the clumsy Republic into a working constitution; and in these efforts he even once or twice allowed conciliation to get the better of political principle. Work had to be done; there was but a year to do it in; obstruction and opposition confronted him at every turn; yet that work *was* done, and done on the whole by the hand of a real statesman, true to the principles of a great party.

And indeed, as we look back on the work of this year, with the map of the Roman Empire before us, and with the subsequent history of that Empire in our minds, we see the consulship of Cæsar in a new light. His legislation affected the world from the Euphrates to the Tagus. It showed how far-reaching were the duties of the Roman government, and how impossible it was to fulfil them, with discord reigning in the city. To banish such discord permanently, there was but one resource left—the military arm, wielded by an intelligent statesman. Cæsar was beginning to understand this in the year of his consulship; seven years later, the Senate began to understand it also.

CHAPTER VIII.

THE DEFENCE OF TRANSALPINE GAUL.

58 B.C.

FROM the time when Cæsar took possession of his provinces in March, 58 B.C., we have a detailed record of his active life, with the exception of the few brief intervals when he was at Rome in the years of his supreme power. It is true indeed that we know hardly anything of the business and the studies in which he was engaged winter after winter in Cisalpine Gaul and Illyria, while military operations were impracticable; it is true that the man's real thoughts and aims, as well as his pursuits and methods of government, are thus entirely hidden from us. That inner life of the mind, which in the nineteenth century we fancy we ought to discover in a biography, is in Cæsar's case not to be explored. But where Fortune has been singularly gracious to us in one particular, it is well not to call her niggard in another; the more so, as we are apt altogether to undervalue the gift we already possess. It takes a scholar,—one, that is, who knows how precious is every fragment of the best authors of antiquity, how great the perils attending the transmission of ancient books, and how vast and varied were the writings that are now irrecoverably lost,— to appreciate the singular good luck that has preserved all Cæsar's military writings to our own time in a tolerably sound condition. And it is only when we have ranged freely over Latin literature, and are familiar with all the great Roman writers of prose, that we can turn back to Cæsar's "Commentaries," which most of us forsake after our earliest boyhood, and feel the truth of Cicero's judgment, that no historical writing could surpass them in the charm of their pure and lucid brevity.*

We may indeed with justice lament that in writing his three books of the Civil Wars he did not tell us more of his acts and views of government, and that his lieutenants who composed the extant histories of his later wars in Africa and Spain should have limited themselves entirely to his military operations. The result is, as will be seen later on, that we are much in the dark as to the very details we most need to know, while we have full information on events which are not really of world-wide interest. But we are concerned at present with the Gallic War only, and here it is impossible to appraise our good fortune too highly. No great conqueror has

---

* Cic., Brutus, xxxv., 262.

left behind him such a perfect record of his work; no war so far-reaching in its consequences has ever been so well described. Though never quite completed by Cæsar himself, it yet forms a complete whole, containing almost every element which is even now looked for in a military history. It places the reader in possession, with little trouble to himself, of an account, from Cæsar's own point of view, of the reason and justification of the war, of military details in every important district, of the nature of the country and its inhabitants, of the character of the peoples who lay beyond it and were in contact with it as enemies or as traders. We gain also a perfect picture of the tactics and the mechanism of a Roman army; we become familiar with its engineering resources, its methods and difficulties of supply. And if to-day we are apt to reckon lightly of military history, we shall do well to reflect that it is precisely in war that the practical ability of a people is best seen, their true temper tested, their scientific intelligence discovered.

But this invaluable work is much more than a mere account of military operations. Cæsar's book is at once a record of war and administration and a tale of adventure and discovery; it is not only the work of a consummate general, but of a man of literary and scientific tastes, and of an unerring artistic feeling for what was pure and suitable in language. It was written in haste,* and probably with the im-

---

* Probably in the winter of 52–51 B.C., when the rupture with Pompeius was beginning. The haste is expressly alluded to in Hirtius' preface to Book viii. (ch. 1., sec. 6).

mediate political purpose of justifying the conquests it describes, and of explaining to the Roman people the independence of home authority which its author had allowed himself; but neither hurry nor policy was suffered to affect either its literary or its scientific value. Cæsar's inquiries into the social and political condition of this new world of which he threw open the gates, though confined to a few brief chapters, are still the chief basis of our knowledge of the subject; every sentence is valuable, and the whole has been proved to be as correct a picture as the best observer of that day could be expected to produce. This constitutes what may be called its scientific merit; its literary merit is still more obvious. In spite of the fact,—known to us not only from the passage of Cicero quoted above, but from the testimony of the author of the eighth book,—that it was not intended as a finished historical treatise, but rather as material for others to work upon, it remains the most perfect specimen we possess of pure and unaffected Latin prose. It is as far removed from the roughness of Varro on the one hand, as it is from the refinements and artistic devices of Cicero on the other. Its Latin is in itself perfect, a genuine Roman product, with the neatness of the best Attic Greek, but wholly independent of Hellenic adornment. It may give the reader some idea of its position in Roman literature, if we compare it with that stratum of pure English writing which lies between the "learned" English of Milton and Sir Thomas Browne, and the Latinised English of Johnson. Swift, Defoe, Addison, and Bolingbroke are our best examples of the happy adaptation of a genuine native tongue in the purest form to the various purposes required of it. Their language, like Cæsar's, is uniformly simple and natural; it is appropriate rather than choice, so that while no individual sentence may linger long in our memory, the whole composition has exactly the desired effect.

One word more must needs be said before we pass to a summary of the operations by which Cæsar secured the Transalpine province against invasion from the north. What idea does his book give us of his own character and personality?

The answer seems paradoxical, but is none the less true. Though Cæsar keeps himself, his personal feelings and experiences, most carefully in the background while he tells his story, his book is yet far the most valuable evidence we possess as to his character and intellect. He is there, indeed, inseparable from his army—an individual unit, though the chief and guiding one, in an irresistible combination of forces. In reading the book we are placed, as it were, on some commanding height, looking down on the plains of Gaul, and seeing armies in motion below; we rarely get a glimpse of the personal details of military life, the hardships, the anxieties, the incessant vigilance and toil. The one cool head which guides all operations seems untroubled by any obstacles, and lifted clear above the petty details either of disappointment or success. The tale moves on, with hardly an attempt to rouse the imagination or stir the blood, even in an age when all rhetorical devices were at the command of every educated man. But it is this very quality of the book which shows us the nature of the man far better than the biographies of later generations, confirming the little we know of him from the writings of his own contemporaries. The absence of sensitiveness, of egoism, and of passion, are characteristic both of the book and the man. Even in the most perilous moments, and in the most adventurous undertakings, we can see as we read that he was a man of facts and not of imagination; or at least that the special kind of imaginative power which every great conqueror and explorer has in some degree possessed—Alexander, Hannibal, Cortes, Clive, Napoleon,—was in him kept in strict subordination to reason and to the exigencies of every day.

Other features, some of which have been already incidentally noticed, will be apparent to the careful reader. The language, almost always clear as crystal, reveals an unclouded intellect and an unhesitating will. The courtesy and kindness for which he was noted, are seen here in the absence of all severe comment on the mistakes of his officers. In his very first campaign, a decisive victory was snatched from his grasp by the blunder of an old soldier in whose experience he had confided; but he contents himself with noting that Considius was frightened, and had reported what was fancy and not fact. In telling the story of the most terrible disaster that ever befell his troops, he does not bear hardly on the unfortunate officer who was responsible. He comments briefly on the mistakes liable to be made by *all* men who are forced to take counsel at the critical moment instead of beforehand, and on the necessity in warfare of keeping in mind not only the rules of the military art, but the moral effect on your own troops and on the enemy of every step you take in an emergency. And lastly, it will be admitted that, on the whole, the book carries conviction with it, and bears the stamp of truth. It must be judged on this score almost entirely by internal evidence, for there is hardly any other means of criticising it. Written indeed as it was with an immediate political purpose, it was inevitable that some things should be suppressed which would give a handle to his enemies at home, and others perhaps of which it might be impolitic to remind his own officers: for that Cæsar was blameless throughout so long and so trying a command was neither possible nor true. But what he does tell us, we may believe to be true, in perhaps a greater degree than we can trust any historical work of antiquity ; and in their clearness, their force, their self-restraint, the " Commentaries " remain an imperishable monument of the true Roman type of mind, of which, as was hinted earlier in this volume, Cæsar was perhaps the last and certainly the greatest example.

We may now turn our attention for a brief space to the state of affairs in Gaul, which called for active and instant measures in the spring of 58 B.C. To give an account of the inhabitants of Gaul, their religious, social, and political organisation, would occupy a whole chapter, and is not possible in this volume. We must be content here with a summary of the circumstances which led to the Gallic War.

With the Celtic race, to which the inhabitants of Gaul for the most part belonged, the Romans had come into contact at a very early period. A considerable part of Italy had probably at one time been peopled by them, and their settlements remained in Umbria and the valley of the Padus. In the fourth century B.C. they had overrun Italy, and taken and burnt Rome itself; but before the end of the third century almost all the Gallic tribes south of the Alps had passed under Roman dominion, and so remained, in spite of their temporary defection during the invasion of Hannibal. Since then their territories in north Italy had been regularly governed from Rome; they served in Roman armies, and their strong and weak points were well known to Roman generals and authors. But the great mass of the Celtic stock inhabited at this time the magnificent territory which we now call France, together with the Netherlands up to the Rhine, and the greater part of Britain; and no part of this population had been disturbed by the Romans until less than a century before Cæsar's consulship. Rome had been too fully occupied in Spain and in the East to seek for complications elsewhere. And she had a very real interest in keeping on good terms with the people of southern Gaul, for her land communication with her Spanish provinces depended largely on the good-will of these tribes towards herself and also towards her old and faithful ally, the powerful Greek city of Massilia. It was, in fact, this alliance which was the primary cause of the movements leading to the formation of a Roman province beyond the Alps.

It was inevitable that Massilia should come into collision with the people whose seaboard was occupied by herself and her colonies on the coast; and she drew the Romans into her quarrels without any unwillingness on their part.

The first collision with the Gallic tribes in this district took place in the year 154 B.C., but it was not till 125 B.C. that any definite policy was adopted at Rome. In that year the consul Flaccus, a leading member of the Gracchan party, was sent to operate against the hill tribes of the Salyes, of whom the Massiliots were then rightly or wrongly complaining. After defeating these he was easily led farther, and his work was carried on by other generals of the Gracchan period : Sextius, who founded Aquæ Sextiæ (Aix); Fabius Maximus, who first defeated the Allobroges and the powerful Arverni; and Domitius, the constructor of the great road from Massilia to the Pyrenees. In 118 B.C. was founded, on the coast west of the mouth of the Rhone, the *colonia* of Narbo, which was destined to be the capital of the newly acquired territory and to supersede Massilia; and about this time or somewhat later the whole district was formed into a Roman province. The communication with Spain was secured ; a vast and wealthy trade-route was opened up ; while the province was protected by the Rhone from Geneva to Vienne, and by the chain of the Cevennes, which stretch from the basin of the Rhone in a southwesterly direction towards the Pyrenees. Its frontier town on the west was Tolosa (Toulouse). Its shape was like that of a boot, of which Tolosa was the toe, the Pennine Alps the heel, Geneva the top, and the Gulf of Marseilles the instep.

But this new province, even guarded as it was by the usual Roman methods—the *colonia*, fortress, and military road—was for several reasons in a very insecure state. Its wealth and fertility laid it constantly open to the envy of the tribes to the north of it; and these tribes were at this time continually threatened with invasion from the wilder German people of the far north and west. Vast hordes of these had already, within the memory of men still living, descended upon the plains of Gaul, pierced the Pyrenees, beaten and destroyed Roman armies within the boundaries of the province, forced the barrier of the Alps, and only succumbed at last within a few days' march of Rome. The panic which the Cimbri and Teutones had caused had long ago passed away, but these peoples of the north were still restless, and no adequate measures of permanent defence had been taken. Torn by internal conflict, harassed by the pirates and by Mithridates, the incapable Roman government had allowed the Transalpine province to develop itself in its own way without paying any real attention to its precarious situation. It was now fast becoming Romanised; it swarmed with Roman traders and money-lenders; it had been the refuge of the democratic party in the Civil Wars, and contained, perhaps, a greater number of Latin-speaking persons than most of the provinces of earlier origin. Yet in spite of all this, it had been not only neglected but ill-treated. The democratic party had tried to hold it under the influence of

Sertorius, but had been rudely driven out by Pompeius; and Pompeius had left behind him a governor, Fonteius, whose savage cruelty is perfectly apparent to us even from the fragments of the unworthy speech in which Cicero afterwards defended him. The Allobroges, the most powerful Gallic people within the limits of the province, had been shamefully oppressed. All their efforts to get reparation had been in vain, and after rising in open rebellion in 61 B.C., they had only been put down by force of arms. The two chief towns of Massilia and Narbo were indeed comfortable and contented; but the whole native population was in a state of suppressed mutiny, and this, added to the danger from the north, made the position here a very critical one in the two years immediately preceding Cæsar's appointment as governor.

Throughout the year of his consulship, Cæsar must in fact have been aware that there was likely to be a severe struggle for Roman supremacy beyond the Alps. The alarming nature of the news that was coming in from that quarter is hinted at in Cicero's letters of the period, though neither Cicero nor the ordinary Roman of the day, perhaps not even Cæsar himself, really understood how grave it was. The reader will be able to appreciate it if he will study the accompanying map, with the following brief account of the causes and events of the campaign of 58 B.C.

The map will show that the Roman frontier was closed in by three Gallic tribes; the Arverni beyond the Cevennes to the north-west, who had once been

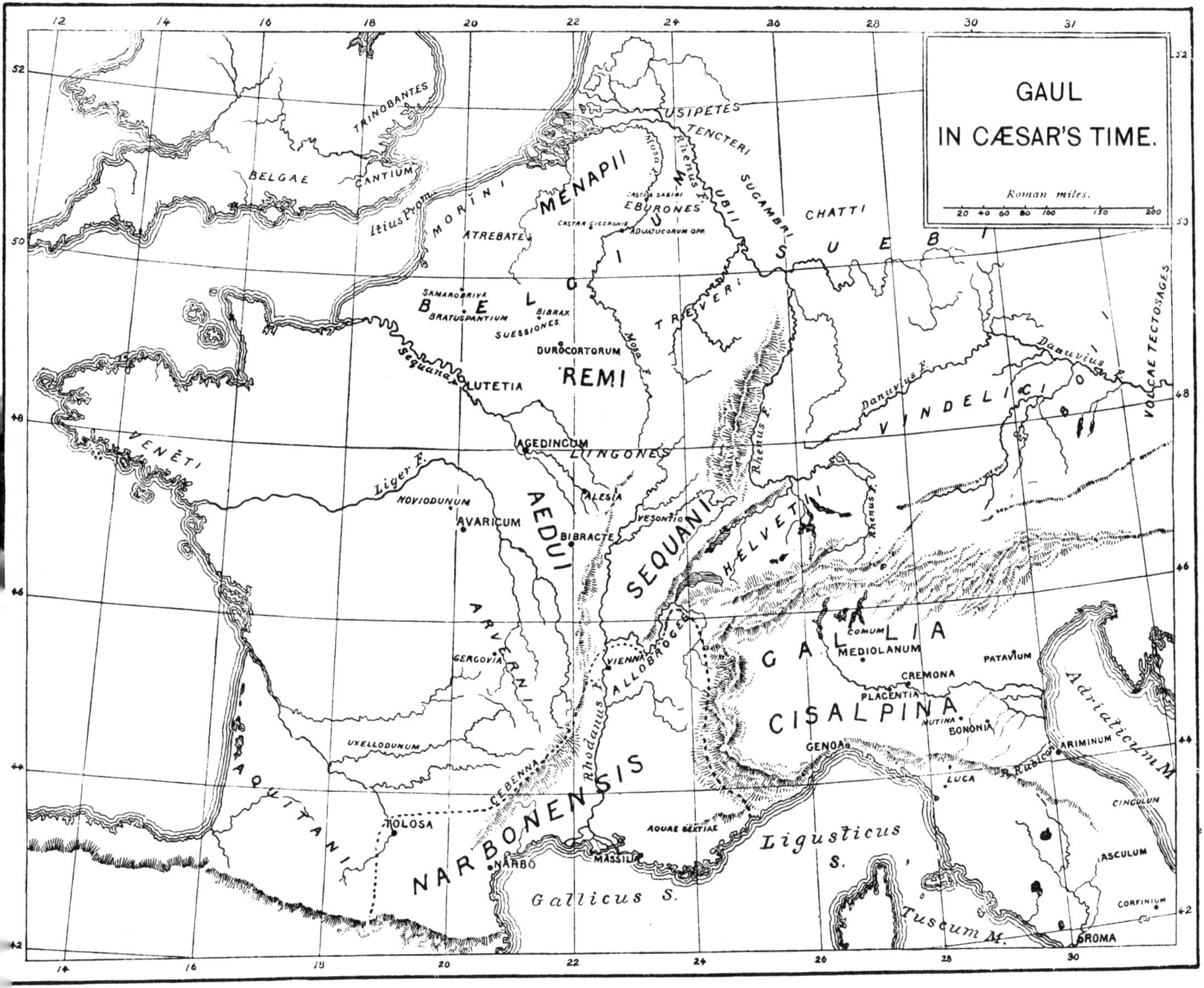
GAUL
IN CÆSAR'S TIME.
Roman miles.
20 40 60 80 100 150 200
TRINOBANTES
BELGAE
CANTIUM
Itius Prom.
MORINI
MENAPII
ATREBATES
EBURONES
CASTRA SABINI
CASTRA CICERONIS
ADUATUCORUM OPP.
USIPETES
TENCTERI
SUGAMBRI
UBII
CHATTI
Mosa F.
Rhenus F.
S U E B I
B E L G I U M
SAMAROBRIVA
BRATUSPANTIUM
BIBRAX
SUESSIONES
DUROCORTORUM
TREVERI
REMI
Sequana F.
LUTETIA
AGEDINCUM
LINGONES
VENETI
Liger F.
NOVIODUNUM
AVARICUM
AEDUI
ALESIA
VESONTIO
BIBRACTE
SEQUANI
HELVETII
Rhenus F.
Danuvius F.
VINDELICI
BOI
VOLCAE TECTOSAGES
ARVERNI
GERCOVIA
VIENNA
ALLOBROGES
Rhodanus F.
COMUM
MEDIOLANUM
GALLIA
CISALPINA
PATAVIUM
CREMONA
PLACENTIA
MUTINA
BONONIA
GENOA
ARIMINUM
R. Rubicon
LUCA
Adriaticum M.
CINGULUM
ASCULUM
CORFINIUM
ROMA
UXELLODUNUM
CEBENNA
AQUITANI
TOLOSA
NARBONENSIS
NARBO
MASSILIA
AQUAE SEXTIAE
Ligusticus S.
Gallicus S.
Tuscum M.

the most powerful people in Gaul; the Ædui to the north, on the west bank of the Saone; and the Sequani between the Rhone and the Saone, in the rich plains of what we now call Burgundy. The Arverni had, as we have seen, been in conflict with Rome, and had been partially subdued; with the Sequani the Romans had had no direct dealings of importance. But the Ædui, as lying between these two formidable peoples, and because they could be successfully played off against the beaten but dangerous Arverni, had been taken into a close alliance and "friendship," and, backed by Roman influence, had attained a power beyond their natural strength, and claimed now to be the leading state in Gaul.

The result was just what might have been expected. The Arverni, ever jealous of the Ædui, allied with the Sequani to crush them, and called in the aid of a German tribe, the Suebi, which, under its energetic chief Ariovistus, had already crossed the Rhine, and was seeking a settlement to the southward. If the Roman government had been as energetic as the German chief, they would have succoured their clients the Ædui, and either declared war on Ariovistus, or at least strengthened their own defences in that direction. As it was, they left their allies in the lurch, the Ædui were conquered, and the province was practically open to an invasion at any moment by a combination of Gauls and Germans. It was thought at Rome that the German chief could be put off by flattery and negotiation; and at Cæsar's own suggestion (so it is said) he was recognised as king, and declared " the friend and ally of the Roman people. It is needless to say that, once established in Gaul, he declined to give up his advantage; and then the Sequani, in whose territory he was, as much perplexed as their former enemies the Ædui, had no resource but to appeal to Rome. Thus, in the beginning of 58 B.C., Rome and the Germans were brought actually face to face. Ariovistus was beginning to be felt at Rome as a really formidable enemy. The Transalpine province was in danger, for there was but a single legion stationed in it; and once in possession of the province, Ariovistus might cross the Alps, like Hannibal, and work havoc within the very bounds of Italy.

It was with this enemy that Cæsar was expecting to have to grapple, when news suddenly arrived of a danger still more pressing. For two years past the inhabitants of what is now northern and western Switzerland, the beautiful country between the Rhine, the Rhone, and the Jura, had been meditating a complete migration into the warmer and roomier plains of Gaul. The Helvetii, themselves apparently a people of Celtic race, were suffering, like the Ædui, from inroads of the restless Germans, and probably from other causes unknown to us. They had heard that far away at the foot of the Pyrenees there was a splendid territory where they might find a home, and they resolved to make their way thither, peacefully if possible, through the tribes that lay between. The modern traveller in Switzerland may well be astonished that any people should be dissatisfied with such a land as that which he passes through on his way from Basle to Lucerne, or from

The Defence of Transalpine Gaul. 139

Geneva to Berne. But much of this was in those days probably forest and swamp; and in any case these vast migrations are the most striking historical features of the age, and constituted the most real and urgent danger for the Roman Empire, and for civilisation. If the Helvetii were allowed to migrate as they wished, the disturbance among the other Gallic peoples on the Roman frontier would be very serious; the Aquitanian territory, which they wished to occupy, was divided from the province by no natural defence ; and the country vacated by them would be at once occupied by the Germans, who would thereby be brought into immediate contact with the Roman frontier at Geneva. It was the moment for a soldier-statesman to act with rapid and unhesitating energy, and to show the real strength of the Roman state. That strength had never really been shown in this quarter since the days of Marius. It was, indeed, rather the weakness and disunion of Rome that was known to the barbarians. If the Empire was to enjoy quiet on her frontiers, some decisive blow must be struck at once: and such quiet was now absolutely necessary to the re-organisation and development of the wearied and worn-out Republic.

How far these weighty considerations were in Cæsar's mind at the outset of his command, does not appear from his own concise narrative. Probably they grew upon him in the course of his first campaign, and as he found them falling in with his own interests and love of enterprise. But for the moment there was no question as to what was to be done. The Helvetii must be stopped, at all hazards, and the German invader must also be watched and checked. Whatever question may arise later on as to the political morality of Cæsar's dealings in Gaul, no reasonable man will deny that in this year 58 B.C., his activity was justified and necessary.

The story of the campaign must be told here even more briefly than he tells it himself. The Helvetii would leave their own land at Geneva, the only point where it was then possible for so great a host to penetrate into southern France; for the Jura mountains, which bound Switzerland to the west, offer no other easy passage but that which is formed by the issue of the Rhone between this chain and the mountains of Savoy. The left bank of the river was the boundary of the Roman province; the right bank was in the hands of the Sequani. There was a route skirting each bank; but that through the land of the Sequani was very narrow and difficult, and the Helvetii decided to take the other, and to force their way through the Roman province, relying on the good-will of the Allobroges, who occupied the country, and had much reason to hate their Roman rulers. They burnt their twelve towns and all their villages, and were to concentrate at Geneva on a certain day about the middle of April.

With that rapidity which was so often to strike terror into his enemies, Cæsar hastened to the threatened spot, ordering a general levy throughout the province. He cut down the bridge which crossed the Rhone below Geneva, gained a short delay by giving an evasive answer to a Helvetian embassy

1. SLINGER. 2. LIGHT-ARMED TROOPS. 3. SOLDIERS OF THE LEGION.
4. CAVALRY.

which came to ask his leave for passage through the province, and instantly set the one legion he had with him to fortify the Roman bank of the river for a distance of some ten miles south-west of Geneva. The object of this work will be apparent to any one who has travelled by rail from Paris or Lyons to Geneva, or who will study the map and text of " Bädeker's Switzerland " which relate to this district. For these ten miles the river is here and there fordable, and the left bank is not protected by rocks; but beyond this the hills close in upon it, and it begins to run in rapids. If the Helvetii were to cross it at all into the Roman province, they must cross it at some point above the rocks and rapids; and Cæsar's fortification would enable the Romans to defeat any such attempt. This work completed, he was in a position to tell the invaders, when their envoys returned according to agreement, that he could not permit them to cross, and would resist any attempt to do so. Several times they essayed to break through his defences, but were in each case beaten back with loss; and then, giving up the attempt, they began to negotiate with the Sequani for permission to use the more difficult route which led through the territory of that people between the Jura and the Rhone. The negotiation succeeded, through the mediation of Dumnorix, the ambitious leader of the anti-Roman party among the neighbouring Ædui; and there was nothing now but the difficulty of the route to delay the migrants in forcing their way into the very heart of Gaul.

The crisis was an exceedingly urgent one; and in order to understand it the reader should grasp, as Cæsar did, not only the military danger of the moment, but the political situation which resulted from the *laissez-faire* policy of recent years. The map will show that there was nothing to protect the Roman province from the invaders, when once they had passed the defiles of the Jura, but the river Rhone, there flowing with a gentler stream; and rivers, as is well known, if undefended, are no serious obstacle even to barbarian armies. There was no force in that part of the province; the Helvetii might be expected in a very few weeks, and nothing but the fact that they were a whole people, as well as an army, could prevent their arriving there much sooner. The Sequani were now on friendly terms with them ; the Ædui farther to the west were divided into two factions, one of them hostile to Rome ; and both these tribes, as well as the Arverni, the ancient enemies of the Romans, were more or less under the influence of the German Ariovistus, whose star was now in the ascendant in Gaul.

The position of this great foreign chieftain is in fact the real key to the situation. He was in Gaul as a conqueror ; the Romans were weak and on the defensive. Only the Ædui and Sequani lay between him and the province, and as Rome had given these tribes no help against him, his prestige with them was naturally overwhelming. They accordingly now showed their readiness to neglect Roman interests by allowing the Helvetii to pass through their territories. Thus the almost defenceless province was

1. IMPERATOR. 2. LEGATUS. 3. CENTURIO. 4. LICTOR. 5. SIGNIFERI.
6. BUCINATOR. 7. TUBICEN. 8. VEXILLUM. 9. AQUILA.

confronted along its whole boundary by disaffected and hostile tribes, backed up by a northern invader whom they no longer dared to challenge. No wonder that they were unwilling to stop the migrating Helvetii, in spite of Cæsar's decision, of which they must have been well aware, that this people could not be suffered to settle on the Roman border. It was absolutely necessary to restore the weight of Roman influence ; and this could only be done either by a strong defensive policy, *i. e.*, by strengthening the frontier in its whole extent, and massing forces at all weak points ; or by boldly taking the offensive, stopping the Helvetii, re-establishing Roman influence among the Ædui and Sequani, and letting it be seen that Ariovistus was not to have it all his own way.

This latter policy was practically forced on Cæsar, though it doubtless also fully coincided with his own active and adventurous nature. There was no time to build up an elaborate system of defence ; he had given his word that the Helvetii were not to be allowed to carry out their intentions ; and he had no choice but to pursue them with all the forces he could raise and turn them back to the country they had left. By this plan, if successful, the frontier tribes would in any case be quieted for the present, and Cæsar might be free to check Ariovistus himself, should he still prove formidable and aggressive.

Leaving his able lieutenant Labienus with the single legion * in charge of the works at Geneva, he returned with all possible speed to Cisalpine Gaul,

---
* This was the famous tenth, of which we shall hear more.

to bring up the three other legions which had been granted him with his province. At the same time, in view of the immediate danger, he anticipated the senatorial sanction, and ordered two new ones to be levied. With these recruits, and with the three legions which had wintered at Aquileia (near Venice), he hurried back over the Alps, probably by the pass of the Mount Genèvre, the best known and most direct route to the Transalpine province, and in spite of sharp opposition from the Alpine tribes, made his way to the Rhone while it was still early summer. Then without hesitation he took the important step of crossing the river and thus passing beyond the limits of his province. He was joined here by Labienus and the tenth legion ; and thus every available trained soldier under his command was brought to bear upon the threatened point. The rapidity with which this concentration was effected was then almost unprecedented in military history, and would be remarkable even at the present day. Its boldness, too, was only justified by success, for it left the whole of the Alpine frontier of Italy bare of troops. But just as the political campaign of the previous year had shown the idlers of the forum that a man had arisen who would not be turned aside from his path by any petty obstacles, so this campaign against the Helvetii taught the whole body of disaffected Gauls that they had a Roman to deal with whose like had not been seen since Marius.

The operations which followed, and the final defeat of the Helvetii, are described by Cæsar in chapters

1
SOLDIER
OF GAUL.

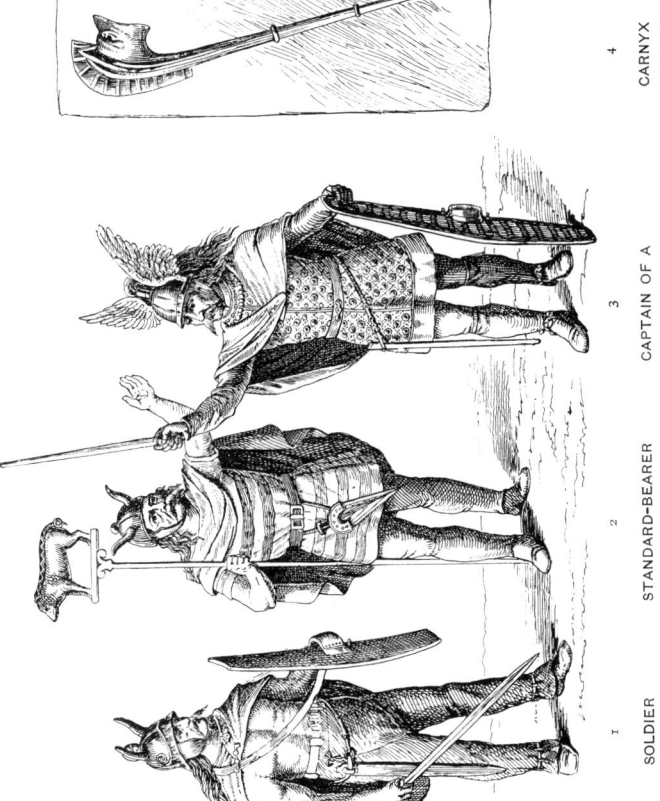

2
STANDARD-BEARER
OF GAUL.
FROM THE TRIUMPHAL ARCH IN ORANGE (ARAUSIO). [A.D. 21.]

3
CAPTAIN OF A
GALLIC TROOP.

4
CARNYX
OR TRUMPET.

twelve to twenty-nine of his first book, with self-evident candour and modesty. Both he himself, his lieutenants, and his troops were only learning the business of really critical warfare, and when he wrote this account some years later he must have looked back on these few weeks as a time of repeated danger and disappointment. His officers were many of them quite worthless and inexperienced, and even some who were old soldiers were frightened by the new and formidable enemies they had to face. His troops were unseasoned, and the real brunt of the work had to be often borne by the one legion on which he could wholly rely; in cavalry in particular he was very weak, and the raw levies which he raised in the province and among the Gallic tribes were at first of little use. His enemy, though encumbered by women, children, and baggage, was reckoned at more than 90,000 men capable of fighting; and perhaps the greatest difficulty of all was the arduous task of feeding his troops in the disaffected country into which he now had to plunge.

The Helvetii had moved very slowly, and had occupied twenty days in bridging the Saone, which was the first considerable obstacle they met with in their progress westwards. They had not all crossed, when Cæsar overtook them and destroyed one of their tribes, the Tigurini, who had in former years signalised themselves by defeating and capturing a Roman army under L. Cassius. He then threw a bridge over the river in a single day, turned the enemy in a northerly direction, and pursued them with great caution into the interior of the country. A cavalry skirmish, and a cleverly conceived ambush were alike failures; provisions began to fail; time was spent in negotiations, both with the enemy and with the Ædui, in whose territory Cæsar now was. He had been all this time marching northward through the plains of Burgundy, to the west of the familiar line of railway now running between Dijon and Macon; and finding himself within a few miles of the Æduan capital Bibracte (now Autun), he felt compelled to leave the pursuit and turn to the city for supplies. The Helvetii, emboldened by what they fancied was a retreat, became the attacking party; Cæsar was forced to take up a strong position in three lines on a hill not far from the town and await their assault. The critical nature of his position, and his want of absolute confidence in his troops, are indicated by the fact, recorded by himself, that he had his own horse and those of all his chief officers taken to the rear, in order to show the legionaries that they were to conquer or to die together. The battle began about midday and ended at sunset. The attack of the Helvetii was repulsed, and the Romans followed them down into the plain; but here they were themselves taken in flank and rear by some 15,000 of the enemy's rearguard, who had only just arrived on the scene of action. Against these, like Napoleon at Waterloo against the Prussians, Cæsar had to form a new front with his third line, and to fight the rest of the battle without reserves. The struggle was intense and prolonged; not one Helvetian, Cæsar expressly

THE CAMP OF A LEGION.

tells us, was seen to turn his back throughout it. Far into the night the enemy sustained all attacks on the fortress of wagons to which they had at last retreated; but by daylight this too was carried, and the whole host was flying.

This great battle of Bibracte, in which some 130,000 men were engaged, had an instant and decisive effect on the whole political and military situation. None of the Gauls dared to disobey Cæsar's order, now at once issued, that no support was to be given to the fugitives; and the result of this was that the vanquished lost no time in submitting themselves to the Roman whom they had defied. The main body was sent back to its old home in Switzerland, henceforward to be the obedient clients of the Roman state on the German frontier; and the Allobroges were ordered to supply them with provision on their journey. The tribe of the Boii, who had been long wandering homeless,* were settled among the Ædui at the request of the latter, and were in due time incorporated with them. Thus long before the summer was over every danger seemed to have vanished on the frontier; the enemies who had menaced the very existence of the Transalpine province were converted into bulwarks against the barbarians of the regions farther north. Cæsar's genius, showing itself no less in diplomacy than in the combined daring and caution of his warfare, had made him in three short months the arbiter of southern Gaul.

---

* B. G., i., 6 and 28.

CHAPTER IX.

THE DEFEAT OF THE GERMANS.
58 B.C.

THE position in which Cæsar now found himself, at the head of a victorious army in the heart of Gaul and out of reach of all immediate control by the Senate, could not but suggest to him the advantage of completing without delay the work he had begun. It was pointed out in the last chapter that it was not only the attempted migration of the Helvetii—an accidental circumstance, though one of a kind liable to occur at any time,—which placed the Roman province in jeopardy. The real and permanent danger was the attitude and temper of the Gallic tribes on the frontier—the Arverni, Ædui, and Sequani. These would become friendly so soon as the Roman power was felt and understood, and would be hostile so long as they were witnesses of a feeble frontier-policy, and believed Rome itself to be hopelessly weakened by internal strife. Thus they had encouraged the Helvetii, and given no aid to Cæsar until they found out his strength; and before this, as has been already pointed out, the Arverni and Sequani had turned upon the Roman party among the Ædui, and had called in Ariovistus and the Germans to help in crushing them.

But Cæsar's victory had again revolutionised their policy. Like all semi-civilised peoples, they followed in the wake of the victor of the day. Among the Ædui the Roman party, with its able chief Divitiacus, at once resumed the lead; and it was probably by their influence that a proposal was made to hold a general representative council of Gallic peoples to deliberate on the state of affairs. As a mark of deference to Cæsar, and in recognition of his supreme position among them at the moment, an embassy of notables came to ask his sanction to this step, which was readily granted.*

When the council had been held the same embassy returned and with much show of humility laid before Cæsar a definite statement of their unenviable position. Divitiacus was the speaker, and he more especially represented the feeling of the Ædui and the Sequani. Both these tribes had been beaten and ill-treated by Ariovistus the German invader; they were indeed themselves chiefly to blame, and they seem to have been well aware of it. But there were other facts of which a victorious Roman general

---

* This at least is Cæsar's account, B. G., i., 30.

could hardly fail to take advantage. The Ædui, allies of the Roman people, had been forced to give hostages to an invading enemy, and to swear that they would in future ask for no aid from Rome; the Sequani, whose territory bordered the province for the whole distance from Geneva to Lyons, had had one third of their land confiscated, and were now called on to show their obedience still further by giving up another third to a German tribe which had lately joined Ariovistus from beyond the Rhine. They declared that this rude and cruel German was treating them as his slaves, and that they had no recourse but to submit unless Cæsar chose to interfere; that the whole of Gaul would ere long fall a prey to the barbarians, who had long wished to exchange their own forests for the rich and cultivated plains of the south.

The question then immediately before Cæsar at the moment was whether he or Ariovistus was to be obeyed by the Gallic tribes which lay between them; and to that question at least there was only one possible answer. Rome had indeed hardly more claim to their obedience than the German; but a civilised state will always claim rights over uncivilised states, and conceive of its own interests as the interests of humanity. Whether or not such ideas are consciously entertained by the civilised state, or justified by the circumstances of the case, it is at least certain that they are habitually acted upon. We may aptly remember that one of the gentlest and most righteous of British provincial governors did not hesitate a few years ago to make demands on a Zulu king more exacting by far than those which Cæsar was now to address to Ariovistus, and that they were applauded at the time by the majority of the English people.

Yet, in Cæsar's account of his action in this crisis, it is very plain that he was not only ready, but anxious, to gain his object without an appeal to arms. It was not his interest to run another serious risk without due cause; he had done quite enough for one summer, and his army, as events showed, was not yet thoroughly to be depended on. He must have wished to keep up the continuity of the diplomatic policy adopted towards the king during his consulship; for the Germans were well known to be most formidable warriors, but possessed of certain frank and chivalrous qualities which might render them open to honourable negotiation. He therefore sent to Ariovistus, asking for a personal interview. To this message a curt answer was returned: "Cæsar might come to him, if he pleased; it was not convenient for him to go to Cæsar, nor did he understand what the Romans were doing in a country which he had himself lately conquered." Cæsar now formulated his demands; Ariovistus must bring no more Germans across the Rhine, and must return the hostages which he had taken from the Ædui and Sequani.

A personal interview might have smoothed down the unpleasantness of such an ultimatum, and have ended in mutual admiration and at least a temporary adjustment; but Cæsar's envoys were not Cæsar, and the answer they brought back was no more than he could have expected. It was a point-blank refusal, a direct claim to rule over the two Gallic tribes, and a challenge to try the valour of troops who for fourteen years had never passed a night under a roof. Further intelligence of German progress southwards came in at the same time with his answer; a hundred Suebic communities were ready to cross the Rhine into northern Gaul, and the Harudes, who had been already complained of by the Ædui, were now actually ravaging their territory. Cæsar instantly provisioned his army, and hastened to meet Ariovistus.

Where the German king then was, he does not seem to have known when he started; but after three days' march news came in that the enemy was pushing in full force for Vesontio (now Besançon), the capital of the Sequani. Well aware that whichever army reached this town first, would have a great advantage in the abundant supplies stored there, as well as in the strength of its position, Cæsar marched day and night till he reached it; and occupying it without hearing anything more of the enemy, he devoted a few days to completing his commissariat. Throughout his military life his vigilant care for the physical well-being of his soldiers is most striking; and he writes of it as if he fully realised what was then far more than now a leading principle in all such warfare, that civilised troops are at an immense disadvantage in fighting with barbarians, unless they are in the best possible condition. At the present day inequality in weapons may lessen this disadvantage; but in the hand-to-hand fighting of antiquity the Italian soldiery was

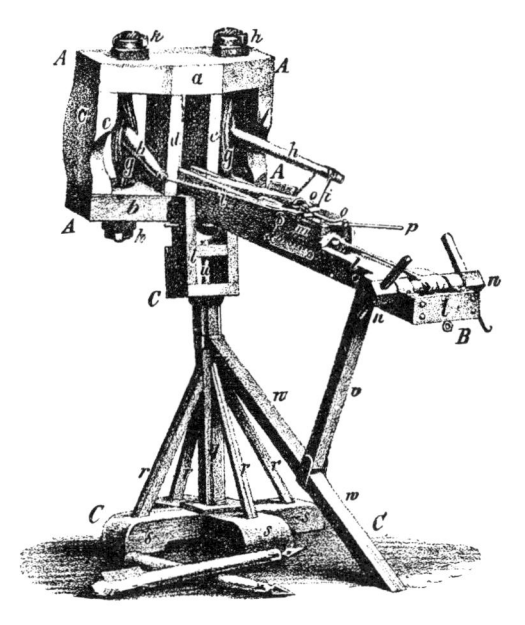

CATAPULT.
USED IN SIEGE OPERATIONS.
(*Baumeister.*)

naturally ill-matched against the hardy and powerful German, and even against the more civilised and less vigorous Gaul.

And Cæsar had now to learn that his soldiers were only too well aware of their physical inferiority. At Vesontio the army was stricken with a panic, caused by the novelty of their position in a country hitherto utterly unknown to them, and by the exaggerated accounts of the enemy brought in by native traders from the north. It seems to have begun with the effeminate officers who had followed the general to Gaul simply in expectation of spoil, after the common Roman fashion; many of these made excuses and departed, while others who had a remnant of shame in their degenerate minds remained to weep in their tents over their miserable lot. The picture that their general has left us of this panic, contained in a very few sentences of suppressed scorn, is one of the most striking in his whole work, and every word of it, as well as of Cæsar's own speech, which follows, should be studied by all who wish to understand how one man's genius can breathe fresh life into a decaying civilisation. What Cæsar achieved on this occasion with his army is a type of what he did afterwards with the Roman state.

The panic spread and threatened to affect the centurions and the rank and file; throughout the army men were *making their wills;* it was even expected that the soldiers would refuse to march when ordered to do so. He took the unusual step of calling a council, which included not only the higher officers, but the whole of the centurions; and made them a speech in which there is not a single harsh note, and every point of which must have gone home. The words cannot, indeed, be exactly those he used at the time, but the concluding sentence must have been held fast in his own memory and in the minds of all who heard him. " If no one else will follow me, I will go on with the tenth legion alone ; on that legion at least I can depend, and I will entrust myself to it as a body-guard." These words must have been speedily communicated to the whole army, and their effect was instantaneous. The tenth legion sent to thank him, the rest to explain and repudiate their shortcomings. The spirit of mutiny vanished without the infliction of a single punishment, and Cæsar was able to march at once with greater confidence than he had felt since he crossed the Alps.

The country they were now traversing, in which the battle was to be fought which put a stop to German invasion and made Cæsar master of eastern Gaul, is not unfamiliar to many Englishmen and Americans. The traveller from London to Basle, when he wakes in the early morning, finds himself passing through a rich undulating plain in the neighbourhood of the great stronghold of Belfort. To the north he may see the outskirts of the Vosges, and to the south the range of the Jura, the two great natural ramparts which defend the plains of France from an invader; but between these two walls of mountain there is a gap,—a weak point in the line of defence ; and it is this gap that the fortress commands. This opening Ariovistus must naturally use in entering Gaul from the valley of the Rhine ; and this too at the present day has offered easy access to railways, which can only be constructed with difficulty through the defiles of the two mountain ranges. To-day, the express trains, soon after passing Belfort, leave the open country and enter the picturesque valley of the Doubs, in order to strike the Rhine at Basle by a shorter though more difficult route; and this route was open to Cæsar also, had he chosen to avail himself of it. But it was for several reasons a hazardous one, and offered great advantages to an enemy well acquainted with the ground. He therefore took a longer route in the open country which lies around Belfort, and stretches northwards towards Mühlhausen and the Rhine. The modern traveller can follow closely on his track by taking the railway from Belfort to Mühlhausen; on his left lies the scene of the movements that ensued, in the comparatively narrow space between the Rhine and the outskirts of the Vosges.

After seven days' continuous march, Cæsar's scouts discovered the German army about fifteen miles distant, near the Rhine, not far from Mühlhausen. Ariovistus now sent to propose a conference; an offer which, as Cæsar clearly means us to understand, was intended to cover a treacherous design. If he tells the truth, Ariovistus had even been tampered with by certain enemies of Cæsar in Rome, and did not hesitate to own it at the conference. The interview was a failure, for by this time things had gone too far for accommodation. If there had ever been a chance of agreement, it was now destroyed; for the conversation was cut short by the threatening attitude of the German cavalry, which compelled Cæsar to retreat to his own guard. It was well for him that this guard was composed of his own legionaries, mounted on horseback, instead of the Gallic horse which Ariovistus evidently expected. What followed showed how foolhardy it would have been to trust his person to the good faith of barbarians with no escort but one composed of new and doubtful allies. Ariovistus sent to ask for a second interview. Cæsar naturally declined it, but sent a young officer, a Roman citizen though by birth a Gaul, to negotiate with the king in the Gallic tongue, with which the latter was well acquainted. No sooner had he entered the king's presence than he and the comrade sent with him were instantly seized and put in chains as spies. It was now obvious that nothing but a pitched battle could decide the quarrel; and Ariovistus appeared to challenge such an issue by moving his army along the spurs of the Vosges, until it was within an hour's march of Cæsar's camp. Next day, still apparently keeping under shelter of the hills, where he could not be attacked but at disadvantage, he marched past the Roman camp, with the obvious intention of cutting off Cæsar's communication with the corn-supplying country to the south. This Cæsar allowed him to do unhindered; probably because the nature of the ground forbade him to risk a general action at that moment.

But in order to place himself in Cæsar's rear, Ariovistus must have descended to the more open ground towards the Rhine; and battle was at once offered him. He declined it for five successive days, and with the instinct of a true general, tried to wear out Cæsar by constant attacks of his cavalry, mingled with swift-running esquires on foot. The situation was becoming awkward for the Romans; not only would their supplies soon begin to fail, but (though Cæsar does not tell us this) they must have been aware that on the first rumour of a reverse, the Gallic tribes would go over to Ariovistus. Cæsar accordingly on the sixth day marched out with his whole force, and using his two front lines to ward off attack, succeeded in forming another smaller camp close to that of the enemy; here he left two legions and a force of auxiliaries, and with his other four legions returned to the larger camp. Next day he again offered battle in vain; only the smaller camp was attacked, and no general engagement could be brought on.

Prisoners had told Cæsar that the reason why Ariovistus would not fight was that the German women, who were regarded as having prophetic power, would not promise a successful issue before the new moon. But it was becoming hazardous to wait; the enemy must be frightened, and forced into an action. With this object Cæsar adopted a ruse which showed his resource as a commander. With his six legions, each at the most but 5,000 strong, he could not venture to attack a greatly superior force, so long as that force remained in its camp; but he now made use of his light-armed troops, recruited probably from the Gallic population of the Transalpine province, and dispensing for the time with their aid as skirmishers, drew them up in front of his lesser camp in battle array, and in two divisions, so as to resemble two regular legions. With the whole of the rest of his forces he then marched straight for the enemy's camp. Ariovistus thus found himself menaced in front by Cæsar's main force, while two entire legions appeared to threaten his right flank and rear. At last he accepted battle, and drew out his forces in order of tribes, with regular intervals between each tribe. In the rear and on the flanks were ranged the carts and waggons, with the women placed upon them, weeping and imploring the warriors not to abandon them to the enemy.

Cæsar had alarmed Ariovistus by the ruse of the two supposed legions on his left wing, and knew that the German right was on this account unduly strengthened, while their left was proportionately weak. He accordingly fell with overwhelming force upon this left wing, and after a hard struggle put it to flight. The quality of his soldiers was fast improving. He has put it on record, that when the Germans locked their great shields together, and so formed an apparently impenetrable defence, there were legionaries bold enough to spring upon this shield-wall and tear it down with their hands. The battle was now won on his left, but on the right the numbers of the enemy were beginning to tell; and the third line or reserve had to be brought up. This was done by young Crassus, the son of the triumvir, who now and afterwards showed himself a capable officer, worth a better fate than to perish miserably

TESTUDO OR SHIELDS INTERLOCKED FOR THE STORMING OF A FORTRESS.
FROM TRAJAN'S COLUMN.
(*Baumeister.*)

The Defeat of the Germans.

in his father's ill-starred invasion of Parthia. He was in command of the cavalry, and was better able than the general to perceive what was needed ; for Cæsar, so far as we can gather from his account, had dismounted as at Bibracte, and was again giving the moral force of his presence to the main attack. To Crassus he gives the full credit of restoring the action by bringing up the reserve, feeling perhaps that but for the young officer's prompt action without orders, the result of the battle might have been different. As it was, the victory was complete ; the Roman cavalry, whose services had not been needed in the battle, cut the Germans to pieces as they fled to the Rhine, which was about five miles distant, and but few escaped across the river. Among the latter was Ariovistus himself ; but two of his wives and one daughter perished, and another daughter was taken alive. The German king disappears from history, the German pretensions to the possession of Gaul were put an end to for several centuries, and Cæsar, representing Rome, remained the sole arbiter in the politics of the eastern Celts.

It is not often that Cæsar in his " Commentaries " alludes to his own personal feelings , he appears in them, as we have already said, rather as a great governing force, than as a human being with feelings and affections. But he finds a place at the close of his account of this battle, to refer to an incident which, as he tells us, gave him as much pleasure as the victory itself. This was the recovery of the young Romanised Gaul Valerius Procillus, whom he had entrusted with his last message to Ariovistus, in full confidence that he would not be ill-used. The king had loaded him with fetters, and in this condition he was being dragged along in the flight of his captors, when Cæsar himself, pursuing with the cavalry, accidentally came upon him. The genuine feeling with which he tells the story, though it occupies but a few lines, helps us to understand the secret of Cæsar's wonderful influence over other men. He felt himself responsible for the fate of his own envoy, in this case evidently a personal friend, and tells almost with a shudder how the prisoner had three times escaped a terrible death at the hands of his captors, while the lots, which were drawn in his presence, each time decided that his fate was to be reserved for another occasion.

No further trouble being expected on the Rhine, the army was sent into winter quarters in the territory of the Sequani, probably at Besançon; and Cæsar himself, indefatigable as ever, set out to perform the work of a peaceful administrator in his other province of Cisalpine Gaul.

CHAPTER X.

THE CONQUEST OF NORTH-WESTERN GAUL.

57 B.C.

"THE troops were withdrawn for winter-quarters into the country of the Sequani." Cæsar wrote these few words in his usual quiet and matter-of-fact way, at the end of his first book on the Gallic War, as if there were no special significance about them. Yet he must have very well known that this act of his was the declaration of a new policy, and full of meaning alike for Gauls, Germans, and Italians. So far he had been acting as the champion of Gallic tribes against barbarian invaders, in order to secure the Roman frontier, and to push back the elements of discord. But to keep an army for a whole winter in territory which was not Roman, meant something more than this—it meant that he was going to extend the frontier permanently, and to trust no longer to the weak and crumbling barrier of Gallic population which separated him from the Rhine and the Germans.

The very sight of the Rhine, never till then seen by Roman soldiers, must have acted strongly on his adventurous spirit, and have suggested that new and useful strategic frontier which he bequeathed to a long line of Roman emperors. But still more irresistible, we may imagine, was his new experience of those undulating plains of eastern Gaul, in which the greater part of the summer had been spent. This was not a land of swamp and forest, like the Germany into which he afterwards penetrated, but one flowing with milk and honey, a veritable land of promise; inhabited by a settled and industrious people, active and intelligent, good traders, and, with the necessary training, good soldiers also. Cæsar had already begun to note the characteristics of this people, their strong and weak points, their political and religious institutions. He saw that they were hopelessly divided amongst themselves, and that their disunion would render their conquest easy and certain. He saw that the mass of the people were oppressed by an upper class of priests and princes, that they were little better than serfs, deep in debt, and ready for " new things." And above all he saw that in this splendid country—such a country as the Romans had never yet reached in their career of conquest,— there was a new and boundless field for the better side of Roman civilisation. What his predecessor Sertorius had done in Spain, might be done even better in Gaul. In the plains of Burgundy, far removed from the petty strife of the forum and the senate-house, Cæsar breathed in fact a fresher air; his mental vision was quickened, the range of his ideas widened ; the great chance he had been looking for so long seemed at last to have come. He was free to act as he pleased ; no one at Rome interfered with him. He was no more troubled by restrictions from a home government than was Cortes in Mexico ; his army was now ready to go with him anywhere and do anything at his orders ; it was as impossible for him to stay where he was, as it was for the British in India in the last century, and for the Russians in Central Asia at the present day. So he planted his army unhesitatingly on Gallic soil, and passed the winter in the assurance of some fresh chance occurring for further enterprise and advance.

The Sequani well deserved to have the legions quartered on them. They were really to blame for all that had happened in the last two years; they had conspired with the Arverni to crush the Romanising Ædui, they had called in the Germans to help them, they had allowed the Helvetii to pass through their territory, and had finally turned again to worship the rising star of Cæsar. They now did what they could to make amends. Through them and the Ædui it must have been that in the course of the winter news came to Labienus, who had been left in command of the army, that the powerful race of the Belgæ, occupying the whole territory to the north-west of them, was in confederation against Cæsar. Labienus at once wrote to his chief, who raised two new legions in Cisalpine Gaul, and sent them in the spring under a *legatus* across the Alps. He had already heard enough about these Belgæ to be sure that they would be formidable antagonists, and that if he was to conquer Gaul, they must be the first people to be dealt with. They boasted, he tells us, of German descent ; a fact which, though in itself apparently improbable, shows at once their contempt for other Gauls, and the reputation in which the Germans were held. They owned the whole country from the Seine on the south to the Rhine on the north, and had crossed the sea and occupied a large part of southern Britain. They were divided into a great number of tribes or cantons, and the disunion which was so fatal to the other Gauls might be expected to work their ruin also ; but this winter they were engaged (so Cæsar learnt) in patching up a strong alliance, and in exchanging hostages for the observance of good faith. When Cæsar arrived in camp, he was informed that their forces were being concentrated ; and with his usual rapidity, after organising his commissariat, he was on the borders of their territory in a fortnight.

His march was direct and unopposed from Besançon to what is now the famous Champagne country lying to the south and east of Rheims ; here dwelt the Remi, the most easterly of the Belgian cantons. Cæsar's swiftness, now as so often, had its due effect in striking terror and saving effusion of blood. The Remi forthwith surrendered themselves, and gave valuable information. They put Cæsar in possession of a complete list of the forces of the Belgæ, and told him of a rumour that the Germans in the far north had crossed the Rhine to assist them. The two most powerful Belgic peoples were the Suessiones (round Soissons), and the Bellovaci (about Beauvais), and between these two there appeared to be some kind of rivalry. Acting on this information of the Remi, Cæsar persuaded his friend Divitiacus the Æduan to make an inroad with his people into the country of the Bellovaci, and so to keep them occupied ; while he himself went straight on with the whole army until he struck the river Aisne at a point half-way between Rheims and Laon, just where is now the village of Berry-au-Bac. Here, as in the former campaign, the Anglo-Saxon tourist may still easily follow him ; for the now favourite route from Calais to Basle crosses the Aisne near this village, which lies on the present high-road connecting the two principal towns of the district.

At this point there was a bridge, of which Cæsar took possession. He then crossed and entrenched himself in a camp on the other side. Sabinus, one of his *legati*, who, like young Crassus, was afterwards to meet with a sad fate, was left in charge of the bridge with a strong detachment. Cæsar is careful to tell us that he fortified his camp strongly ; this alone would have justified him in taking up a position with a river in his rear crossed by a single bridge. The reader of his "Commentaries" must bear in mind that in the Roman system of warfare a well-fortified camp was all but inexpugnable, and that with a well-organised commissariat, an army so entrenched could for some time dispense with a regular base of operations. But in this case the communications also were secured by the bridge, and the river protected the camp from an attack in the rear.

Some few miles to the north-west, on a lofty ridge, which in 1814 was the scene of the bloody battle of Craonne, was a frontier fortress of the Remi, called Bibrax. The whole Belgic army, now on their way to meet the Romans, fell upon this place, and all but took it; word of this was sent to Cæsar, who despatched thither by night his most valued light-armed troops, from Crete, Numidia, and the Balearic Islands. He wisely refrained from dividing his main force, and these skirmishers proved sufficient to divert the enemy from the town. The Belgæ now came on against Cæsar, burning and ravaging on their way, and encamped opposite him on the other side of a little marshy stream, now called the Miette ; " their encampment, he says, appeared to be several miles in length. Cæsar was never given to despising his enemy, and his tactics here show admirably that combination of caution with confidence and daring which marks the consummate general. He would not at once offer to fight a pitched battle, but contented himself with feeling the strength and valour of the Belgæ in cavalry combats, until he was assured that he was a match for them. Then he drew out his six old legions on a hill which sloped gently to the swampy ground, leaving his two new legions as a reserve in the camp. The enemy, however, declined to fight, but made a vigorous attempt to cross the Aisne and take him in the rear. This attempt was checked without much difficulty; and then, finding the Roman position impregnable and their own supplies failing, the Belgic chiefs decided at a council of war to return to their several cantons, and to re-unite for the defence of whichever should be first attacked. They broke up, therefore, and their forces ceased to be a united army. The retreat began in the night, and it was daybreak before Cæsar appreciated its meaning; he instantly despatched his cavalry after them, followed by three legions under Labienus. The result was the total discomfiture, with terrible slaughter, of at least a large portion of the Belgic force, the whole of which was thus broken up and dispersed with hardly any loss to the Romans.

Before the cantons could concentrate their strength a second time, their untiring enemy bore down upon them one by one. He swooped upon Noviodunum, the fortress of the Suessiones; though its entrenchments were too strong to be carried at a first assault, the appearance of his artillery* effected an immediate surrender. From Noviodunum, the modern Soissons, he went on to Bratuspantium (Beauvais), and received a like submission from the Bellovaci; thence to the citadel of the Ambiani (Amiens), who surrendered themselves as readily. He does not tell how he dealt with this last people; but the Suessiones and the Bellovaci were treated with equal clemency and firmness. The one tribe had

---

* By this word are to be understood the various siege appliances in use at the time, which the Roman engineers had brought to a high degree of perfection ; *e. g.*, the *tormentum* and *ballista* (catapults), and the *aries* or battering-ram.

been the allies of the Remi, the other of the Ædui, and their cause was pleaded in each case by the representatives of the friendly canton. No cruelty was used; but their arms had to be given up, and hostages handed over as pledges for their obedience. The Suessiones gave among others the two sons of their chief, and the Bellovaci, the most powerful among the more civilised of the Belgic tribes, had to surrender six hundred of their citizens. In the case of this latter people, Cæsar made a point of insisting that his clemency was due to the influence of Divitiacus and the Ædui, whose ancient renown in Gaul it was a part of his policy to re-establish.

The reader of the "Commentaries" may be disposed to ask how it was that Cæsar, with a force of little more than 40,000 men, could effect even a temporary conquest by simply marching through the country of the Belgæ. It was done, no doubt, in the first place by the very rapidity of his progress and the perfect organisation of his material; but also in part by the demand for the surrender of arms, and chiefly by the policy of taking hostages as a pledge of good faith. This policy, now obsolete in civilised warfare, had a force which can only be understood by the careful student of antiquity. It is only when we have learnt to appreciate the strength of the ties that bound men together in groups of kin, and the troubles that might arise from a failure of heirs in those groups, that we can feel the binding force of a compulsory surrender of hostages. The claim of blood was the strongest that the ancient Celts knew, and the feeling sur-

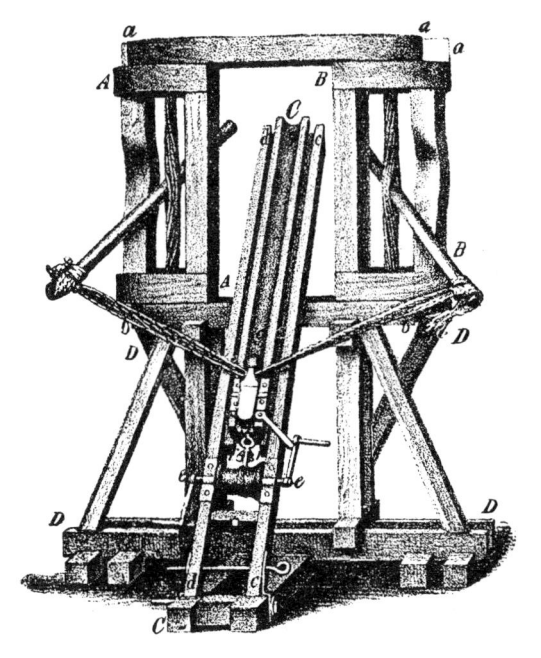

BALLISTA OR STONE-THROWER.
(*Baumeister.*)

vives among them to the present day. To place in the hands of their enemies those on whom the future of their race and their religious rites depended, was to let themselves be fettered by bonds which only the most desperate would ever attempt to break.

From the country round Amiens Cæsar turned in a north-easterly direction, and soon found himself in the territory of a people wilder and more warlike than any he had encountered this year. The Nervii were not to be cowed by the easy submission of their kinsmen, whom they regarded with contempt as traitors and cowards, demoralised by luxury and self-indulgence. They themselves drank no wine, and gave no admission to the traders in such luxuries, who swarmed in every other part of Gaul. They fought on foot only, and were protected from raids of hostile horsemen by the dense wall-like hedges of their country—a feature absent, then as now, from the open plains of central Gaul. This hardy people was now destined to win immortal glory, and to have its valour honourably recorded by the very man whom it so nearly overthrew.

After three days' march without coming in touch with the enemy, Cæsar learnt from prisoners that he was but a short march from the river Sabis (Sambre) and that the enemy were concentrated on the farther bank.* He at once altered his order of march,

---

* The scene of this famous battle has been placed with great probability on the Sambre near the Belgian frontier, a few miles above Maubeuge. The main line from Paris to Brussels skirts the battlefield as it passes the station of Hautmont.

and instead of advancing by successive legions separated from each other by their baggage, he placed the whole baggage in the rear, protected by the two newly raised legions, and led the way with the cavalry, followed by his six other legions under arms and ready to form for battle. It was well he did so: for Gallic informers had given the Nervii a hint that they might surprise him in the former order, and destroy his army, legion by legion, as they came successively up to camp.

When the cavalry came in sight of the river, they found it flowing at the foot of a gradual descent; on the other side the ground rose again at about the same gradient, open for a short space, and covered with wood higher up. A few horsemen were seen on the lower open ground; these were quickly brushed away by the Roman cavalry and light-armed, who easily crossed a stream not more than three feet in depth. The enemy disappeared into the wood, but as quickly reappeared, and a desultory combat went on while the six legions came up, marked out their camp, and set to work upon it. While they were thus engaged with spade and mattock, or in search of the brushwood needed to construct the defences, their helmets laid aside, their shields hanging loose on their backs, there emerged from the wood opposite them the whole force of the enemy, sweeping the Roman cavalry before them, and making with prodigious speed for the river and the unfinished camp.

The struggle that ensued was one of the most terrible that Roman soldiers ever had to go through.

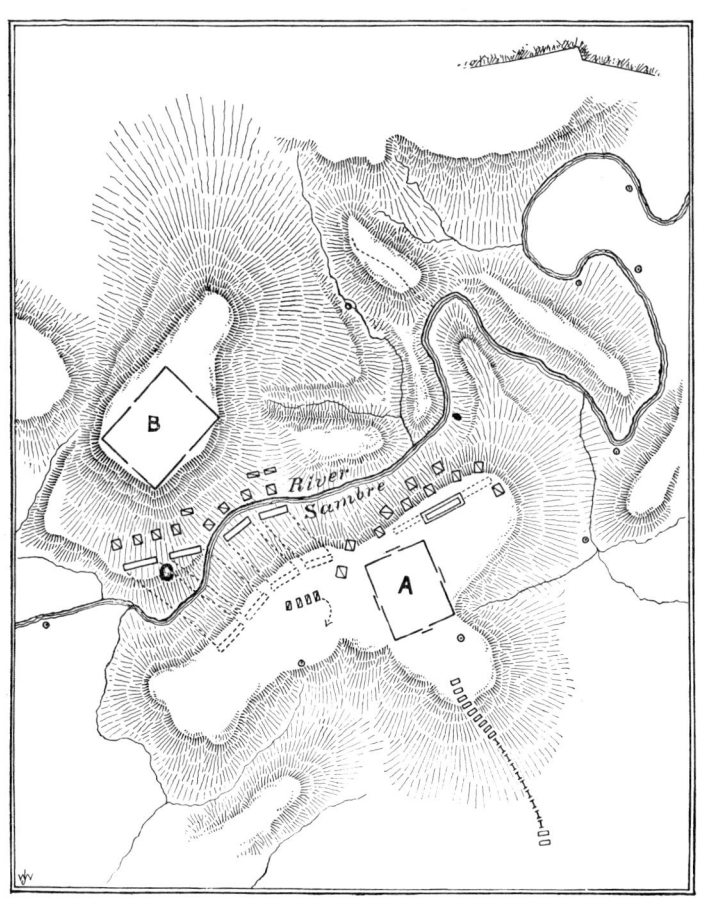

BATTLE OF THE SAMBRE, 57 B.C.

A. CÆSAR'S CAMP.   B. CAMP OF NERVII.   C. LABIENUS WITH TENTH LEGION.

The memory of it lived in Cæsar's mind so vividly that he seems to fight the battle over again as he describes it, in language for him unusually strong and intense. "There was no time to think," he says; "the enemy were no sooner out of the wood than they seemed to be upon us; the general had but a moment to go through the whole process of getting thirty thousand men into such order as the hurry allowed." And it is plain from his narrative that two things alone saved that army from total destruction: the excellent discipline and intelligence of the individual soldier, and the coolness and personal valour of the wonderful man who led them. Every man did his part; each legion was got into some sort of fighting array by its commander; as the men hurried in they took station where they could, and wasted no time in seeking their own companies. Cæsar after giving the first few necessary orders and signals, gave up all attempt to govern the battle, and hurried round cheering and urging his men, well knowing that all tactics were both useless and impossible, and that the day would be decided by sheer hard fighting.

On the left was the famous tenth legion, to which Cæsar had found time to give a few hurried words of exhortation; and these veterans, with the ninth legion, resisted and broke the enemy in front of them, and pursued them down the slope and across the river. Two legions in the centre also stood firm and even gained ground. But on the right there seems to have been a gap in the line, caused partly, perhaps, by the nature of the ground, partly by the advance of the two legions in the centre; and this gap caused the camp itself to be exposed in front and flank. To this point Cæsar now hurried, for the main force of the Nervii was being pushed into the vacant space, and was beginning to surround the two legions on the right. When he arrived defeat must have seemed inevitable ; the cavalry and light-armed had taken to flight, the camp-followers had vanished in a general stampede, and spread the news of a disaster in every direction. The two legions were huddled in a narrow space, without room to fight freely; the twelfth had lost almost all its officers and the standard belonging to one of its cohorts. There was no reserve available, and the fight threatened every moment to become a second Cannæ. Cæsar seeing this as he rode round in the rear, seized a shield from a common soldier, rushed with it to the front, shouting encouragement, and calling on the centurions by name ; and by thus steadying the men for a few minutes, and restoring something of their ardour to do well in the eyes of their general, he found an opportunity of disentangling the crowded companies, so as to give them space to use their swords. This done, he contrived to bring the two legions together, so that they could not be surrounded separately, and further formed them back to back, enabling them to fight at once in front and rear. The dread of being cut off, which often paralyses even the best soldiers, gradually left them, and they began to fight with greater freedom and pluck.

And now the whole aspect of the battle suddenly changed ; discipline had done its work, and was to be rewarded. Labienus, who had pursued the right wing of the enemy to their camp in the wood, sent back the tenth legion in hot haste to the rescue. The Nervii were thus themselves taken in the rear; and no sooner had the tide turned, than the cavalry and even the camp-followers began to return, and did their best to re-establish their credit. Even the wounded struggled and fought, leaning on their shields, and adding their quota to the heaps of dead bodies. Behind these heaps the undaunted enemy still strove to fight, snatching up the Roman spears as they fell among them, and hurling them back at their owners. Their heroism won Cæsar's unbounded admiration; an attack like theirs, he says, on such difficult ground, showed plainly that they fully merited their reputation for extraordinary valour. It is no disgrace to the Roman soldiers that after such an awful struggle and escape, they should have indulged in indiscriminate slaughter; the enemy indeed invited it by the desperate way in which they fought. When the Nervian women sent to implore Cæsar's mercy after the news of the battle reached them, they told him that but three " counsellors " survived out of six hundred, and but five hundred warriors out of a total of sixty thousand. This was of course an exaggeration; but it shows well how this famous battle might be regarded by the Gauls as making further resistance hopeless. In vain the flower of the Gallic warriors had fought against the small Italians, with their rigid discipline, and their wonderful commander. And as Cæsar was ready to receive all into submission, on condition of their giving hostages and surrendering all their arms, the whole Gallic population accepted the position that was forced on them. One tribe alone, the Aduatuci, living probably around Charleroi to the north of the Nervii, though accepting the conditions, rescued secretly a part of their weapons, and made a desperate attempt to destroy their enemy by a night attack. Cæsar, who half suspected them, drove them back into their town, from which he had the previous night (with singular humanity for that age) withdrawn all his soldiers lest they should be tempted to do violence to the conquered; and taking easy possession the next day, he sold the whole population into slavery, to the number of fifty-three thousand.

In such an act he is but the embodiment of the proud Roman policy of the Republic

Parcere subjectis et debellare superbos.

But it was indeed only treachery and rebellion that he punished, not mere resistance. Courage always won his esteem, and it is clear that he admired and esteemed the Gauls, for their courage as for their many gifts. But as a conqueror with a definite object before him, he never relaxed his firmness or shrank from exacting what he thought due; and his firmness is apt to become hardness in our eyes, as our sympathy is roused for a brave and struggling people.

Publius Crassus had been sent early in the summer with one legion to the tribes bordering on the ocean, whose warlike reputation was not supposed to be such as would render a larger force necessary; and he now reported to Cæsar that a number of these cantons had submitted and given hostages. The news of Cæsar's progress and final victory must have sped very swiftly in a country where news of any kind was the thing most desired and enjoyed in every town and hamlet. Even from beyond the Rhine came envoys, promising obedience and hostages from the renowned Germans. But with a lordliness of spirit that showed how clear the way now was before him, and how confidently he could tread it, he ordered them to return home, and come to him again the following spring. He then distributed the army in winter-quarters over the conquered territory, and left for his Cisalpine province, where the news reached him that the Senate had voted him the unprecedented honour of a *supplicatio* or thanksgiving to last fifteen days.

So ended the memorable year 57 B.C.; when the first foundation was laid of that fruitful civilisation of Gaul, of which it has been said by one of its own heirs in this century, that it has contributed more to the education of the European world than any other save that of Greece.

CHAPTER XI.

CONFERENCE AT LUCCA, AND CAMPAIGN IN BRITTANY.

56 B.C.

CÆSAR was fully occupied both in the winter of 57–56 B.C., and in the spring which followed. Each winter, when he had accomplished the long and wearisome journey to Cisalpine Gaul, the general had to take up the rôle of judge, and go his circuits, settling all the arrears of jurisdiction which had been accumulating during the summer. And there was one of his provinces which he had not as yet even visited; that of Illyria, which had been given him along with Cisalpine Gaul by the Lex Vatinia. This was the coast-district east of the Adriatic, the ancient home of pirates and robbers; the Roman government had never as yet taken the trouble thoroughly to reduce and organise it, and it is probable that Cæsar himself was its first regular provincial governor. While engaged here this winter, his attention was distracted by events occurring in the farthest districts of Gaul. News arrived from young Crassus, who had been left with the seventh legion on the lower Loire, that officers sent by him to collect provisions from the neighbouring tribes had been detained and imprisoned, and that a general rebellion was being fomented in the districts bordering on the ocean. Cæsar, at a distance of some eight hundred miles from the scene of these events, at once sent orders for the equipment of a fleet on the Loire, and made up his mind to complete his work in western Gaul the following summer by carrying on the war by sea as well as on land. The Veneti, inhabiting part of modern Brittany, were known to him already as the most formidable of the peoples on the coast, and the most skilled in naval warfare. He knew also that they kept up a close relation with the Celts of Britain, the island beyond the ocean which, as Cæsar was well aware, served as a refuge for the more independent spirits among the conquered Gauls, and as the hotbed in which fresh rebellions were nourished.* Already, we may fairly guess, he was projecting an invasion of this island; not only from reasons of policy, but stimulated doubtless by the spirit of adventure and discovery which had been growing in him since he had first touched the Rhine and the ocean.

* See *e. g.*, B. G., iii., 9.

But during the spring of 56 B.C. events at Rome made it obvious that he would be this year later than usual in getting to his distant army. Ever since the one real leader of men had left Rome, the influence of the triumvirate had been growing weaker. In 58 B.C., Clodius as tribune had reigned supreme in the streets, while Pompeius, who should have controlled him, was living in retirement with his new wife Julia, to whom, as we saw, he was passionately devoted. Crassus, who had never had any cordiality to spare for his former rival, was rapidly becoming estranged from him, and did nothing whatever to restore order in the capital. That year Cicero had been exiled, and all attempts to secure his return had been baffled, in spite of an opposition street-rabble under the leadership of Milo and others, whose frequent collisions with the Clodian mob must have made life almost intolerable for decent and orderly Romans. The hopelessness of realising any of the blessings of order and security which we are used to associate with civilisation, except under a new and stronger form of government, must be apparent to everyone who wades through the wretched story of the anarchy and confusion of these two years.

In August 57 B.C., after many fruitless efforts, Cicero was recalled from exile; a step which was brought about with the consent of the triumvirate, after they had exacted a promise from Quintus Cicero that he would be responsible for his brother's conduct. Cicero at once attached himself to Pompeius, acting (as he himself put it on record),* on the

---

* Ad Fam., i., 9, 14.

old vain hope that he might guide the counsels of this witless politician, and might even, through his influence, transform Cæsar himself into a good servant of the Senate. But such a hope was from the outset fallacious; and Cicero, who ought to have known this already, failed to understand it till after the bitter experience of many years. To support the republican constitution from genuine conviction of its excellence, never had been, and never could be, the interest or the policy of Pompeius. At this very moment his thoughts were turned in quite a different direction; he was a soldier tired of inaction, and anxious to get some work to do by which he might counterbalance the enormous prestige Cæsar had been acquiring in Gaul. To this desire Cicero could only respond by supporting a law which gave him a five years' commission for supplying the capital with corn; and this Pompeius accepted, but it was not what he wanted. A project for the occupation of Egypt, under pretext of restoring the banished king, Ptolemy Auletes, was more to his purpose; but this Cicero was forced to resist, for it would have probably ended in the division of the Roman world into two great military powers in East and West, and would have precipitated the result that came about seven years later. It was evident that Cicero and Pompeius could never work together, and for the time Cicero seems to have abandoned the idea. The only other policy open to him was to try and reconstitute a republican party; and this was just as hopeless as the attempt to reduce Pompeius to orthodoxy. The fact was that the republican party, so far as it existed or deserved the name, entirely declined to be reconstituted by Cicero. There was no hope for him of renewing the former policy of the agreement of the orders. The triumvirs had won over the equites in 59 B.C.; and even if this had not been so, Cicero could not have gathered a senatorial party together to combine with them. Again and again in his private letters of this period he complains of hostility and jealousy on the part of those degenerate nobles who would not act themselves nor allow another to act for them. They hated him as narrow aristocrats are always liable to hate new men; they hated him because he was clever, witty, sarcastic, and pushing, and more than all because he was so firmly convinced, and never scrupled to let them know his conviction, that neither they nor the Republic could possibly get on without him.

In spite, however, of his lack of any hearty following, Cicero did not scruple to attack the triumvirate with all the vigour he was capable of, and thereby rushed upon his fate. In defending Sestius, a tribune who had rioted on his behalf during his exile, he set himself to review the political history of recent years in a sense unfavourable to the triumvirs; and in cross-examining the witness Vatinius, one of Cæsar's agents, he let fly all his pent-up wrath, not so much at the individual rulers, as at their instruments and methods. Sestius was acquitted early in March, 56 B.C.; and he now thought he might venture even further. At the beginning of April, he asked leave, as we should say, to bring the question of the Campanian land before the Senate on the Ides of May, *i.e.*, to reconsider the settlement of Pompeius' veterans, and, in his own language, to attack the very centre and citadel of the enemy's position.

To this the Senate consented. Crassus went at once to Lucca, a frontier town of Cisalpine Gaul, whence Cæsar was watching affairs at Rome; Pompeius went to Sardinia and Africa on business connected with the corn-supply, and then hastened to join Cæsar and Crassus at Lucca. Thither all the *élite* of the popular party were assembled; 200 senators are said to have been in the town, and 120 lictors, attending Roman magistrates, showed the world what it had to learn a few years later as a permanent lesson, that the unmanageable capital was no longer the only place in which the powers of government could be exercised. Cæsar entertained his guests with magnificence; the wealth of Gaul was exhibited to their wondering eyes; and from this time forward it became evident to all that in the material resources of power, as well as in the qualities that make a ruler of men, Cæsar had far outstripped both his antagonists and his allies.

A few days sufficed to change the whole situation of affairs. It was arranged that bills should be brought before Senate and people, 1st, to give Cæsar a new term of five years' government to complete his work in Gaul; 2d, to give Pompeius the government of both Spanish provinces for five years also; 3d, to secure the succession of Crassus to the government of Syria, in order to make war on the growing strength of the Parthian Empire beyond the

Euphrates. It was also agreed that the two latter should have the consulship for 55 B.C., a result which could easily be secured by Cæsar's wealth and by the votes of his veterans; and that the utmost pressure should be put upon Cicero to prevent his bringing up the question of the Campanian land in the Senate. Pompeius went off to Sardinia, where Q. Cicero was acting for him in the matter of the corn-supply; they had a long interview, which resulted in a promise from Quintus to secure his brother's support for the new arrangements; and, strange as it seems to us now, Cicero himself yielded without a struggle. This is not a life of Cicero, and it is not necessary here to explain this sudden and complete submission to the power which for months he had been doing his best to overthrow. It is sufficient to notice that for some time to come the old and natural friendship between him and Cæsar was allowed to re-assert itself; that they corresponded in affectionate terms; and that Cæsar lent him the money he had been sorely in need of since his exile. A few weeks later he signalised his conversion by a vigorous speech in the Senate, in which we still admire the glowing tribute to Cæsar's great work in the West, and the singular grace and tact with which he sketches the history of his relations with a friend whose acts had often strained, but never destroyed, his good-will and esteem.*

The proceedings at the conference of Lucca are differently explained by the historians and biographers, for the obvious reason that they were secret in so far at least as the three principals were con-

---

* This was the speech " de provinciis consularibus."

cerned. What astonishes us in them is that Cæsar should have so readily consented to arrangements which might seriously prejudice his position ere many years had passed, and might turn his coadjutors, who had so far been quiescent if inactive, into dangerous military rivals. But we may interpret Cæsar's action with confidence by the light of his one leading characteristic as a man of action. He never put his hand to a piece of work without carrying it through to the end; work was to him so absorbing and so necessary that he could entertain no visionary plans while it was still unfinished, and was content to let things take their course elsewhere, provided he himself were allowed to go through with what was before him. To some, and even to the penetrating genius of Mommsen, the astonishing career of Cæsar mounting upwards step by step, and mapped out before us as we look on it as a whole, suggests the irresistible temptation of accounting for it by ascribing to him a clear, far-reaching vision capable of planning out his whole route, from the base to the summit of the difficult crags that must be scaled. But this, we may venture to believe, is wholly to mistake the character of the man. He may have believed in his destiny, but assuredly he took no great trouble to control it. He was a climber who doubtless believed that he might reach the highest peak; but his whole energy as he climbed was given to making his footing firm where he stood. Leaving the future of his relations with his rivals and enemies to take care of itself, he turned back to join his legions on the inhospitable coast of Brittany.

The campaign of 56 B.C. is not one that need detain us. His own part in it was not a personally successful one, and he contents himself in his third book with giving an account, accompanied by ungrudging praise, of the more fortunate efforts of the lieutenants under his direction. Labienus in the far distant country of the Rhine and Moselle, young Crassus in Aquitania under the Pyrenees, and Titurius Sabinus in what is now Normandy,—all had their successes chronicled by the general-in-chief. But the chief merit lay with the energetic young officer whom Cæsar had placed in command of his fleet on the Loire, and left to his own resources in grappling with the formidable navy of the Veneti in the open ocean. Decimus Brutus was one of those active and single-minded officers in whom Cæsar came to repose entire confidence, and who followed their master's fortunes with unswerving loyalty and friendship until the last few weeks of his life. On this occasion, fighting through a long summer's day against a vastly superior fleet, under the cliffs whence Cæsar and his army were watching the unequal combat with anxiety, he succeeded in totally destroying his enemy by means of a new invention for cutting their rigging, and so disabling them as to make them an easy prey. The Veneti, who were almost wholly relying on their navy as a defence, surrendered themselves unconditionally, and had to pay a heavy penalty for imprisoning Roman envoys; all the members of their council were put to death, and the rest of the male population were sold as slaves.

This is the first example we meet with of what must seem to us deliberate cruelty on Cæsar's part towards a population struggling bravely for liberty; hitherto we have only had to remark his singular clemency, and the protection he extended to defenceless women and children. His own explanation is clear and brief.* He decided that a heavy punishment must be inflicted, in order that the barbarians might learn for the future to be more careful of the inviolability of envoys. On this it has been remarked, that the military tribunes who had been detained in chains by these tribes during Cæsar's absence, were not ambassadors in the proper sense of the word, but only officers sent to make requisitions for corn. It is possible of course that they may have been arrogant in their mission, though that is a conjecture for which we have no evidence; but from Cæsar's point of view, whether or no they were wanting in tact and courtesy, they were at least his *legati*, dealing with people who had nominally submitted to the Roman power, and who had given hostages as a pledge of obedience. And more than this, the corn-supply was a matter of the most vital importance to Cæsar, as has been already pointed out; he was entirely dependent on it for the very existence of his army, and the only way in which he could make it secure was by vigorously holding the conquered to their pledges, and by maintaining the inviolability of his foraging parties. Lastly, the violation had been followed by an open rebellion and an extremely dangerous and difficult campaign; and Cæsar was now beginning to

---
* B. G., iii., 16.

feel that dread anxiety of revolt, which has so often driven conquerors to make a terrible example in order to save themselves from repeated annoyance and continuous bloodshed. These were Cæsar's reasons for an act which is abhorrent to our modern feeling of justice, and which enlists all our sympathies on the side of the struggling victims of Roman conquest.

By the end of the summer, Cæsar and his generals had been everywhere victorious, and Gaul from the Pyrenees to the Rhine appeared to be reduced to obedience. Two tribes, the Morini and Menapii, dwelling on the coast of modern Picardy and Flanders, were indeed still in arms and had made no submission; and to these Cæsar turned his attention for a while in the early autumn. His expedition was not a success, for the country was covered with wood and swamp, and these wild people fled into the forest, leaving their empty dwellings at his mercy. Heavy rains also checked his progress; and after ravaging their cultivated land, and burning their villages, he gave up the attempt to reduce them, led his army back to Normandy and Brittany for the winter, and returned himself to Cisalpine Gaul, in order to discharge his civil duties.[*]

---

[*] B. G., iv., 6, 1.

CHAPTER XII.

INVASIONS OF GERMANY AND BRITAIN.
55–54 B.C.

THE fourth book of the Gallic War is of far greater interest than the third. It introduces us for the first time in history to two hitherto unknown peoples, the Germans of the lower Rhine, and the inhabitants of Britain. In this year, 55 B.C., these barbarians first saw the army of a civilised power in their land, and learnt that science and perseverance can overcome all natural obstacles, and defeat untrained courage.

Cæsar begins with an account of the manners and customs of the Suebi, to whose power and pertinacity the German campaign was due. He starts with their social economy, as we should call it, and in a few condensed sentences gives his reader a rational explanation of their formidable character as neighbours, based on what he had observed or learnt of their agricultural system, their mode of life, and their education. A modern writer would have spread this information over half a volume; Cæsar tells it in two very short chapters, and subordinates it strictly to the matter he has in hand. These chapters, and those more famous ones in the sixth book which describe the social state of the Gauls, are the very choicest product of the best type of Roman mind, and stand out in striking contrast to the dreariness of the Greek professed historian of this and later ages, and even to the long-winded wordiness of the modern traveller.

These two chapters seem by Cæsar to be meant to explain the events which followed, by showing his reader the really formidable nature of the German peoples; their hardihood, abstinence, courage, and above all their refusal to admit traders, and dislike of all neighbours. He wishes it to be seen that an invasion of Gaul by a whole German tribe was a thing he could not possibly permit, and had firmly determined to resist, ever since he had rolled back Ariovistus and the Suebi across the upper Rhine. Examining carefully his account of this people, we see that he looked upon the Suebi as at the bottom of all disturbance along his new frontier of the Rhine; it was they who set other tribes in motion, by refusing to have them as neighbours, turning them bag and baggage out of their homes, and destroying their crops wherever the unfortunates settled. The Ubii, a powerful people on their northern border, could not be thus rooted out of their settlements, though they were forced to pay tribute; but two other tribes, the Usipetes and Tencteri, were entirely dislodged by the Suebi, and sent wandering hopelessly about Germany, to find a home at last, as they thought, on the lower Rhine, not far from its mouth. Cæsar in fact plainly means to impress on us that he had a series of hornets' nests on his frontier ready to swarm upon the plains of Gaul whenever the strongest among them should drive the others out; that they would give the milder Gauls no peace if once they settled in Gaul; and that these Gauls themselves, with their love of news and of change, their mobile and uncertain temperament, would inevitably be shaken in their allegiance to Rome by any such event.

The two homeless tribes, victims of Suebian bullying, succeeded by a ruse in crossing the Rhine and occupying part of the territory of the Gallic Menapii in what is now northern Belgium. This drew Cæsar upon them at once. As he had expected, the Gauls of the valley of the Meuse invited them to advance, doubtless as future auxiliaries against the Roman power. He therefore advanced rapidly along that river (the course of which he pauses for a moment to describe), after summoning a meeting of Gallic chieftains and assuming the position of their protector and champion. Soon an embassy met him from the Usipetes and Tencteri, demanding freedom to settle in the lands they had won. Cæsar answered that he could not permit it, adding that he would use his authority with the Ubii beyond the

Rhine to allot the wanderers a portion of their own territory. At the same time he refused to stay his own advance as they requested, because he knew that they had sent a large force of cavalry away to forage and merely wished to delay the inevitable struggle till the return of this detachment. They were to return in three days; meanwhile he would continue his march.

On the third day they met him on his march and begged for a further three days to ascertain whether the Ubii would be willing to receive them. This demand Cæsar again chose to consider as a subterfuge, and it may be that he was right; for if we are to accept as correct his statement that he was still on or near the Meuse, it must have been impossible for envoys to go to the Ubii and return in the short space of three days. He declined their request, but promised only to advance a short distance that day to a spot where there was water, and bade them come again next day in larger numbers to consider the whole matter. This was equivalent to a suspension of arms; and Cæsar sent express orders to his cavalry in front not to attack the enemy.

Upon this unsuspecting Gallic cavalry of his, however, the Germans made a sudden treacherous attack with a much smaller force, and utterly routed them, killing seventy-four, and among them a valued Gallic officer, whose sacrifice of his own life to save his brother is related by his chief with evident admiration and sympathy. After this reverse Cæsar determined to strike at once. A whole German tribe, in all (as he says) 430,000 strong, was in his

Invasions of Germany and Britain.

front, the impressionable Gallic population ready to rise in his rear. To negotiate further with a people who had already tricked the Menapii, and were now plainly trying to deceive himself, was "the height of folly," nor could he wait till they had gathered their whole strength. When next day a numerous embassy of chiefs and others came into his camp, as he had requested, for further negotiations, he·detained them as prisoners on account of the late breach of truce; and then making a forced march upon the German camp, where the whole mass of men, women, and children were unsuspectingly awaiting the return of their leaders, he let loose his legions upon them, slaughtered a great multitude, and drove the rest into the Rhine, near the angle of its confluence with the Meuse. His narrative seems to imply that the whole 430,000 perished in various ways, and this has been the general inference of historians; he does not, however, say this directly, and it is not in itself probable. But it is certain that he repaid treachery in its own coin; and though this was done under great provocation, and in circumstances of greater danger than we can probably estimate correctly, yet we must lament that he should here for once have violated his own honourable nature. His enemies at home did not lose the chance thus offered them, and Cato as their mouthpiece actually proposed in the Senate that the conqueror of Gaul should be given up to the Germans, as a reparation for the crime committed against them. However we ourselves may judge of Cæsar in this matter, we may be quite sure that Cato's was a bitterly prejudiced opinion : and it is as well to remember that this purist had but lately returned from carrying out, as a rigorous agent of Roman unscrupulousness, one of the most unjustifiable acts of robbery ever committed by the Roman government.* *Quis custodiet ipsos custodes ?*

Not content with the destruction of this invading host, Cæsar now determined to turn the tables on the Germans, and show them that a Roman army could not only defend Gaul, but carry the war into the country of the invaders. The German cavalry, which had been absent foraging on the day of the battle, had escaped across the Rhine to the territory of the Sugambri, which we may place with tolerable certainty in the country to the east of Cologne and Düsseldorf. Cæsar sent to the Sugambri, demanding the surrender of the refugees who had dared to invade Gaul, and received a haughty answer; the Ubii, on the other hand, who were wedged in between the Sugambri on the north and the Suebi on the south, asked him for support against their untoward neighbours. He decided to cross the Rhine, to frighten the Sugambri, and to give a moral support to the more civilised and friendly Ubii. The latter promised him a supply of boats ; but, to use his own words, "he did not think that method of crossing sufficiently secure, or in keeping with his own dignity or that of the Roman people." He wanted in fact to impress these wild peoples with a sense of the vast power which the arts of civilisation place in the hands of a determined man, and at the

---

* The plundering of Ptolemy, King of Cyprus.—Plutarch, Cato, 34 foll.

same time to run no risk from the treachery with which he clearly credited his German enemies.

In ten days a bridge was completed, probably not far from the modern Bonn, where the river-bed is softer and the current less strong than higher up the stream. It was a triumph both of engineering and industry. Cæsar does not mention the names of his engineers, nor does he say how far he himself had a hand in the design; but he was able more than three years later to write an exact account of it, from which the nature of the structure can be understood, even without the help of diagrams, by any careful and intelligent reader. The interest for us perhaps lies not so much in the simplicity of the design, or the care taken to reckon duly with the force of the current, but in the extraordinary speed with which the execution followed on the plan. Nothing can better show us what an admirably organised body Cæsar's army must have been; able and ready literally " to go anywhere and do anything" at the bidding of a chief who devoted all his energies to their well-being, safety, and comfort. The Roman legionary was always trained to turn his hand to any kind of work; but to build such a bridge in ten days —to hew the timber from the forest, to bring it to the spot, to work it into shape, to drive the piles into the river-bed, must have called for an amount of labour and patience on the part of the whole force, which could only have been cheerfully given to a commander in whose star and genius every man believed. The military art is seen here at its highest point of perfection; where the army works, not as a machine, but as an intelligent organism, guided and inspired in the movement of each minutest member by a single master-mind.

Cæsar's object being not to conquer new territory, but to impress the Germans with his power, he only spent eighteen days on the farther side of the Rhine. The Sugambri vanished in their forests, and he did not attempt to pursue them. After destroying their crops and burning their villages, he turned to the land of the Ubii, and promised them aid against the Suebi ; but he was not to be induced to attack that formidable people, who had concentrated their forces in their own territory in expectation of invasion. He had other designs in hand ; and returning to the bridge, which he had left strongly guarded on both banks, he recrossed it, broke it down, and turned his back on the Rhine with a full sense that he had done all that he had intended to do.

He had seen the white cliffs of Britain the year before in his expedition against the Morini. He had been hearing of the island ever since he came to Gaul, and knew it to be a refuge for his enemies and a secret source of their strength.[*] He had now a fleet which could navigate the ocean ; and as he failed to obtain any satisfactory information about the nature and inhabitants of the country from the traders and merchants who alone were acquainted with it, he determined to go and reconnoitre it for himself. Every precaution was taken, for the enterprise was perhaps the most hazardous ever yet undertaken by a Roman general. Volusenus, an officer whose command of the Gallic cavalry made

[*] B. G. iv., 20.

40 FEET ACROSS.

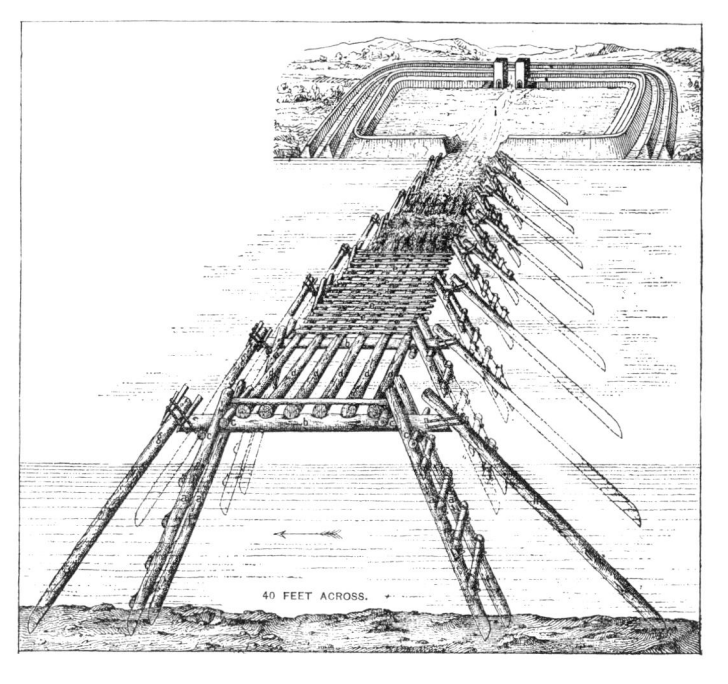

BRIDGE BUILT BY CÆSAR ACROSS THE RHINE.

him a fit person to land on a strange Celtic shore, had been sent with a ship of war to discover a suitable harbour, and to make inquiries as to the strength and warlike capacity of the natives. Envoys sent by British tribes to whom the rumour of Cæsar's coming had floated, were warmly received, and sent back with promises of his good-will and protection; and a Gaul of distinction was sent with them, who was already known in the island and in some degree influential there. This person was one Commius, of whom we shall hear more hereafter. Cæsar had made him King of the Atrebates, and could rely upon his intelligence and fidelity.

Volusenus returned without having ventured to land, and therefore without any very useful information. Cæsar had by this time assembled eighty merchant ships in one port, to transport two legions, and eighteen in another a few miles farther up the coast, to carry a detachment of cavalry. The last dispositions for the protection of the ports and the movements of the rest of the army were completed by August 26th; and on that night, with a favouring breeze, he set sail shortly after midnight with the two legions, having sent orders to the cavalry to follow him from the upper port.

Where was it that this famous crossing of our familiar Channel took place? Whence did Cæsar sail, and where did he land? These are questions that have been discussed with all the aid of classical learning, mediæval history, geology, hydrography, and with a fair admixture of reason and good temper. But in spite of the confidence of some writers on the subject, the questions will perhaps never be finally solved ; and fortunately they do not admit of being discussed here. It is, however, much easier to guess at the port from which he sailed than to make out with any certainty the point on the English coast where he succeeded in forcing a landing. We may fairly assume that both in this and in next year's expedition, he set sail from the harbour of Wissant, now sand-choked and disused. This harbour, which Cæsar calls the Portus Itius, lay some twelve miles west of Calais, and was sheltered from the prevailing south-west winds by Cape Grisnez, the Itian promontory, as it was then named. After a slow and cautious voyage, he found himself at about 9 A.M. under some abrupt cliffs, which we may suppose to have been those between Dover and Folkestone. Only his fastest ships had kept up with him ; and as the Britons occupied the summits of the cliffs, whence they could hurl missiles onto the beach below, he waited here for some hours for the rest of his fleet, and then, finding the tide flowing westwards, turned towards the low shore of Romney marsh, and prepared to effect a landing there. The old belief that he turned eastwards and landed at Deal, cannot, in the present state of our knowledge of the tides, be any longer maintained. But another view of his movements takes him from Boulogne, or some port west of Wissant, and brings him to the cliffs of Hastings, and so to the level shore of Pevensey.*

---

* Much can be said in favour of this opinion ; but if both invasions be taken into consideration, the route by Wissant and Romney seems the most probable. See the controversy between Messrs. Malden and Ridgway in recent numbers of the *Journal of Philology*.

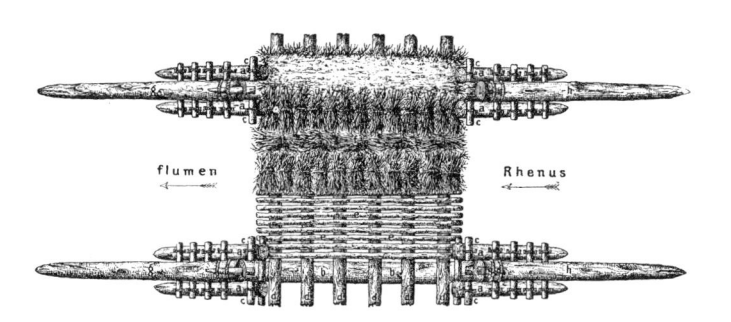

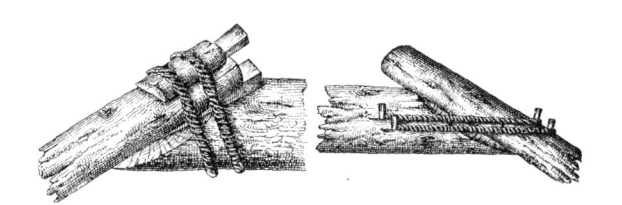

SECTION OF THE BRIDGE, SHOWING METHOD OF CONSTRUCTION.

The scene at the landing is graphically described by Cæsar, and is familiar to most of us. The difficulty was very great, for the Britons were on the beach with their formidable war-chariots, and the ships drew too much water to be brought in close to the shore. But Cæsar had employed the delay near Dover in collecting his principal officers, and warning them of the quick obedience and intelligence needed in such operations as he had now in hand; and it was probably owing to this exhortation that he had forced his way to shore before the August day had ended. The standard-bearer of the famous tenth legion, who was the first to set the example of leaping into the water to his hesitating comrades, has had his words immortalized by his chief: " Come leap ashore, soldiers, unless you would betray this eagle to the enemy. I at least will do my duty to the Republic and my general." When once the example had been set, every ship quickly discharged its soldiery: and Cæsar, by manœuvring with his lighter ships and the boats attached to the heavier ones, was able to give them support, and to help them to get into some kind of order. No sooner were they on dry land than the Britons fled at once, and soon afterwards sent envoys to beg for peace and to promise obedience. Cæsar upbraided them for attacking him, since they had already sent their submission to him in Gaul; but he merely demanded hostages as usual (some of whom they handed over at once), and affected to pardon their rash conduct.

So far so good; but after this everything began to go wrong. The eighteen ships with the cavalry, which had been detained by adverse winds, were on the fourth day caught by a storm in mid-channel; some put back to port, others were carried away to the west, and only reached the Gallic coast again with great difficulty. The same night the gale and a high tide did great damage to the fleet which had carried Cæsar across, as it lay off the landing-place, and swamped the war-ships which had been drawn up on the beach. Ignorance of the nature of the tides had prevented the general from anticipating this disaster, and now he was unable to stir hand or foot to stay it, as he watched the wreckage from the shore. He must have felt himself in a very awkward plight; cut off from all retreat, destitute of provisions, without cavalry, and with an infantry force of no more than seven or eight thousand men. And these, though old and ripe soldiers, were, as he says, of necessity alarmed by the predicament they were in; for besides the ominous fact that they were cut off from retreat, they soon became aware that the Britons had discovered their disaster, and were hoping to put an end to this and all future invasion by the utter destruction of the little army.

For averting a panic there is nothing so good as hard work, and this remedy could be applied at once. One legion was employed in refitting the broken ships with the timber of those which were hopelessly damaged, and the men worked with such good will that all but twelve were soon once more ready to be floated. Meanwhile, the other legion was sent out every day to bring in corn, which would at this time be just ready for cutting. This legion was much harassed by the enemy, who had now gathered in great numbers to fall upon their prey, hiding in the woods, and then bearing down suddenly on the scattered foragers with their chariots. Cæsar at length withdrew the legion into camp, and waited his opportunity during some days of continuous rain. Then, when the foe had gathered round him in still greater numbers, he drew out his force and offered them battle; they were, of course, broken at the first charge of Roman infantry, fled in every direction, and again sent to beg for peace. Cæsar ordered them to send to him in Gaul double the number of hostages he had required before; and then, as the equinox was at hand, set sail by night and reached the Portus Itius safely with all his force but two ships. The soldiers in these landed farther to the west, and though attacked by the Morini and put to great peril, were eventually rescued.

As a reconnoitring expedition, this bold adventure of Cæsar's had not been without result. He had learnt where and how to land, and had noted the British methods of fighting; above all he had accustomed his men to the sight of the sea and of the painted barbarians, and had taught them to believe more firmly than ever in his own boundless resource and good fortune. He had seen enough to make him wish to see more. Before quitting his legions in their winter-quarters in Belgica, he gave explicit orders to his staff for the preparation of a large new fleet and the repair of the old vessels; they were now to be built on a new model, low and with flat bottoms, and broad in the beam, so as to suit the requirements of transport and landing in a sea subject to strong tidal influences. The work was carried out so thoroughly that when he returned from Cisalpine Gaul, after putting an end to the predatory incursions of a barbarous tribe on the frontiers of Illyria, he found the fleet almost ready ; and he did not omit to praise the indefatigable willingness of the soldiery who spent their winter in thus toiling for him. All the ships, some of which were built in the interior and had to be conveyed overland, were to assemble at the Portus Itius, the most convenient starting-place for the crossing, as he here tells us.

Whether Cæsar's judgment was not seriously at fault in thus concentrating his whole strength on another doubtful adventure, may very well be matter of question. He knew well enough that the Gaul he had conquered was not yet reconciled to his conquest. He had evidence on the very eve of setting out that disaffection was abroad, and had himself to take four legions in all haste into the country of the Treveri, who were disobedient and said to be inviting a new German invasion. The dangerous Æduan Dumnorix (see p. 141), whom he was taking with him to Britain, escaped at the last moment, and had to be pursued and killed lest he should foment rebellion in Cæsar's absence. He had as yet had little time to organise the newly acquired territory, to show himself in all parts of it, and to exercise his wonderful personal influence in the work of conciliation. All that he seems to have done as yet in this direction, besides fixing the tribute to be paid, or setting up a new king here and there, was to summon a general meeting of the Gallic chiefs from time to time, at which he no doubt presided himself, directed the proceedings, and, as master of the whole country, demanded supplies or ordered auxiliary troops[*]; and those who failed to come were, like the Treveri, punished as rebels. The Gauls must have so far looked on those assemblies as no more than proofs of their own subjection, and they might even serve as centres of conspiracy. But before disaffection came to a head, it might surely have been possible to avert it by spending at least one whole summer in a general inspection, with a view to more definite organisation, based on the habits and needs of the people themselves.

But Cæsar was induced to put all such considerations aside, if he ever entertained them, by an irresistible desire for further adventure and discovery. The story of this second expedition must be told very briefly. After a delay of twenty-five days, occasioned by continued winds from the northwest, Cæsar set sail at last at sunset with more than six hundred vessels before a southerly breeze. It dropped in mid-channel; and when day dawned he found "that he had left Britain behind him on his left"—*i. e.*, that the tide had carried him to the north-east, and that the Kentish coast was now in his rear. The soldiers set to work, with a vigour which called forth warm praise from the general, to row back to the landing-place of last year; the speed they attained with the transports equalled that of the war-galleys with their trained crews. Every man

[*] See B. G., v., 2, 4; vi., 3, 4, 4, 6.

in the army seems to have given himself up, body and mind, to the service of Cæsar; again and again this year he pauses in his narrative to note their marvellous activity.

The landing was effected this time without opposition; no enemy was to be seen. It was about midday when they arrived; a site for a camp was marked out, but the men must have needed some rest, and the actual spade-work seems to have been postponed. At midnight, or soon after, having received some intelligence of the enemy, Cæsar marched with his main body in search of them, found them in force on a certain river, and dislodged them from a strong position; but forbade pursuit in a country entirely unknown to him. Next day he despatched three columns of mixed infantry and cavalry in the direction of the fugitives; but no sooner had they started than a messenger arrived with the news that his fleet had a second time been caught in a storm and that nearly every ship had been seriously damaged. Recalling the columns, he halted them in position, and instantly rode off himself to the coast. There was nothing to be done, he found, but to repair the damage, and haul the ships ashore. Contingents from all five legions were sent for, and worked night and day for ten days; Labienus, commanding at the Portus Itius, was ordered to set his men to build new ships. And thus this indefatigable man, with his patient and devoted army, made their line of retreat secure at the cost of infinite labour.

Once more free to advance, he found that the

Britons had gathered in great numbers under Cassivelaunus, King of the Catuvellauni north of the Thames, to whom the other chiefs had entrusted for the time a general power. Desultory fighting followed, as the army advanced inland; and much damage was done to foragers and camp-makers by clever and sudden attacks of the enemy, and by their cavalry and war-chariots. Cæsar clearly considered these Britons a more dangerous foe than the Gauls, and is at considerable pains to explain the difficulties of his advance. The legions however never flinched, and reached at last that point on the river beyond which lay the territory of Cassivelaunus. Here they crossed the only available ford in the face of the enemy by a rush, and drove him from his position on the opposite bank, in spite of the fact that the passage was carefully guarded by stakes, both on the farther side and in the bed of the river itself, and that the water was so deep as to leave only the men's heads above the surface. After this defeat Cassivelaunus contented himself with retiring into his forests, and breaking out on the Romans with his chariots whenever a chance was given him.

Cæsar must have now made up his mind that it was no easy matter to conquer Britain, and probably also that it was not worth conquering. He received at this time an embassy from the Trinobantes, inhabiting what is now Essex, which gave him a good excuse for retreat and departure. A young chieftain of this tribe, whose father had been a victim of a feud with Cassivelaunus, and had formerly escaped to Cæsar in Gaul, was with him at this moment.

The Trinobantes asked to have the young chief back, and promised in return entire submission to Cæsar, who graciously acceded, with the usual demand for hostages. The example once set, other tribes followed suit; and from these Cæsar learnt that Cassivelaunus had retired to a fortified camp in the midst of forest and marsh. He at once hastened thither, stormed it easily, and carried off a quantity of cattle and many prisoners. But this powerful chief had meanwhile taken another step, which might have had serious consequences; he had sent a force into Cantium (Kent) to attack the Roman naval camp, and cut off Cæsar's retreat. The force that had been left there as a garrison was strong enough however to repel this attack; and Cassivelaunus, foiled again, sent to offer his submission. Enough had now been done to retire with the appearance of success ; and after imposing a tribute on the country (as a matter of form, we may presume), and giving Cassivelaunus the most positive commands not to molest the young chief of the Trinobantes, Cæsar returned to the naval camp before the summer was quite over, and transporting his army across the Channel in two successive voyages, arrived safely without the loss of a single ship at the Portus Itius.

It was nearly a century before another Roman army crossed to our island. The idea of annexing it was not wholly abandoned; for as Cæsar clearly perceived, the connection between the continental and insular Celts was too intimate to allow the Romans to hold the former in subjection without at least keeping a check on the latter. But neither

Cæsar nor Augustus could afford to wage so distant and difficult a war, without a more ample return, political and material, than could then be expected from it. Unlike Gaul, Britain had yielded little spoil; and soldiers who adventured themselves in distant lands could no more be expected to give their best years to warfare without hope of booty, than the Spaniards who followed Cortes or Pizarro, or the Devonshire seamen who sailed for El Dorado with Drake or Raleigh.

But Cæsar himself, if we can trust the evidence of his own memoirs, had other objects in view besides conquest and booty. As has been already pointed out, the scientific habit of mind was strong in him; he went to Britain not only to acquire wealth, but to extend his knowledge. Of booty he says hardly a word, though writing for a public in whom avarice was a much stronger motive than curiosity; but of the geography and inhabitants of Britain he sets down carefully all the knowledge he had collected. It was scanty enough; it occupies but two chapters; but it comprises almost all we know of Britain, except from coins, down to the time of its final conquest under Claudius. He gained a rough idea of the shape and size of our island. He has preserved the names of several of the tribes inhabiting it,—no easy matter, save for a careful note-taker. On a single sentence of his rests our knowledge of the early invasion of our southern coast by the Belgæ of the continent. He noted the mild temperature of the island, and by means of a water clock discovered that the nights were longer there than on the continent. Of the coinages he met with he had something to say, but unluckily his text is at this point corrupt, and we cannot be sure of what he wrote. He knew of the tin mines in Cornwall, and of iron ore found on the south coast, *e. g.*, in Sussex, and notes the abundance of timber, and the absence of the pine and the beech.* Of the inhabitants he says that the Cantii were the most civilised, having constant intercourse with Gaul; and that in the interior there was little cultivation of the land, but an abundance of cattle. He describes the men as painting themselves with woad, as clothed in skins, and as wearing moustaches but no beards.†

These notes of his are reproduced here, not because the ancient Britons are any part of the subject matter of this volume, but to show that their first discoverer, in a measure beyond any ancient conqueror of whom we have knowledge, was possessed of the desire to know, and of the ability to record his knowledge carefully.

---

* It is, however, almost certain that the beech was indigenous in Britain ; and Cæsar may have meant some other tree by *fagus*, or set it down by an error of memory.

† He adds one or two other particulars, *e. g.*, the practice of polyandry; for a criticism of these, see Professor Rhys' "Celtic Britain," p. 52 foll.

CHAPTER XIII.

THE GALLIC REBELLIONS.

54–52 B.C.

THE retreat from Britain in September, 54 B.C., marks a turning point in Cæsar's life. His happiest and brightest years were surely the first four that he spent in Gaul, when he was far removed from the hurly-burly of party strife in Rome, free to indulge his own love of glory and of adventure, and free to use exactly as he pleased the services of an admirable and devoted army. Hardly a check had occurred to mar the brilliancy of his career; his star seemed ever in the ascendant, his good fortune unfailing. He worked and travelled indefatigably winter and summer in all his three provinces; he was in the full vigour of the ripest manhood, and his bodily health seems to have answered all the calls made on it, and to have profited by the constant change of scene, and by the unbroken activity of a healthy mind. And lastly, a splendid hope lay before him; that when his new conquests were completed and organised, he might return home to a second consulship, and finish the work he had begun in his first. He would once more attempt to consolidate all parties in a rational and active government, to teach men what the Roman Empire had become, and to discover for them the principles on which alone it could be intelligently and happily governed.

But just as in the early afternoon of a brilliant summer day, the face of the heaven will suddenly appear flecked with the clouds that tell of the storm to come, so at this point in Cæsar's life, he became aware of the first warnings of serious trouble. We need not speak yet of his relations with Pompeius, of the death of Crassus in Asia, or of the loss of his only daughter Julia; even in Gaul itself the trouble was beginning, and it is this that must be dealt with in this chapter. But we may say, not without truth, that from this time forwards his life, like that of Cromwell after Naseby, was one long series of struggles against disappointment and vexation. In all these struggles he was victorious, like Cromwell; but in each case the heroic man was carried by them out of the course he would have chosen for himself, and each life was worn out in the long unwearied effort.

The northern Gauls had taken advantage of Cæsar's absence in Britain to organise something like a general rebellion *; they only waited to see

* B. G., v. 27, 5.

how his forces would be disposed in winter-quarters. Unaware of what had been going on, and urged by the necessities of a bad harvest, which made it difficult to feed a large force in one district, he unwittingly played into their hands. The several legions were settled for the winter at a considerable distance from each other; though, with one exception, they were all within a circuit of a hundred Roman miles.* Three of them were in what is now Belgium: one, under Q. Cicero, at Charleroi; another, under Labienus, in the country of the Treveri, not far from Luxemburg; the third was still farther north, at Aduatuca, which is believed to be Tongres, a few miles north of Liege. This last was a newly raised legion from the Transalpine province; but to make up for this, five extra cohorts, or half a legion, were attached to it. Cæsar himself remained with one legion at Samarobriva (Amiens) until he should hear that all were established and entrenched for the winter; three other legions, under Fabius, Plancus, and Marcus Crassus, were within a day or two's march of him. When once all these legions were entrenched and provisioned, he might leave for Cisalpine Gaul as usual, without misgivings as to their safety.

It was fortunate for him that he did not hurry. The troops at Aduatuca had hardly been a fortnight in winter quarters, when they were furiously attacked by the Eburones, the people of that district, under their chiefs Ambiorix and Catuvolcus. Such attacks against Roman entrenched camps were sure to fail,

* See the map in Napoleon's "Jules Cèsar," pl. 15.

and this was no exception; but Ambiorix was a man of many wiles. He asked for a parley, explained that the attack had been forced on him by his army, that he was himself bound to Cæsar's interest by many benefits, and that he felt compelled to inform the Romans that the whole country was rising and the Germans crossing the Rhine, that each legion would be attacked separately, and that their only chance of safety lay in joining Labienus, who was some fifty miles to the south of them. Unluckily Cæsar had in this solitary instance divided the command, doubtless for some reason at which we can only guess, between two *legati:* Titurius Sabinus, who had done him excellent service, and Aurunculeius Cotta, who had also been with him from his first campaign. These now took different views of their situation. Cotta showed himself the better general; he refused to take his measures on the recommendation of an armed enemy. Sabinus took the other view, and urged a concentration with Labienus. Ambiorix offered himself as guide. At last Cotta gave in, after a long argument, which Cæsar, who saw the difficulties of the position as clearly as he saw the right way to surmount them, has described from reports for the benefit of young officers in a responsible station. The little force, some five or six thousand men, left its entrenchments at daybreak, and when night fell only a few stragglers were left alive. Ambiorix led them into a trap, from which escape was hopeless. All day long they struggled for life, and not a man, writes Cæsar with feeling, did anything unworthy of himself. At last Cotta was badly wounded, and Sabinus determined to capitulate. Ambiorix received him and his centurions, ordered them to disarm, and instantly slew them. The attack on the legion was renewed; Cotta was killed with the majority of his men; the rest fled at night to the camp they had left, and, after holding it heroically for a while, slew themselves in despair. A few stragglers only escaped to carry the terrible news to Labienus. Such was the first disaster that had befallen Cæsar's arms; in which the man who was to blame was one of his most trusted generals, and the heroes who died rather than surrender were chiefly raw recruits of Gallic birth.

Had all his commanders been as weak as Sabinus, Cæsar's army might have been now destroyed piecemeal. Ambiorix, after his victory, gathered contingents from all the neighbouring clans, and flung himself with a vast host upon Q. Cicero at Charleroi. Cicero was ill at the time, and his force was surprised; it was with difficulty, even behind entrenchments, that they held their ground at first. But the legion was a tried one, and its commander, though not an ideal officer, had a certain pertinacity and obstinacy of character that served him well now. He worked night and day without rest till his men compelled him to take it. He urged them to superhuman exertions; a hundred and twenty wooden towers were run up in a single night. When Ambiorix, foiled in his first attack and indisposed for a long siege, tried the same trick with which he had deceived Sabinus, and offered the legion a free passage through the country, Cicero simply answered that the Romans were not used to negotiate with an armed foe. He held on to his position with the grip of a bulldog until nine men out of ten in his little force had been killed or wounded, and the huts and all the baggage burnt by fireballs thrown into the camp by the enemy. Meanwhile he sent messenger after messenger to Cæsar at Amiens; but day after day passed and no succour appeared. At last a javelin was found stuck in one of the towers, to which was fastened a paper with a few words in Greek: "Take courage; aid is at hand." Cicero's last messenger, a Gallic slave, had escaped detection and reached Cæsar when the siege had already lasted more than a week. The same day smoke was seen rising in the distance, and the beleaguered force knew that Cæsar was burning the villages to draw the enemy away from their prey. In a few hours the siege was raised; they had been saved by the marvellous swiftness of their chief.

Cæsar had received Cicero's letter one day late in the afternoon; he instantly sent orders to Crassus, who was twenty Roman miles away, to join him by next morning, to Fabius, who was some distance to the north, to meet him with his legion on the march, and to Labienus, to advance towards Cicero, if he could do so with safety. Next morning he started on the news of Crassus' approach, leaving orders that he should remain with his legion at Amiens to take charge of the baggage, stores, and documents which were housed there. Cæsar was joined by Fabius, and thus with two legions only (for Labienus found it wiser to keep in his entrenchments) he made a series

A SIEGE-FIGHT WITH ARCHERS, AND BATTERING-RAM.
FROM TRAJAN'S COLUMN.
(*Baumeister.*)

of forced marches towards Charleroi. The distance is about eighty English miles; he arrived in the vicinity on the fifth day from starting, and on that day was confronted by the vast host which had just raised the siege.

To fight a battle with only eight thousand men was impossible; but Cicero was now safe, and his rescuer could renounce speed for caution. He tried a plan which the impetuous Gallic character readily invited, and succeeded in inducing the enemy to attack his camp under disadvantageous circumstances; waiting till they were on his very ramparts, and even tearing up his palisades, he threw all the gates open, dashed out on them on every side, and dispersed them in hopeless panic. Then he set out, arrived at Charleroi at three that day, and spent the rest of it in inspecting the defensive works, and in thanking and praising Cicero and his officers. Every centurion was addressed singly, and their heroism is glowingly recorded in their chief's own words. Cicero wrote warmly to his brother in Rome of the reception he had from Cæsar, and the immense energy which had saved him from destruction.

It was here that he first heard certain news of the disaster of Sabinus, which is said to have caused him the most intense pain. But the very next day, when he made it known to his army, he so far hid his own grief as to tell them "that they must not lose heart at a disaster which had been caused purely by the fault of a subordinate commander, that the favour of the gods and their own valour had already wiped out the defeat, and that the enemy would not be allowed to exult long over his victory." He then concentrated three legions, his own and those of Cicero and Crassus, round Amiens; sent orders to raise three new ones in Cisalpine Gaul, and prepared, for the first time since he took the command, to spend the whole winter with his troops.

During that winter, he says, he was never for a moment free from anxiety. One after another reports came in of rebellious designs and open outbreaks. At length he summoned a meeting of the chiefs of all the tribes, showed them that he knew what they were about, and succeeded in frightening some and conciliating others. But yet, as spring approached, the rumours of mutiny did not die away; every tribe was under suspicion of disaffection, except the faithful Ædui and the useful Remi. The Senones on the upper Seine expelled a king whom Cæsar had given them; the Treveri stirred up all north-east Gaul, called on the Germans for aid, and attacked Labienus furiously in his winter-quarters. Cæsar's ablest *legatus* was able to defeat his enemy, and even to slay their valiant chief Indutiomarus; but yet everything pointed to the approach of a stormy summer.

The events of that summer are told by Cæsar in his sixth book. They are of comparatively slight interest to the reader as compared with the stirring adventures of the earlier campaigns. No new ground was broken; the season was spent in avenging the late rebellion and in once more crossing the Rhine to overawe the Ubii and Suebi, and to secure the Gallic frontier on that side. Cæsar himself felt that the interest of his Roman reader would flag at this point. Each book so far had had a fresh and stirring tale to tell; the defeat of the Helvetii, the first sight of the Rhine, and the overthrow of Ariovistus, the novel campaign on the great western ocean, the bridging of the Rhine, the two invasions of Britain, the terrible disaster at Aduatuca, and the gallant defence and rescue of Quintus Cicero. And now there was nothing to tell of the summer of 53 B.C. but the reconquest of the Senones, Carnutes, Treveri, and others, tribes which had long ago been conquered, but never yet conciliated. It was to be a tale as much of failure as of triumph, for it showed how easily the work done in any district by force of arms only, could be undone on the appearance of a single energetic patriot. Not even the second invasion of Germany, or the story of a second calamity at Aduatuca, where Q. Cicero's disobedience of orders lost him the reputation he had won at Charleroi, could rescue this book from falling flat in comparison with its stirring predecessors.

And yet this very sixth book is, for the modern reader at least, the most interesting and valuable of them all. With the true feeling of an artist Cæsar inserted in it, at exactly the right point, a digression of some length on the life and manners of the Gauls and the Germans, which not only most happily diverts the reader's attention through eighteen chapters, but is still the foundation of all our knowledge of the religion, the social state, the political institutions of our Celtic and Teutonic ancestors. It is introduced with some abruptness, in his straightforward, soldierly manner, just at the point where he has reached his farthest in his incursion into Germany; and when it is concluded he resumes his narrative by giving his reasons for retreating. Some critics—Germans, it need hardly be said—have insisted that the digression was inserted here simply as it were to cover his retreat from the eyes of the Roman public: " I invaded and I retreated —these must not stand too close to each other."* But there is no need to have recourse to a motive which might not be unnatural in Napoleon, but is utterly unlike Cæsar; who never scrupled to tell a plain tale of defeat when it had to be told, and knew well that a great commander is never so great as when he recognises his own failure and prepares calmly to retrieve it.

These chapters show us how lively was the interest he took not only in the Gauls he had subdued, but in the more warlike race beyond the Rhine whose conquest of Gaul he had frustrated. He seems here to claim the attention of the Romans for these great peoples, as those with whom their future would inevitably henceforward be bound up. In comparing the Gauls and Germans he even seems to hint the belief, to which his policy bears witness, that the one might be a tower of strength, the other a standing danger to the Empire. He saw that the Gauls were on the road to civilisation, and might be met half-way by Rome, absorbed into the Roman state and army, converted into a powerful bulwark of the Empire; he saw also that the Germans were still in a condition of hearty

---

* Drumann, iii., 330.

and healthy barbarism, that their conquest and absorption were hopeless, and that the only available policy was to keep them firmly and strictly within their own territory. Thus it was that he marked out the Rhine as the boundary on which the eyes of all Roman rulers must henceforward be fixed ; a boundary within which Gallic civilisation must be developed to the utmost, and beyond which German barbarism must be left to its own devices. This at any rate is the political lesson of these chapters, and this was the policy which Cæsar's successors ultimately adopted.

His second expedition across the Rhine at once confirmed him in his policy towards the Germans, and put an end to all their hopes of breaking through this boundary. He never again came in contact with them as enemies, and all his activity for the next two years was spent in securing his Gallic conquests—a work which turned out to be the most formidable he had ever yet had to face. In the winter of 53–52 B.C., during his absence in Cisalpine Gaul, the disaffection which he had extinguished in the north broke out again with far greater obstinacy in the central and southern tribes. A real leader at last appeared ; a man who had doubtless learnt much from the Romans, and who knew the hopelessness of rebellion without discipline and organisation. Vercingetorix, the hero of Cæsar's seventh book, is also the hero of the whole Gallic race. He was a young Arvernian of a noble family, whose father had held the chieftainship of the whole of Gaul. Though the fatal jealousy of his countrymen had caused the father's death, his prestige descended to his son. His family would not listen to his anti-Roman designs, and expelled him from their capital city. Thus Vercingetorix became a soldier of fortune, enlisted numbers of the broken and discontented who swarmed in Gaul, and so gathered a force far more formidable in quality than the comfortable Gallic citizens to whom Cæsar was accustomed in the south. He marched in every direction recruiting, and when once the impulsive people had recognised his strength, he showed himself a master both of organisation and strategy. He was made supreme commander; he exercised his power to the full, reduced the Gallic methods of warfare to a system, and punished insubordination with extreme severity. While it was still winter he had thought out a plan of campaign, and at once fell to executing it with a swiftness and secrecy worthy of Cæsar himself.*

This plan was simply to prevent Cæsar from reaching his legions, most of which were quartered on the upper Seine, by barring his way out of the Roman province. Before he could force his way through, if he succeeded in doing so, Vercingetorix would have raised the whole country, and swooping on the legions in their chief's absence, would put an end for ever to the Roman occupation. We have no better testimony than this to the power of Cæsar's name and presence. Rumours had already reached the Gauls that affairs at Rome were likely to embar-

---

* Cæsar does not attribute this plan to Vercingetorix himself (B. G., vii., 1 foll.); but if it was not his own it was admirably developed by him.

rass and detain their conqueror; and the powerful tribe of the Carnutes had gone so far on the strength of these as to rise and massacre the Roman men of business who were already pushing their way everywhere in the country. Enthusiasm was aglow in every direction; even the faithful Ædui were giving way to it, and if Vercingetorix could secure the defection of these, the legions would be entirely surrounded and cut off from their general and from all succour.

The Gallic forces were divided: one division was sent southward to act on the frontier of the Roman province, and to combine with the snow-covered mountains of the Cevennes in preventing Cæsar or any Roman army from forcing a way to the legions. Vercingetorix himself turned his attention to the Ædui, and first of all to their clients the Bituriges. The plot was growing to completion when Cæsar heard of it. It was still winter, but he set out instantly from Italy, after learning that Pompeius had been made sole consul, and that affairs in Rome were quieting down. He saw the dilemma he was in; either the legions would have to fight without their general, or his own safety would be imperilled if he attempted to join them. Never were the resources of his genius shown to greater advantage. He had brought a few troops with him; he collected some cavalry in the province and sent part of it to the northern frontier at Vienne. Then he garrisoned the stations on the western frontier, and with what troops remained he cut his way through the deep snow still lying on the Cevennes, and descended into the plain of the Arverni (Auvergne). This was utterly undefended; no one dreamed that he could force the passes at such a season. For two days he advanced; then, leaving D. Brutus in command, with orders to scour the country and so draw Vercingetorix southward to the rescue, he slipped off almost alone to Vienne. Secrecy was so indispensable that not even Brutus knew his real intentions; he gave out that he was going for re-inforcements and would be back in three days.

At Vienne he picked up the horsemen he had sent there, and rode with them day and night to the two nearest legions, which were quartered nearly two hundred miles to the northwards. He reached them safely, and felt himself once more on firm ground. Messengers flew to the other legions, and the whole army was concentrated once more under their chief, before the enemy was even aware that he was in the neighbourhood. He had completely beaten Vercingetorix at his own game of strategy. The Gallic chief had gone southwards, just as Cæsar intended he should, to protect his own people, the Arverni, from the force which had crossed the Cevennes; and now central Gaul was occupied, not by an enthusiastic host of rebels, but by Cæsar himself at the head of ten admirable legions.

When the news of his presence spread abroad, Vercingetorix turned once more northwards, and attacked a small settlement of Boii who were under obligations to the Romans. In spite of the serious difficulties of supply which he knew he would have to face at that season, Cæsar marched at once to the rescue, took three towns in rapid succession, and threatened Avaricum (Bourges), the capital of the Bituriges. Vercingetorix had now to leave the Boii alone, and do all he could to stay Cæsar's course. He showed his genius for war by the new policy he persuaded his desperate countrymen to adopt. Cæsar must be beaten by famine. He depended on the towns for his supplies, and the towns and all their stores must be burnt; even every village and farm that could give him aid was to share the same fate. Only Avaricum was to be spared; it was the finest city in Gaul, and Vercingetorix yielded to the popular feeling. It was thought to be impregnable, and Cæsar could be starved during the siege. But the young chieftain did not even yet know what stuff the Roman legions were made of, or the endless resources of their engineers. In a few days Cæsar had laid his grip upon the devoted city.

The siege which followed lasted nearly four weeks. Cæsar has described it with even more than his usual care, and recorded with equal admiration the endurance of his own men, and the heroism of his enemy. His strong dislike to operate with an ill-provisioned army made him soon give his men the option of abandoning the siege. So impossible was it to obtain the ordinary supplies with Vercingetorix hanging in his rear, that he took the famished men into confidence, and tells with just pride their unanimous refusal to retreat. They begged him to persevere; they had never yet acknowledged a failure, and they must avenge the blood of the Romans who had been so cruelly massacred by the Carnutes. The siege went on; the engineers pushed their embankment, built of beams and fascines covered with earth, almost to the wall of the city, at the only point where it was not rendered impregnable by streams and marshes. At the end of the embankment were wooden towers from which missiles could be thrown at the defenders; covered ways protected the soldiers who passed to and from the front of the works. Every resource of engineering was employed; but the quick intellect of the Gauls, says Cæsar, had already learnt many of the devices of their enemy. One night when Cæsar was going his rounds, inspecting the works and cheering his men, the timber-work was seen to be in flames; the embankment had been fired by a mine from the city. A furious sortie followed instantly, which was with difficulty checked by the two legions on guard; the Gauls were pushed back, but never ceased fighting. Here it was that Cæsar saw a scene of heroism, which wonder compelled him to hand down to posterity. A Gaul stood before the city gate, throwing lumps of pitch into the fire in the Roman works, to keep it burning; he was killed by a missile from a Roman engine. A second took his place, and shared the same fate, then a third, and then a fourth, and so on till the struggle was ended, and the Gauls driven back into the city.

These heroes now proposed to evacuate Avaricum, and join Vercingetorix, who was not far off, but they gave way to the tears and prayers of the women, who would thus have been left to their fate. They manned the walls again, but with less vigour than usual; and the ever-watchful Cæsar saw his opportunity. He ordered a general assault; the city wall was carried by storm; the Romans spread themselves round the ramparts, and blocked the gates from without. None, says Cæsar, thought of plunder; maddened with privation and the thirst for vengeance, like the English at Badajoz, they spared neither man, woman, nor child. Scarcely eight hundred, out of a population of forty thousand souls, lived to remember that awful day.

The scene changes to Auvergne, that rich volcanic country lying below the northern slopes of the Cevennes, which was the home of Vercingetorix, and of the hereditary enemies of the Romans. Cæsar, though much hindered by dissensions among the Ædui, who had so far been of infinite service to him, and by the obvious growth of an anti-Roman party among them, determined to strike a blow for the possession of the Arvernian capital Gergovia, in hopes of destroying Vercingetorix and ending the war. The Gallic chief, unsuccessful in his operations against Cæsar at Avaricum, set out by forced marches to throw himself into his native stronghold; he knew that he was no match for his enemy in the open field, and that Gergovia was all but impregnable. He hurried along the western bank of the river Allier, which flows from the Cevennes to join the Loire; he broke down all the bridges, and Cæsar, who had been detained by the affairs of the Ædui, was too late to overtake him. When the legions arrived before Gergovia, it was already occupied by a vast array from all parts of Gaul, and a single reconnaissance convinced Cæsar that it could not be taken by storm. He resolved to try a blockade, though his troops were not really numerous enough for his purpose.

This famous stronghold, which is still called by its ancient name, consists of a single lofty and almost isolated hill, nearly an English mile in length, flat at the top, oblong in shape, and descending steeply on all sides but one to the lower ground. On its western side only it is joined to outlying hills by a ridge, lower in elevation than its own level, and offering no easy opportunity of assault. Cæsar's only hope seems to have lain in the possibility of cutting off the besieged from water and provisions; for there is but little water at the top, and some at least would have to be fetched from one of the two streams which flow at the foot of the hill. Between the southern stream and Gergovia there is a lower hill, with steep sides, now called La Roche Blanche, which was occupied by the Gauls. This was taken by assault, and two legions were at once entrenched upon it. It was then connected with the larger camp, which had been pitched on the eastern side of the fortress, by a double entrenchment. But this plan did not immediately succeed. The blockading force was clearly too small to cut off all the water supply. Cæsar had, in fact, only six legions, some 25,000 men, with him; the other four were operating under Labienus against the rebellious tribes on the Seine.

Meanwhile, the expected defection among the Ædui had taken place, and a force of 10,000 men, whom Cæsar had ordered them to send him, had renounced their fidelity on the march, and were

SIEGE SCENE.
FROM TRAJAN'S COLUMN.
(*Baumeister.*)

intending to join his enemies. Cæsar had to leave Gergovia with four legions and all his cavalry, and catch them on their way. He was but twenty-four hours absent, but he returned with the Æduan army penitent and obedient, and the news of their submission decided the fate of the hostile Æduan faction. But it was clear that he could not stay at Gergovia while such perilous intrigues were hatching elsewhere; and finding on his return that his camp on the Roche Blanche had barely escaped from a vigorous sortie by the enemy, he began to consider whether it would not be advisable to abandon the siege. But a sudden movement of the enemy decided him to make one last effort to get at least a tighter hold upon his prey.

The ridge which connected Gergovia with the neighbouring heights was felt by the besieged to be a weak point in their defence*; and as they had failed to recover the Roche Blanche, they feared that Cæsar might seize this in addition, and shut them up on all sides. The reason why he had not already seized it was, no doubt, want of sufficient troops; but they determined in any case to forestall him, and moved large bodies in that direction from the slope of the hill where they were encamped. Cæsar saw this, and made a strong demonstration towards the ridge in order to complete their illusion. Ger-

---

* The English reader who happens to have visited the great entrenched camp called Maiden Castle, near Dorchester, will be able to realise not only this weak point, but the whole position of Gergovia, by simply doubling the height, length, and breadth of the hill which it occupies.

govia itself seemed bared of troops. The enemy's attention was fixed on the ridge and the supposed attack on it. Meanwhile the two legions on the Roche Blanche had been strengthened stealthily by parties of men ordered to steal quietly over from the larger camp; and when a sufficient force was collected there, it was sent swiftly up the only part of the hill where the ascent is possible for soldiers. A wall, which had been built half-way up by the Gauls, was reached and surmounted; three almost empty camps of Gallic contingents were captured. The wall of the city itself was now not far ahead; and the excited legionaries pressed on, regardless of the efforts of their officers to restrain them, and unable to hear the trumpet-call by which Cæsar, who was with the tenth legion below, endeavoured to stay their advance. Some few actually got within the ramparts; but they sacrificed their lives by their temerity. Suddenly the enemy poured out on the breathless Romans, forced them down the hill, and pursuing them into the plain, were only checked by the veteran tenth legion. So complete was the *mêlée*, that Cæsar himself is said to have been for an instant in the hands of the enemy. He does not mention this himself, nor does he describe the moment as a critical one; but he owns to the loss of forty-six centurions and nearly 700 men, and implies the complete failure of his combinations. The fact was that on this occasion, chiefly owing to the nature of the ground and their own ardour, his men were not well in hand. The fault was doubtless partly his; but in addressing them next day, as became a general who must be wholly trusted by his men, he laid it chiefly upon them, blaming them for rashness while he praised their valour. He ended by cheering and consoling them; and then drawing up the whole army in a good position, offered Vercingetorix battle. But this was, of course, declined; and next day he set out, defeated for the first time, on his retreat to the wavering Ædui.

Never were his prospects at a lower ebb. The work of eight years must have seemed wholly undone. He was far away from his four legions on the Seine, under Labienus, and the intervening country was in open insurrection. The news from Gergovia, too, had produced a new revolution among the Ædui; they revolted, armed, and seized the town of Noviodunum in their territory, where Cæsar had left all his hostages and prisoners, his munitions of war, and supplies. The hostages were released, and all the magazines plundered or destroyed. Even the Roman province itself was open to attack, and the troops there were few in number. A weaker general would have retreated to protect it, and Cæsar says that the thought passed through his mind; but he could not desert Labienus, whose position gave him grave anxiety. He contrived with difficulty to ford the Loire, the frontier of the Ædui, who had destroyed all the bridges. He found ample supplies on the right bank, provisioned his army, and set out to effect, if possible, a speedy junction with Labienus. It was in this district that eight years before he had won his first great victory over the Helvetii; and he must have felt with chagrin as he traversed it, that the conquest of Gaul was no nearer to completion than it was on that eventful day of triumph.

But he had taken the right step, and in spite of the universal spread of insurrection, and of the genius with which Vercingetorix organised it, from this moment his position began slowly to mend. Labienus, by some clever manœuvring and one hard-fought battle, had disentangled himself from the network of insurrection that surrounded him on the Seine, and the junction of the armies was effected. Cæsar had now at the lowest computation 50,000 men under him ; to these he added a contingent of German cavalry which he had sent for—a somewhat humiliating confession of weakness—from beyond the Rhine. And now rightly judging it his best course to keep up his communication with Italy, to secure a base of operations in Roman territory, and so doubtless (as the summer was not far advanced) to begin the task of conquest afresh, he turned in a south-easterly direction towards the country of the Sequani, intending to put himself in touch with the Roman province, on the northern frontier of which that people dwelt. He was just upon their borders, when he was caught in his march by Vercingetorix, who, after a general Gallic council at Bibracte, had again been appointed general-in-chief, and had organised a powerful cavalry to pursue his policy of cutting off his enemy's supplies. The legions had to fight in marching order, but Cæsar was equal to the emergency, suited his tactics to the novel situation, shook off the enemy with the help of his German horsemen, and turned their retreat into a rout. Then Vercingetorix, despairing once more of success in the open field, threw himself with all his forces into the neighbouring fortress of Alesia; a name for ever famous in the annals of warfare.

The traveller who takes the railway from Paris to Dijon, on his way to Switzerland or the Riviera, passes near this ancient stronghold as he enters the Burgundian Côte d'Or, between Tonnerre and Dijon. It is an isolated hill, shaped not unlike that of Gergovia, and nearly a mile in length; as you ascend it, you find the slope moderate until you near the summit, where you are confronted by a steep wall of broken rock. This extends round a great part of the hill, and makes it almost impregnable to assault. And this rocky summit is not connected, like that of Gergovia, with the neighbouring hills, by anything that can be called a ridge; but stands almost as much alone as does the Acropolis of Athens. To the westward, it overlooks a considerable plain; but to north, south, and east, as may be seen in the annexed plan, other hills are grouped around it at no great distance. On the north and south they are separated from it by two valleys about half a mile in breadth, down which run two streams to join the river Brenne in the plain to the westward; but on the eastern side the ground is higher, and forms in fact a low watershed between these valleys. Though modern artillery could command it from any of these heights, it was undoubtedly a place of immense strength in Cæsar's time; when he reached it, it was occupied by a force more than sufficient to defend it at all points, provisioned for thirty days, and supplied with abundant water by natural springs on the hillside. He saw at once that it could not be taken by storm, and that to blockade it would be a work of stupendous labour. Nevertheless he resolved to try this last method. Could he but succeed, the war would be practically ended ; and as he was master of the largest and most experienced army he had ever yet worked with, failure, in any serious sense, was not to be thought of.

In order to gain an adequate idea of the vast extent of the work now undertaken by Cæsar, the reader must not fail to examine the plan carefully, with the following explanations in his mind as he studies it. The length of the summit of the hill is about one mile, its breadth at the widest half that distance ; but the circumference of its base is fully six miles. To draw a line of works around this base would alone have been a heavy task for an army of 50,000 or 60,000 men ; but it was necessary also to occupy the adjoining heights where they approached nearest to Alesia, in order not only to command a view of the city and the proceedings of its defenders, but to guard against an enemy advancing from without.

What Cæsar actually did, he has recorded with great exactness in three chapters of his seventh book ; and these have been completely verified and explained by the excavations made by order of Napoleon III. in 1862. First of all, four camps were formed, two on the hill to the south (Mont de Flavigny), and one on that to the north-east ; these were occupied by the greater part of the infantry.

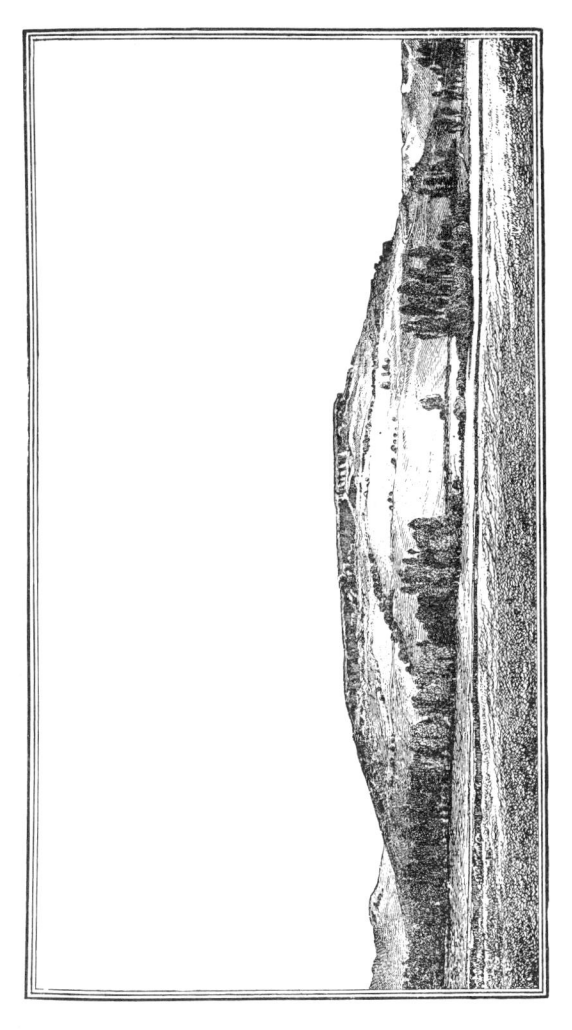

ALESIA, SKETCHED FROM MOUNT BASSY.
(From Napoleon's "César.")

In another camp, at the *foot* of a hill to the northwest (Mont Réa), two whole legions were stationed; this was the weakest point in the whole line, for the crest of this hill was too far from Alesia to be brought within the lines of blockade. In the plain near the river Brenne, the cavalry was quartered in three camps, and a fourth was placed at the extreme north, where now stands the village of Grésigny. All these camps were strongly fortified ; and in front of them, *i. e.*, between them and the base of the hill, was carried a double ditch with a rampart and palisade behind it, 11,000 paces, or some eight miles in length. This was strengthened by twenty-three forts (*castella*) at intervals of about a third of a mile ; and further by an elaborate series of devices to embarrass an attacking force, consisting chiefly of branches and trunks of trees fixed in the ground, and of holes or traps dug and then covered over at the top to deceive the eye. Lastly, on the western side, in the plain, a ditch twenty feet deep was dug at the very base of the hill, with almost perpendicular sides; this was some distance within the line of investment, and was meant to embarrass the enemy during an attack, and to give the Romans time to concentrate at any threatened point.

The works had hardly been begun, when Vercingetorix made a vigorous attack on them with his cavalry. These were beaten, and pursued right up to the city gate by Cæsar's German horse ; and Vercingetorix, wisely judging that cavalry would be of no further use to him, and would only consume his provision, sent them off, before he was entirely hemmed in, to summon the tribes in every direction to the rescue. They did their work well ; and before the garrison was actually starved out, an enormous host, computed at 240,000, made up of contingents from almost every Gallic people, had arrived on the scene and turned the tables upon Cæsar, who was now invested in his turn. But from prisoners and deserters he had heard what was going on in time to construct an outer line of defence, on the same elaborate plan as the inner line of investment ; and thus he now occupied a position, unique in military history, consisting of a narrow fortified ring, with a numerous and furious enemy both within it and without. Surely never was the strength, goodwill, and obedience of any army so severely taxed, as in the construction and defence of these extraordinary lines, which Cæsar describes with his own peculiar *sangfroid*, as though they were all in the day's work.

Great indeed was the joy of the besieged when they saw this great host approaching. They were already almost worn out by famine. Voices had even been heard proposing surrender ; others wished for a last sortie, while they yet had strength to fight. One Arvernian chieftain urged them to hold on to the last, and to resort even to cannibalism rather than submit. Into the mouth of this man, Cæsar, contrary to his custom, has put a speech of some length, to rouse the feelings of his reader to the intense horror of the situation ; and from this point to the end of the siege he has abandoned his usual cool and quiet style, and told the story in vigorous and

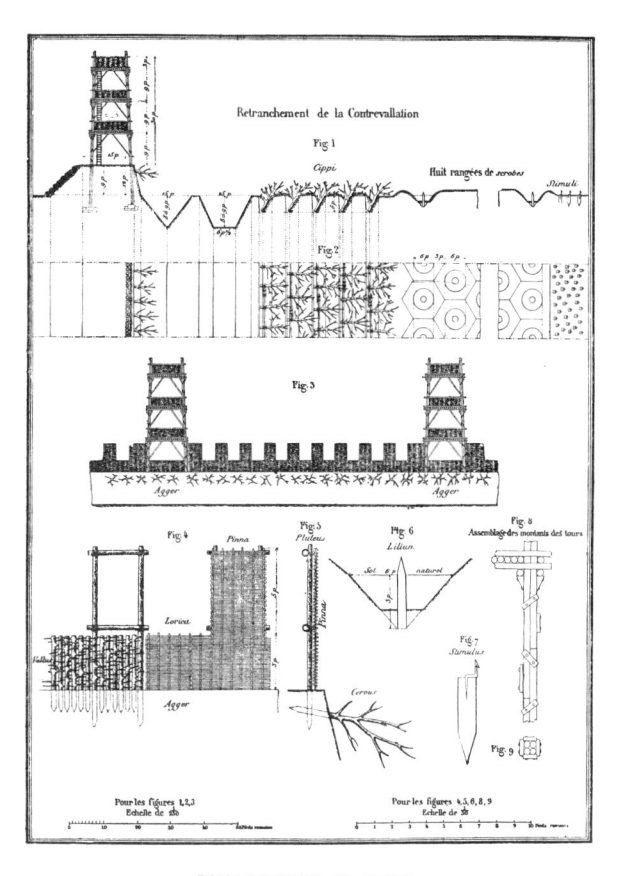

ROMAN WORKS AT ALESIA.
(*From Napoleon's "César."*)

graphic sentences, rising in intensity till the last terrible crisis is reached, and showing how keenly he recognised that this struggle must decide his own fate, as well as that of Gaul.

Two terrible combats followed the arrival of the new Gallic army: the first by day, which lasted from noon till nightfall; the second by night, after a day spent by the enemy in collecting material to fill up the ditches of Cæsar's outer line. Both attacks were repulsed, though the second one was assisted by a furious sortie from the town. Then all three armies gathered themselves together for one last mighty struggle: every Gaul knew, says Cæsar, that defeat meant destruction; every Roman, that victory would put an end to all his toil.

There was, as we saw, a weak point in Cæsar's lines, where, at the foot of Mont Réa on the north, two legions had been established. Here the line of circumvallation could not be carried over the summit of the hill without a *détour* too long to be thought of; and it ran along the slope above the camp of the two legions. The Gauls of the relieving army saw that here, if anywhere, the lines could be broken through; and a force was sent by night round in the rear of this hill, which, after resting till mid-day, crossed the summit, and descended upon the fortifications and camp below them. At the same time the besieged made a last furious sally, and the rest of the relieving force attacked the lines at every point. The Romans had to fight in front and rear at once, and it was with the utmost difficulty that they held their own on a line of such unparalleled length. Cæsar, like a modern general, took up a position whence he could see the whole action, and, keeping a reserve in hand, sent aid repeatedly to every point which seemed specially hard pressed.

It soon became evident that the lines would be forced at the weak point under Mont Réa; and Cæsar sent Labienus thither with 3,000 men, with orders to withdraw the whole force at that point, if he could not hold it, and then as a last resort to dash out of the lines and take the enemy in flank and rear. Leaving his own watch-station, he hurried round the works to cheer the men and urge them to end their labours by this supreme effort; a step which shows that the crisis had indeed come. In the plain the lines were strong, and the Gauls from Alesia, despairing of victory there, rushed up the slopes of Mont Flavigny which Cæsar had just left, and attacked the slighter defences on that side. Cæsar despatched first Brutus with succour, then Fabius; but still the attack was unwearied. At last he called up his reserve, which had not yet been engaged, and after beating the enemy off at that point, rode away once more to the scene of the struggle at Mont Réa. Labienus, hopeless of holding his ground there, had collected every man he could lay hands on, and was preparing to take that step which Cæsar had ordered as a last resource. An aide-de-camp flew with the news to Cæsar, who swiftly gathered a few cohorts from the forts in the plain, and ordered some squadrons of cavalry to ride round outside the lines and take the enemy in the rear.

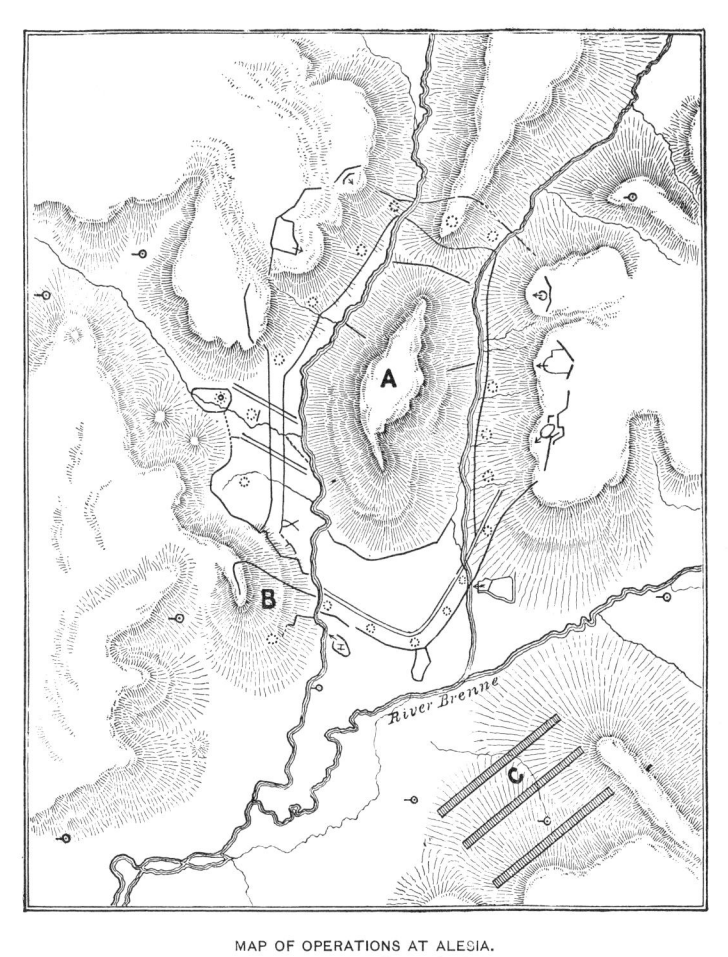

MAP OF OPERATIONS AT ALESIA.
AFTER NAPOLEON III. (JULES CÉSAR).

A. Alesia. **B.** Mont Réa. **C.** Gallic Army of Relief.   Cæsar's Castella Connecting his Lines.

When the Gauls on Mont Réa recognised him by the purple mantle of the proconsul which he wore in action, and saw him bringing up his last available troops, they knew that the supreme moment had arrived. For a few minutes they renewed the fight with fury; then, before Labienus had carried out his desperate task, the cavalry sent by Cæsar appeared in their rear, and they began to fall back. They were met by the horsemen and cut to pieces. This decided the battle; all the rest was capture and slaughter. Seventy-four standards were taken; hardly a man would have escaped, if the Romans had not been utterly worn out. As it was, the cavalry sent in pursuit broke up the whole army, and after a terrible slaughter, returned with multitudes of prisoners.

Next day Vercingetorix called a council of chieftains, and proposed submission as a sheer necessity. "I myself," he added, "have not been fighting for my own ends, but for my country. My work is now over, and I offer myself as a victim to appease Cæsar's wrath. Kill me, or surrender me,—whichever you will." They decided that he should surrender himself, and appeal for them to Cæsar's well-known clemency. But to Roman eyes things had gone too far for mercy. The scene which followed is only just alluded to by Cæsar himself, but the account of it in later writers bears the stamp of truth. "Vercingetorix went out of the gates excellently well armed, and his horse furnished with rich caparison accordingly, and rode round about Cæsar, who sat in his chair of state. Then alighting from his horse, he took off his caparison and furniture, and unarmed himself, and laid all on the ground, and went and sat down at Cæsar's feet, and said never a word. So Cæsar at length committed him as a prisoner taken in the wars, to lead him afterwards in the triumph at Rome." * He is said to have been led along the Sacred Way in Cæsar's great triumph six years later, and to have been put to death in the ancient dungeon at the foot of the Capitol, while his conqueror offered his thanks and prayers in the great temple above.

So died the hero of the most heroic struggle ever fought out by the noble Celtic race. Nineteen centuries later, a monument was erected to his memory on the hill which will ever be associated with his name. But no colossal mound or breezy barrow among his native hills was to mark his last resting-place; his body must have been cast out into some vile refuse-heap in the great imperial city, and only the memory of his deeds survives. But they survive in the words of his conqueror; so much at least has Cæsar done for the most formidable of all his foes. He has told us enough of Vercingetorix to show us that he was one who embodied all the finest qualities of his race, and added to them a steadiness of purpose and a power of organisation rare among the Gallic peoples. In Cæsar's pages he stands out as the only man who could overcome all the petty dissensions, the suicidal jealousies, which had made his countrymen so long a prey to every invader; who not only fired his people with the love of liberty, but taught them how to fight for it with sanity, discipline, and perseverance.

* North's Plutarch, "Life of Cæsar," ch. 26.

And on the conqueror who showed no mercy, what judgment are we to pass? Like his victim, he was a man in whom all the best instincts of his race were united; like him, too, he joined with these others which his countrymen rarely possessed. The Romans never forgave their most deadly enemies; yet Cæsar, as he showed again and again in the last years of his life, could both forgive and put unshaken trust in the forgiven. Still he was a Roman, and to a Roman the heroic never did or could appeal, but when the hero was himself a Roman. He might admire, but his admiration would never be stirred into the warm glow of generous impulse. And so much is indeed wanting in the character of Cæsar, which some have wished to paint as perfect beyond the poor measure of perfection to which human nature can attain—that he was a true Roman at heart, and as a Roman could not always reach that highest level of perfect justice where cool head and warm heart work together in blameless harmony.

A ROMAN HEAD

CHAPTER XIV.

PACIFICATION OF GAUL AND OUTBREAK OF CIVIL WAR.

52–49 B.C.

THE fall of Alesia decided the fate of Gaul. Henceforward that splendid country with its gifted population was to exercise an ever-increasing influence on European history; an influence on the whole for good, and one which, in some ways at least, has surpassed that of every other European race.

Great indeed were the sufferings the Gallic people underwent, before by becoming embodied in the Roman Empire they could attain the position for which their genius fitted them. We may, if we choose, call up before our minds a dismal picture of ruined homesteads and wasted crops, of population thinned by war and famine, of domestic and civic morality disintegrated by war and passion. Undoubtedly Cæsar's name was terrible in the land, and some stubborn tribes had seen him in no other guise than that of a ruthless conqueror and stern master. Even the year that followed the siege of Alesia (51 B.C.), the events of which must be here omitted, saw the lands of rebellious Belgic peoples ravaged again, and the whole heroic garrison of Uxellodunum sent to their homes with their right hands cut off. The fact was that the conqueror's anger was thoroughly roused; his prize had all but slipped from his grasp, his term of command was rapidly drawing to an end—a fact his enemies knew only too well,[*]— and he put forth without scruple all the force of his will. The result at least answered his expectations. The last year of his government was a comparatively peaceful one, which he could devote to a general pacification. The Romanising tribes, the Ædui and others, who had been seduced from their allegiance only by the genius of Vercingetorix, remained henceforward loyal subjects; the rest submitted to the will of fate and Cæsar. No attempt was made, even after he had finally quitted Gaul, to rise against the governors whom he appointed; and the land had rest, so far as we know, for nearly seventy years.

When the last struggles for liberty were over, Cæsar had still a year to devote to those victories of peace, without which, as he very well knew, all his work would be thrown away. Unluckily his officer Hirtius, who wrote the eighth and last book of the Gallic War, has devoted only a few lines to this most important part of his master's work, and we can add

[*] Hirtius, B. G., viii., 39.

to them but a few stray hints drawn from later writers. Hirtius says that Cæsar spent the winter of 51 B.C. in the country of the Belgæ, bent upon the task of conciliation, so as to leave no further room for fresh appeal to arms. He laid no heavy burdens on the tribes, made handsome presents to their chiefs, and now at last found his opportunity for using his rare gifts of courtesy and gentleness. " Gaul, worn out with a long series of disasters, was thus easily kept in peace, by providing it with happier opportunities of obedience than it had enjoyed in the previous years." Henceforward, so far as he had time to attend to Gallic affairs, this policy was steadily acted on. He had enrolled one whole legion, besides cavalry and auxiliaries, from among the conquered peoples; and this legion, which was to do him much good service, and was known by the name of the " Lark " from the crest on their helmets, eventually by his good-will received the full Roman citizenship. It is even said that he later introduced a few Gauls into the Roman Senate; and whether this be true or not, the fact that it is told of him serves to show the direction which the world believed his thoughts to be taking.

Of Cæsars organisation of his conquests we know hardly anything. They were no doubt at first simply added to the existing Transalpine province, and were for some years ruled, as he had ruled them, by a single provincial governor. But before his death in 44 B.C., he had divided them between two governors, the one taking the whole of the south, excluding the older Narbonese province, and the other the whole of the north, henceforward to be called Belgica. This in itself shows a certain progress towards civilisation, for it implies an increase of civil business beyond the powers of a single ruler. Augustus, following on the same lines, divided southern Gaul into three provinces; and from his time the whole territory from the Mediterranean to the ocean and from the ocean to the Rhine, was administered by four provincial governors. No attempt was made by Cæsar to drain the resources of the country into the Roman treasury; he knew that the people had suffered terribly, that they had been in debt before he conquered them, and that he and his staff had already sufficiently enriched themselves at their expense. Tribute had of course to be paid; but it was to be paid in one lump sum, was to be levied by the Gauls themselves, and does not seem to have been excessive in amount.

One word more before we enter on the next act in the drama of this great life. What was the effect of these long campaigns, this absence of nine years from the capital, on the character and capacities of Cæsar himself?

Enough has been said in former chapters to show the deteriorating influence of life at Rome on the character and conduct of men naturally well-meaning. Enough has also been said to point out the narrow view of politics—of the duties of Rome to her vast empire, of the rights of humanity against her—which a continued life in the forum, like that of Cicero, seemed necessarily to bring with it. Cæsar had indeed always, so far as we can discern, held wider views on these subjects, derived from his democratic predecessors; but he, too, might have been swept away in the whirlpool of party fury and selfishness, but for his long sojourn in a foreign land, relieved by visits to Cisalpine Gaul, the home then of all that was best in Italy. We know too well even in these days how hard it is to keep steadily and honourably to great principles in the heat of party strife. It was far harder to do so then, in an age when self-restraint was the rarest of virtues, and political quarrels knew no such thing as compromise. But Cæsar in Gaul must have learnt to keep his mind steadily fixed on one great end, the re-constitution of the Empire on a rational and humanitarian basis. We have no direct evidence of this, but we can be certain of it. In Gaul he had leisure to watch the phantasmagoria of politics at home, and to see through the blind folly of it; while at the same time he mixed daily with men who were young in civilisation, and whose moral and political vitality was not yet spent. And everywhere he saw the value of absolute command in ordering a disunited state, and the value of implicit obedience as a discipline; at every turn he learnt that he had the requisite force within him to make men obey him willingly, and by degrees he learnt also how much patience, gentleness, and persevering hard work are necessary to the successful and permanent use of that force. And so it was that when the last year of his government arrived, his political insight was clearer than ever, and his capacity for enforcing his will was ten times greater than it had been. As his conduct afterwards fully showed, he had learnt not only the duties of government and the art of war, but the great secrets of humanity—good faith and justice. He had once or twice strayed from the right path, and had probably repented it. He never again left it ; and if in the last six years of his life we find in him an unparalleled combination of hard work and strong will on the one hand, and of high aims and true humanity on the other, we may account for it by supposing that a nature, in itself noble and humane, had gained yet more of strength and self-restraint from a long period of labour in a bracing political air, and chiefly from the last few years of constant toil, anxiety, and disappointment.

We must now return for a brief space to the course of events at Rome since the re-construction of the triumvirate at Lucca in May, 56 B.C. By that arrangement, as we saw, Cæsar gained a five years' prolongation of his command, and a law was passed the following year which probably made March 1, 49 B.C., the limit of his tenure. Pompeius and Crassus were to be consuls for 55. Pompeius, on his part, obtained the governorship of both Spanish provinces for five years from the close of his consulship, and Crassus in the same way the governorship of Syria. Crassus left Rome for his province at the end of 55 ; but Pompeius was to remain, contrary to all precedent, in spite of the fact that he was commanding an army and was actually a provincial governor. To him, therefore, once more fell the task of keeping the city in good order, and of defeating the inevitable struggles of anarchical tribunes and electioneering clubs.

During the year of their consulship no special opposition was offered to Pompeius and Crassus, who contrived to get the laws passed which concerned their interests and that of Cæsar, and added one or two others of a generally useful character. But no sooner was Pompeius left alone than the enemies of this self-constituted and irresponsible government began to take advantage of his isolation and weakness. Bribery was of course rampant on both sides, both in elections and in the law-courts, and letters of Cicero's dated July, 54 B.C., show the utter political profligacy of the time in the most glowing colours.* The existing consuls made a private contract with two of the candidates to obtain their election, while the juries convicted the innocent and acquitted the guilty. The elections were postponed again and again, so great was the excitement, and so incompetent was all authority to control the mobs. Almost absolute anarchy prevailed for twelve months, and the consuls for 53 B.C. were only elected in July of that year. A dictatorship was freely talked of, and men naturally looked to Pompeius. Crassus was defeated and killed in Parthia this year; Cæsar was engaged in his deadly struggle with the revolted Belgæ, and had no choice but to carry out the work to which he had put his hand. Pompeius stood quite alone; for the third time he had the fate of the Empire and his own in his hands, should he but choose to seize the opportunity. He had his two Spanish provinces, and an army in Italy, with which he might master the capital if he pleased. Nothing more was necessary

* " Ad Att.," iv., 15 and 18.

to make him absolute, except the consent of Cæsar—and this consent, strange as it may seem, he actually obtained.

The situation at the beginning of 52 B.C. was a very critical one. The three rulers were reduced to two, and of those one only was in a position to govern. The two survivors were on good terms, each content that the other should be where he was; but the one bond that had promised permanently to unite them had been rudely snapped. Cæsar's daughter Julia, the dearly loved wife of Pompeius, had died the year before; and her loss was irreparable. For five years there had been no difference between the two men, and this was universally ascribed to her influence. In vain Cæsar tried to fill up the gap she left by proposing to marry Pompeius' daughter, and offering him the hand of his own grand-niece. These offers were declined; and from this time we may probably date a certain want of confidence between the two, which ripened, as Cæsar's prolonged absence drew to an end, into alarm and suspicion, and even into underhand dealing, on the part of the weaker of the two. We must briefly trace the growth of this new phase in their relations to each other.

At the beginning of 52 B.C. there were no consuls; as we saw, the elections for 53 had been postponed so long that they only took place at the time when the consuls for 52 should have been elected. Everything was at a standstill; the notion of a dictatorship took a stronger hold than ever on men's minds. Cæsar was far away and could exercise no direct personal influence on Roman politics. For a short time this miserable state of affairs dragged on, till an accident brought on a crisis suddenly. On January 13th Clodius and Milo, the two free lances of the streets, met on the Appian Way, and in a sudden brawl Clodius was killed. The history of these men for the last few years does not concern us here; it was not the murder of an unprincipled demagogue that was in itself important, but the events which followed from it. The body was brought to Rome, and the excitable mob broke out into open riot at the loss of their old favourite. Inflamed by the funeral speeches, and by the sight of the corpse, they burnt down the senate-house and used it as a funeral-pyre. Milo, the senatorial candidate for the consulship, and Lepidus the *interrex* who should have conducted the elections, were besieged in their houses; it was much as if the Houses of Parliament were to be burnt down, and all government offices closed by a London mob.

To re-establish order was now absolutely necessary. The task fell, as it had always hitherto fallen, to the Senate; and the Senate appointed as their executive officer the only man who had the means of compelling obedience. They proclaimed martial law, and directed Pompeius to raise a new army in Italy; they declared the rioters guilty of high treason; and, finally, after a lapse of some weeks, they nominated him sole consul, without the form of popular election. This last step was proposed by Cæsar's old colleague and enemy Bibulus, the most obstinate of the senatorial party; it was practically the same thing as giving Pompeius the dictatorship, and it was accomplished by the same senatorial procedure. Thus the bewildered triumvir found his only help and counsel in the Senate he had so long despised. He became its nominee and its sole executive officer on the motion of its most pronounced aristocrat. In reality, however, he became its master, and the Senate, by appealing through him to the military arm, practically acknowledged that the days of a constitutional republic were over. He brought troops to Rome, saw the trial of Milo carried through under an armed guard, and fairly mastered the unruly element in the city populace. In the summer he nominated his father-in-law Metellus Scipio, to be his colleague, but remained master of the situation for the rest of the year.

How did Cæsar regard these startling proceedings and this new alliance between his colleague and the Senate? He had returned to Cisalpine Gaul after punishing the Belgic tribes (p. 217) and had there heard of the murder of Clodius, and of the decrees of the Senate. He took advantage of that one which ordered an Italian levy, to raise new troops in the Cisalpine province. He must have had communications with Pompeius, but we know nothing of them save that he made no opposition to his colleague's elevation to supreme power, or to the use he made of it. The fact was that his hands were tied. Vercingetorix was beginning his great rebellion, and he must leave Pompeius and the Senate to take care of themselves, or be content to see the whole of his work in Gaul utterly destroyed. All that he tells us is that, when he left north Italy to begin that last terrible campaign, he had learnt of the restoration of order in Rome, and considered it to be due to the virtus, i. e., the firmness and courage of Pompeius.* The struggle with Vercingetorix detained him till the autumn, and the following winter he passed in Transalpine Gaul; nor did he once return even to his Cisalpine province until the spring of 50 B.C. He was intent on finishing his own work, and knew that it was on this that his own future and that of the Empire depended, far more than on the caprice or blunders of Pompeius and the Senate.

When at last he did return, he found serious difficulties in front of him. Pompeius had drifted into a position in regard to him which can at the best be described as an armed and suspicious neutrality, while the senatorial party, now trusting to the aid of Pompeius, even if it had to be won at the cost of their own liberties, was openly determined to achieve his ruin. Cæsar, ennobled and strengthened in character by adversity, and trusting in himself and his resources, in his agents at Rome, and perhaps in his star, made no threats, and left almost his whole army in the distant province. But plain as it is that he sought no open rupture, and that the last thing he wished for was civil war, he could not sit still and see ruin staring him in the face, the moment he should have resigned his provinces and his army; and thus arose that famous quarrel, which shook the world to its foundations, and went far in its results to solve the problems of the Roman revolution. It is called, in the language of scientific

* B. G., vii., 6, 1. This was probably written in 51 B.C.

history, the question between Cæsar and the Senate ; it was really a question between old ideas and new ones, between forms and realities, between the ancient and worn-out government of the city-state, and the one man whose genius and destiny were driving him towards the creation of an entirely new system.

To put the case for either party in this quarrel in a few words is by no means an easy task, much less to sum it up impartially. All that can be done here is to state the facts as far as we can know them, and to draw the inferences which seem legitimate.

The plot laid for Cæsar's destruction was a perfectly fair one from the point of view of an honest enemy. In order to remain a power in the Empire it was indispensable for him to be either proconsul or consul—to govern a province or to govern in Italy. There must be no interval in which he should hold neither office. In such an interval he would be merely a private man, unprotected by office from the assaults of his enemies ; he could be tried for extortion or high treason, his conviction might be secured by the help of bribery and political clubs, and he would have to go into exile and die a political death. To this political extinction the only alternative would be civil war. And even if he were not likely to be convicted, the time of his trial might so be arranged that he would be disqualified, as an accused person, for candidature for the consulship. Now Cæsar's proconsulship of Gaul was to terminate on March 1, 49 B.C., and the consular elections would take place at the earliest in the following summer.

There would therefore be an interval between the two offices, and he would be exposed to the utmost peril if he gave up province and army on March 1st.

But he had of course long ago foreseen this. His agents in Rome kept him fully informed of the outspoken hatred of his foes,* and he had taken steps to secure himself against it. When the law was passed in 55 B.C., which added a fresh term of five years to his government, Pompeius seems to have inserted in it (doubtless in accordance with a previous promise to Cæsar) a clause prohibiting the discussion of a successor before March 1, 50.† At that time it was the rule, as it had been since Sulla had regulated the succession to proconsular governments, that the Senate should select the provinces to be governed in any year by proconsuls, before the election of the consuls who after their year of office would succeed to proconsulships; thus the consuls elected in 50, who would serve their consulship in 49, would only succeed in 48 to those provinces which the Senate had chosen before their election as consuls. If Cæsar's provinces were not to be open to discussion in the Senate till March 1, 50, he could not be superseded except by the consuls of 49, and these would not be able to succeed him till January 1, 48. He would thus be able to retain his army and his government throughout the year 49.

But there was another difficulty to be foreseen

---

* Suetonius, Cæsar, 30.

† This important point is made almost certain by comparing Cælius' words, (Fam., viii., 8, 4, and 9) with Hirtius, B. G., viii., 53.

and overcome. As the law stood, he would have to come in person to Rome to profess himself a candidate and to canvass for the consulship. He had had to do this in 60 B.C., as we saw, and had given up his triumph in order to comply with the regulation. But the imperious necessity of self-preservation forbade him to yield a second time; and he took a step which will perhaps be only thought justifiable by those who understand the deadly nature of the conflict he wished to avoid. Through the agency of a united body of friendly and probably well-paid tribunes, he had a law promulgated early in 52 B.C., which relieved him from the necessity of canvassing in person. Pompeius supported this law; to oppose it would have been an open breach with Cæsar, for which he was neither willing nor ready. Even Cicero seems to have used his influence in its favour, and to have induced his friend Cælius not to oppose it; he had met Cæsar lately at Ravenna, and was for the time under the spell of the magician.* The law of course was passed, and Cæsar might feel himself secure. He would retain both army and provinces throughout 49, and would not be forced to return to Rome until he was safe from prosecution as consul. During his consulship, he might, as in 59, obtain by a special law another provincial command.

But on his return to north Italy in the spring of 50 B.C., he found all the defences broken down which he had been at such pains to construct. Pompeius and the Senate had combined to alter the whole legal

---
* Cic., Fam., vi., 6, 5; *cp*. Phil., ii., 10–24.

machinery for appointing provincial governors, by a law, bearing the name of the sole consul, and passed not long after that one which dispensed with Cæsar's personal canvass. There was now to be an interval of five years between a consulship and a proconsulship. The first obvious result of this would be to prevent Cæsar, even if he were duly elected consul in 49, from obtaining a fresh provincial governorship until five years from the end of 48. But it struck a much more direct blow at his interests than this. When the bill became law, there would be an interval of some years before any consuls would be qualified under it for provinces; and to fill up the governorships during the interval, the Senate was authorised to appoint any persons of consular rank who had not as yet succeeded to proconsulships. This they might do at any time, without regard to any previously existing regulations; and thus they now had it in their power to supersede Cæsar on March 1, 49, *i. e.*, to demand his resignation both of his army and his provinces. To complete the work, by this bill (or another one) it was expressly re-enacted that a personal candidature for the consulship should henceforth be indispensable. This was almost an open declaration of war; and Cæsar's friends pointed out to Pompeius that he was contravening the vested interests which Cæsar possessed through the tribunes' law passed earlier in the year. Pompeius then appended a clause to the bill, on his own authority, as it seems, and after it had been formally passed by the people, saving the interests of anyone who had previously been excepted by law from its provisions.

Outbreak of Civil War.

Such a clause, it need hardly be said, was legally mere waste paper.

This bill came into force in 51 B.C., and already in that year the Senate became eager to act upon it for Cæsar's destruction. In September the question of superseding him was first formally discussed [*]; but Pompeius himself interfered, with the objection that by the law under which Cæsar held, the matter could not be dealt with till after March 1, 50 B.C., and the obedient Senate contented itself with resolving to take it as the first business after that date. But when the day arrived, nothing was done; so well did Cæsar's agents do their work, and so half-hearted was Pompeius in his opposition to them, that after two or three adjournments the question was again allowed to drop. And even up to the last day of that year no definite resolution had been taken.

But if the Senate had taken no decisive step, the political current was none the less setting strongly towards civil war. It was becoming every day plainer that the question was one, not so much between Cæsar and the Senate, as between Cæsar and Pompeius. The mist was lifting, and the real combatants were becoming visible to all men. They could see Cæsar, now politically almost defenceless, but with an apparently irresistible army, and fast being driven to desperate action by the absolute refusal of his enemies to admit what must in all fairness be considered his legal rights. They could see Pompeius, on the other hand, master of Italy by

---
[*] The matter had been touched on in July, but adjourned till the indispensable Pompeius, who was at Ariminum, should return.

means of the army which the Senate had allowed him to raise, and governor at the same time, contrary to all precedent, of the Spanish provinces; and they knew that this military power of his was guaranteed him by a law for no less than five more years. Between this Scylla and this Charybdis— between Cæsar's desperation and Pompeius' military absolutism—it was all but impossible that the old and shattered Republic could be safely steered. And the hopelessness of the situation is only made the clearer if we can believe, as we have every reason to do, that neither Cæsar nor Pompeius had any real desire to resort to civil war.

In the summer of 50 B.C. Cæsar let it be known in the Senate, through a fickle but able young tribune who had lately come into his pay, that he was willing to resign his army and provinces if Pompeius would simultaneously do the same; and the Senate voted a resolution in this sense by a majority of 370 to 22. The consul Marcellus broke up the meeting in anger, crying out that they were voting for Cæsar to be their master. About the same time, or earlier, a scheme was suggested for sending Pompeius to the East, and so ridding themselves of King Log; and in view of this Cæsar was required to send home a legion which he had some time previously borrowed from Pompeius to help in the Gallic rebellion, and to contribute another himself. He at once obeyed the order; but the legions were detained by Pompeius in Italy, and the Parthian War was quietly dropped. These two facts—the vote in the Senate, and the retention of the legion—show plainly enough that the Senate was afraid of both the rivals, and that it was entirely at the mercy of the one whom it least dreaded.

So the year wore on, and the actual crisis was still delayed. The consular elections were hostile to Cæsar, though, on the other hand, two of his officers, M. Antonius and Q. Cassius, were elected tribunes of the people. On Lentulus Crus and Claudius Marcellus, the new consuls, must rest the immediate blame of the Civil War. No sooner had they entered on office on January 1, 49 B.C., than it became obvious that the difficulty would shortly come to a head. On that day Curio once more presented proposals from Cæsar, in the form of a letter to be read before the Senate by the new consuls. What these proposals were cannot be determined with certainty, owing to the loss of the last few lines of the eighth book of the Gallic War; but it is highly probable that they were those extreme concessions which Suetonius mentions as having been already submitted at an earlier date, before Cæsar finally left his Transalpine province in the autumn.* They startle us by their marvellous moderation, and hardly an historian has been found to give Cæsar the credit of honesty in venturing on them. He declared himself willing to give up the Transalpine province and eight of his legions, if the Senate would allow him to retain Cisalpine Gaul with two legions, or that province and Illyria with one only. And he only asked that this arrangement should continue until after he had been elected consul; after his election he would

---

* Suet., Cæsar, 29 and 30.

resign everything, and thus place himself at the discretion of his enemies during the last months of the year.

Cæsar's letter was read, after some opposition. What followed, he has himself described, no doubt from accounts given him by Curio and Antonius, in the first chapters of his work on the Civil War. In the main they must represent the truth, though obviously written in indignation and anger. The consuls would not allow the proposals to be considered. Lentulus even hinted that he would go over to Cæsar unless decisive action were taken. Pompeius, roused at last, let it be known through his father-in-law, Scipio, that if the Senate wished for help from him, they must act now or never. All attempts at delay were roughly put aside; the majority that had voted some months before for a general disarmament, frightened by these threats and by the presence of Pompeius' soldiery in the city, now passed a decree ordering Cæsar to give up his provinces and army by a fixed date (possibly by July 1st, the last day on which he could become a candidate for the consulship), on pain of being proclaimed a public enemy. Antonius and Curio put their tribunician veto on this decree. Several days were spent in discussing the legality of this veto, during which every attempt to communicate with Cæsar was frustrated. At length, on January 7th, the decisive step was taken. The consuls were authorised, by that once terrible decree under which Cicero had put to death the conspirators fourteen years before, to see that the Republic took no hurt. A state of war was then

MARCUS ANTONIUS.
FROM THE BUST IN THE UFFIZI GALLERY IN FLORENCE (*Visconti*).
(*Baumeister.*)

declared, and Cæsar's tribunes were no longer secure of their lives. They fled to their master at Ravenna, and the Senate immediately proceeded to appoint successors to the Gallic provinces, to order fresh levies and supplies, to place the whole resources of the state in the hands of Pompeius. On that day the Senate sealed its own fate ; and though the great Council had yet in the future much valuable work to do, it never met again, save for a few short weeks in the winter that followed Cæsar's death, as the independent ruler of the civilised world.

ROMAN LICTOR.

CHAPTER XV.

CIVIL WAR IN ITALY AND SPAIN.

49 B.C.

CÆSAR had made no preparations for such a contingency as a declaration of war. Hirtius, who knew him well and was an honest soldier whose word can be relied on, says that Cæsar fully believed that as soon as the Senate could regain its freedom of action, it would approve his cause.*
He refused to listen to unpleasant reports about Labienus, whom he had set over the Cisalpine province during his last visit to Further Gaul; and for some time this strategical key to Italy was actually in the hands of a man who was secretly plotting against his chief, and was soon to be his bitterest enemy. And when at last Cæsar arrived

---

* Hirtius, B. G., viii., 52.

and superseded him, he brought only a single legion with him, though the year was drawing to a close, the consuls elect were hostile to him, and Pompeius had actually been entrusted with the task of raising levies throughout Italy. Those who think that everything Cæsar did was the result of deep calculation must find it hard to explain these facts.

But anyone who can fairly divest his mind of the notion of Cæsar's craft, and can read without prejudice the books on the Civil War, will not be likely to find himself forced to retreat on his old belief. Those books, with the whole story of the rest of Cæsar's life, seem to tell another tale. An extraordinary confidence in his own good fortune, leading to serious rashness and risk, an almost blind belief in the faithfulness of all his friends and helpers, and a persistent desire to avoid shedding the blood of Roman citizens,—these are the characteristics which astonish us again and again in the last years of Cæsar's life. He was no deep calculator; his habit was to act for the immediate exigency. He was no suspicious enemy, but a perfectly frank and honest friend whom simple men loved.* He not only shunned civil war till the very last moment, but then only entered on it because to submit would have ruined not only himself but all his hopes for the Empire, and would have undone all the work of his party since the Gracchi. He stood firm as a rock when it became clear that he must fight or be destroyed; but never in any civil war has victory

---

*Such men were Matius, Decimus Brutus, Hirtius, Oppius, and other intimate friends.

been used with such clemency, or enormous strength wielded so gently.

When Antonius and Cassius, or couriers despatched by them, reached Ravenna with the decisive news, Cæsar addressed the thirteenth legion, the only one he had with him. He explained the determination of his enemies to ruin him, and asked the soldiers to defend him. Their loyalty ascertained, he sent orders for the rest of his army to march at once from Further Gaul,* and set forward himself for Ariminum, the frontier town of Italy, as it was then politically defined. For a proconsul to pass beyond the boundary of his province was high treason to the state, and the boundary here was the little river Rubicon, flowing from the Apennines into the Adriatic. The moment of crossing the Rubicon was therefore the turning-point of his life. Asinius Pollio, who afterwards wrote memoirs of him, was with him at the time, and it is perhaps to his book that Plutarch owed a story of Cæsar's doubt and hesitation when he reached the banks of the stream by night.† He may well have stayed for a moment to brace himself for the task before him; but the die once cast, he went straight on to Ariminum, and never hesitated again for the rest of his life.

At Ariminum, which he occupied without opposition, he found Roscius, a prætor, and a young con-

---

* This is his own statement. Colonel Stoffel has made it seem probable that an order of this kind must have been sent three or four weeks earlier. (Histoire de Jules César, i., 205 foll.)

† Plut., Cæs., 29. Cp. Suet., Jul., 31. If we could be sure that this and the other tales of this night are not really legends which gathered round a famous event, they might be worth inserting.

nexion of his own, with a friendly message from Pompeius, excusing himself and urging Cæsar to abate his anger. He sent them back with a last proposal for peace, which is quite as astonishing as his former one, and would hardly be credited from Cæsar, if it were not amply confirmed in a letter of Cicero's.* " Let Pompeius retire to Spain ; let both parties simultaneously disarm, and allow the constitution to work once more without terrorism ; and I will then give up every point in dispute." To this he added an earnest request for a personal interview.

Meanwhile Pompeius and the consuls had abandoned Rome in haste, making for Capua, where were the only two legions which were complete and ready for action ; no vigorous preparation for war had been made, and they despaired of staying the enemy's advance at any point north of Rome. Before they reached Capua Cæsar's messengers overtook them, and two days later (January 27th) an answer was despatched after serious deliberation. Cæsar must return to his province, and there disband his army; when that was done, Pompeius would join his own legions in Spain,† and the Senate might meet in Rome for a general settlement. To such a demand no reply was possible but instant action. Antonius was despatched to occupy Arretium, and hold the main road from Rome to the Cisalpine province, so as to protect Cæsar's flank

---

* Cæs., B. C., i., 10. Cic., Ad Fam., xvi., 12, 3.

† Cicero (*l. c.*) omits the point of which Cæsar naturally complained, *i. e.*, the dismissal of his army. Cicero's letters of this time are often hasty and reckless of the truth ; and as he here puts the conditions, it would have been difficult for Cæsar to refuse them.

and rear; the rest of the troops were launched upon the road that follows the Adriatic coast southwards, and three coast towns were successively taken. Auximum, Cingulum, and Asculum opened their gates, and some Pompeian officers fell into Cæsar's hands. They were courteously dismissed; and Cingulum, though it was a foundation of Labienus, who had now deserted Cæsar, met with no ill-treatment.

Pompeius had fixed his head-quarters at Luceria, a town in Apulia near the high road which his enemy was pursuing; it was his object to concentrate his troops here, and then to retreat along the same road to Brundisium, in order to evacuate Italy and cross to Epirus. We need not stop to criticise his strategy; we have his own word for it that he could not trust his soldiers, and that the work of concentration in midwinter was slow.* That he was right, is shown by the fate of Domitius, who had been collecting troops for him at Corfinium, some eighty miles north-west of Luceria. Though urged by repeated orders and entreaties from his chief, he delayed too long. On February 14th Cæsar was upon him. He had left the coast-road with this object, knowing that with his small force he could not afford to leave Domitius in his rear. Italy, if we are to believe Cicero, was against Cæsar; and if Domitius were left in a strong position in central Italy, he might gradually raise a powerful force, cut off Cæsar's legions which were following at intervals, and even occupy Cisalpine Gaul. Cæsar's resolution

---

* Four of Pompeius' despatches are preserved in Cic., Ad Att., viii., 12, A, B, C, D.

was justified, though it cost him a delay of seven days, which had other serious consequences. Corfinium was invested, and the conduct of Domitius' troops showed that Pompeius had rightly judged the situation. Believing that their commander was about to make his escape alone, on February 20th they opened the gates; the next day the senators and equites who had gathered there surrendered to Cæsar, who after a short speech released them all unconditionally. He protected them from all insult, and returned to Domitius a large sum of money which had been entrusted him for military purposes. The captured troops enlisted in his ranks, and took the oath of obedience to him. The same day he set off with all speed towards Luceria; but Pompeius had already evacuated that place and was on his way to Brundisium.

If we may judge from Cicero's letters, which abound in these weeks, Cæsar's clemency and courtesy at Corfinium had an extraordinary effect on all waverers in Italy. Up to this time Cicero had written of him in terms of intense hatred and fear; now his whole tone changes. Cæsar found time as he hurried southward from Corfinium, to send him a hasty note, which is still preserved; and about this time he also wrote a letter to his private friends and agents, Balbus and Oppius, which was probably meant to be copied and sent to various acquaintances as a declaration of policy.* In this remarkable document, which is also preserved, he states in explicit terms his determination not to imitate the

---
* Cic., Ad Att., ix., 7 C. and 6 A.

cruelty of Sulla and other conquerors in previous civil wars. " My method of conquest shall be a new one; I will fortify myself with compassion and generosity. He lays the blame of the war, not on Pompeius, but on the Senate, and expresses his ardent desire for a reconciliation with his great rival. From this time forward Italy was on the whole on his side; and there was need of it, for all the provinces but Gaul were as yet occupied by the troops of the Senate or of its supposed champion.

On March 9th he reached Brundisium with six legions, three of his old ones, and three newly formed. Pompeius was still in the town, but a part of his force, under the two consuls, had already sailed for Epirus. Caesar instantly set to work with two objects: first, to blockade the port; secondly, to bring Pompeius to a personal interview. Moles were constructed at the entrance of the harbour, and negotiations were attempted through common friends, as well as through a certain Magius whom Caesar had captured. But Pompeius successfully counteracted the moles, and steadily refused the interview, maintaining, according to Caesar, that in the absence of the consuls he had no authority to treat.* Such an answer was under the circumstances absurd, and it is not hard to guess its real motive. He dreaded Caesar's personal address and persuasiveness as much as Caesar himself trusted in it; he had perhaps begun to realise his opponent's greatness as he had never realised it before, and felt that he must now fight or lose his old position as "the first citizen of the

---

* B. C., i., 26. Letters of Caesar in Cic., Ad Att., ix., 13 A and 14.

A SEAPORT TOWN.

state." He exerted himself with unwonted alacrity, and by skilful dispositions he contrived to escape on March 17th, with the loss of only two ships, which ran against one of Cæsar's moles and were captured with all on board. Had his enemy not been delayed at Corfinium, it is quite possible that he might either have been forced to surrender with all his troops, or at least have voluntarily come to terms and abandoned the Senate.

Pompeius had escaped ; and to follow him at once was impossible, for there were no transports at hand. Cæsar determined on a plan which, on a much smaller scale, Napoleon so often adopted with brilliant success. He stood in Italy between two hostile peninsulas; between Pompeius in Epirus with one army, and the *legati* of Pompeius in Spain with another. If allowed to concentrate strength, these two armies would combine to crush him, and as commanding the seas, they would be able to blockade Italy ; but if the one were with all speed destroyed, he could take the offensive against the other with his rear clear of enemies, and with his whole available force. The Spanish army was largely composed of veterans, and was far more formidable than that of Pompeius was likely for some time to be ; this accordingly was to be the first object of his attack. To prevent a blockade of Italy, he sent one of his *legati* to Sardinia with one legion, and Curio to Sicily with another; and they had no difficulty in occupying those islands, and so securing a corn-supply for Rome. Cato, who was in command in Sicily, fled to Epirus in despair, after uttering bitter reproaches against Pompeius for plunging into war without any adequate preparation ; and it is characteristic of the total want both of union and discretion among Cæsar's enemies, that Cicero is equally bitter in his complaints against Cato for so hastily evacuating a most valuable province.*

Cæsar set out towards Rome, on his way to Spain, immediately after Pompeius had escaped. The Senate and consuls had been swept out of Italy, and some provision must be made for the government; there would be no time to organise a constitution, but some first steps might be taken, and negotiation might be renewed. His first object was to bring together all the members of the Senate who were still in Italy; among these was Cicero, and if Cicero could be induced to be present, his example would have a good effect. At Formiæ, on his way to Rome, he had a friendly but unsatisfactory meeting with the friend of his early days, which Cicero duly reported to Atticus. † Cicero declined to appear in the Senate, unless he could speak his mind freely, and his views, uncertain as they were at this time, could not be made to suit Cæsar's. They parted with a promise from Cicero that he would take time to consider the matter, and did not meet again until Cæsar was master of the world. The two noblest characters of the age were destined to be continually in conflict ; the one looking ever backwards, the other ever at the facts before him; the man of letters clinging fondly to a broken constitution,

---

* Cic., Ad Att., x., 16, 3. Cæs., B. C., i., 30.
† Ad Att., ix., 18.

the man of action forced henceforward in spite of himself to treat it as no longer capable of repair.

On the last day of March Cæsar arrived in Rome. The Senate was legally summoned by the tribunes Antonius and Cassius, and Cæsar addressed it in a speech of which he has given us the heads. He began by stating his own case in the present quarrel, pointing out how Pompeius and the Senate had combined to deprive him of advantages, especially the right to stand for the consulship in his absence, which had been bestowed on him by the people; and he went on to contrast the many attempts he had made to obtain peace, with the reception those attempts had encountered. Then he came to the point. Would they unite with him to carry on the government? If they feared to do so, he would be no burden to them, but would carry it on by himself. Lastly, he invited them to select envoys to send to Pompeius; not as a confession of weakness, but as a matter alike of justice and equity.

The last proposal was agreed to, but no one would go, as Cæsar tells us, from fear of Pompeius, or, as Dio Cassius has it, because they doubted whether he was in earnest. Seeing them to be hopeless he began to act for himself. They met him with the tribunician veto[*]; he brushed it aside, and, as the story runs, even removed a tribune, Metellus, from the door of the inner treasury, when he interposed his person to prevent its violation. He took all the money contained in it, and, making up his mind to waste no more time, left the city, after a stay of a

[*] Cælius to Cicero. Ad. Fam., viii., 16, 1.

very few days, on his way to Spain. But before leaving he appointed a prætor to govern Rome as prefect of the city, and a tribune, with the title of pro-prætor, to command the troops in Italy. These were M. Æmilius Lepidus and M. Antonius, afterwards two members of the second triumvirate. The third member, Cæsar's grandnephew, C. Octavius, afterwards called Augustus Cæsar, was this year a boy of fourteen.

These appointments, and in fact all Cæsar's acts since the crossing of the Rubicon, were of course entirely unconstitutional. When he left his province he became guilty of high treason, and unless that act can be justified, all that he did afterwards must be reckoned as a wanton violation of those sacred principles of constitutional order under which all free political societies agree to live. Such a principle at Rome was that of senatorial government; it was almost a necessary law of the Roman mind. To attempt to make conditions with the Senate, as Cæsar had done, and then to disobey it, to make war on it, and to drive it and the magistrates out of Italy, was to break utterly with one of the most deeply rooted traditions of government in the mind of the ordinary Roman. But we have tried to make it plain in this volume that there was another principle, of later growth, and rooted in the great changes of recent times, which was of far graver importance to the human race than the idea of government by an assembly of Roman notables. This was the principle of the development of Italy and the provinces by means of Roman institutions; and of this Cæsar was the rep-

THE YOUNG AUGUSTUS.
FROM THE BUST IN THE VATICAN.
(*Baumeister.*)

resentative. Were the two principles incompatible? Was it really necessary to overthrow the Senate in order to govern and develop the Empire? The only way to answer these questions is to study impartially the whole history of the relations between Rome and her dependencies, first under the Republic and then under the Empire; and such a study must almost always lead to an affirmative answer. The Senate had failed to do the work that had to be done; it had resisted every project of reform; it was tied down by the selfish interests of a permanent majority; it was unable to control its own provincial governors, and the strongest of them for the time being must always be its master. Thus, when Cæsar crossed the Rubicon in January, and when in April he told the senators that he was prepared to take the government on himself, he was justified to himself by the past, and he is justified to us also by the result.

Cæsar left Rome on or about April 5th on his way to Spain. His wrath cooled down on the journey, and on the 16th he wrote a kind and friendly note to Cicero, urging him for their old friendship's sake to remain in Italy and abstain from all partisanship.* On arriving at Massilia, he made precisely the same appeal to fifteen of the leading citizens, whom he summoned to meet him; and with a temporary success, as in Cicero's case. But the arrival of a fleet under that unworthy Domitius, who had been taken

---

* Ad Att., x., 8 B. This is a very interesting letter. It seems to have been written by Cæsar in his carriage, and shows obvious signs of haste. He appeals, it is noteworthy, first to his good fortune, and then to his past life, to induce Cicero not to side against him.

and released at Corfinium, caused the Massiliots to change their mind; while Cicero, on the first news of a disaster to Cæsar's arms, turned against him and joined the real enemies of the state.

There was no time, however, to dally before Massilia. Cæsar built a fleet with wonderful rapidity, put it in command of D. Brutus, his admiral of former days, and hastened over the Pyrenees to deal with the Pompeian armies in Spain, which were now concentrated north of the Ebro under Afranius and Petreius. He had already sent on six legions under Fabius, and now joined them with nine hundred cavalry at Ilerda on the Segres. The basin of this river, which descends from the Pyrenees to join the Ebro some sixty miles from its mouth, was now to be the field of the most brilliant campaign in all Cæsar's military life. It is a short and exciting drama in three acts or phases, lasting in all only forty days. The story, which must be here told as summarily as possible, occupies the last half of the first book of the Civil Wars, and is written with every appearance of truth.

The first phase of the campaign opens with Cæsar's arrival before Ilerda on June 23d.* The town, now called Lerida, stood on the right or western bank of the Segres on a hill close to the river, commanding the main road from the Pyrenees to the Ebro. Afranius and Petreius were encamped on another hill somewhat to the south-westward, and between them and the town was another lower eminence. At Ilerda there was a bridge, so that

---

* These dates are those of the unreformed calendar. They are given here with the view of showing the rapidity of Cæsar's movements.

by holding the town they could command both banks of the river, and gather supplies in every direction except to the north. Cæsar also had two bridges four miles apart, made by his officer Fabius before his arrival; one of these had been broken by a storm. As soon as it was repaired Cæsar offered battle, but it was declined, and he set to work to fortify a camp in the plain near to that of the enemy, in order to watch his opportunity.

On the 27th, seeing the importance of the little hill which lay between Ilerda and the enemy's camp, he determined to seize it, and so to cut him off from the town and its bridge, and from communication with the left bank of the river. But the attempt was a signal failure, though made with picked men; the enemy's troops reached the hill first, and fighting in loose skirmishing order, drove the Cæsarians before them, and compelled the whole legion to which the attacking party belonged to retreat to the nearest high ground. This surprising result disheartened the whole army. The ninth legion was sent to the rescue, but only succeeded in making matters worse. They at first repulsed the enemy, but in pursuing them up to the city wall, were stopped by a sudden steep rise in the slope they were following, from the top of which rise the enemy could discharge missiles on them at his leisure. This slope and the sharp rise at the upper part of it were enclosed between two rocky spurs or ridges, which projected from this southern side of the hill at a considerable angle. The farther Cæsar's men pressed up the ascent the more closely they were hemmed in between the steep walls of these spurs; and when they were stopped by the sudden rise they found themselves crowded in a narrow space where they could no longer advance or manœuvre, or retreat without bringing the enemy down on them with headlong force. The attacking column was now worse than useless, for it blocked up the way for supports, which could not reach it on the flanks owing to the steep sides of the ridges between which it was wedged. The column, however, stood its ground bravely, though severely handled by the enemy above; and Cæsar contrived to keep it there during five hours by sending fresh troops to take the place of the wounded and fatigued. At last when all missiles were spent, the men drew their swords and rushed up the steep rise above them, driving the enemy under the city wall and thus making a free space for their own retreat. This was further secured by the valour of the cavalry which pushed up under the steep sides of the ridge, and interposed themselves between the retreating column and the enemy. This day's work cost Cæsar heavy loss; and though he says that both sides claimed the victory, it is plain that it was a defeat for him at every point, and that the ninth legion must have been utterly routed, and perhaps destroyed, had they once given way on the ridge and begun to retreat with the enemy close upon them.*

In this first act of the campaign the famous Gallic troops had been fairly beaten, but even worse was

---

* The real nature of this fight has been for the first time fully determined by Colonel Stoffel's personal examination of the ground. See his work, vol. i., 52; Cæs. B. C., i., 45, 46.

in store for them. During the fighting the river Segres had risen and overflowed its banks, owing to heavy rain and the melting of snow on the Pyrenees. Fabius' two bridges were carried away, while the high stone bridge at Ilerda stood firm; Cæsar was cut off from the left bank, while Afranius could still operate there and prevent any new bridge being built. Worse still, another river, the Cinga, thirty miles to the west, was also flooded and impassable, so that Cæsar was confined in a narrow space where all supplies were already exhausted, and the growing corn was very far from ripe. The Pompeians had ample supplies in Ilerda, and were free to forage on the left bank of the Segres, and with their abundant light troops, accustomed to swim rivers, they could cut off all Cæsar's foragers and intercept all convoys. Corn in the camp rose to the extraordinary price of fifty denarii the modius; a disastrous retreat into Gaul was inevitable if this went on, and the news of it would utterly destroy Cæsar's prestige in the Empire. Rumours had already been flying about of Pompeius' approach from the east to end the war, which showed how the wind was blowing, though they were utterly unfounded. In this crisis news reached Afranius of a large convoy of supplies which was on its way to Cæsar from Gaul and was unable to cross the river so as to reach him; it was protected by Gallic archers and cavalry, but was heavily encumbered and without discipline. He made a vigorous effort to capture it and end the war, and Cæsar saw clearly that he must save it or succumb.

The expedient by which he extricated himself

from such peril shows the immense advantage possessed by a general whose troops are trained to turn their hands to all kinds of work. He set his men to build boats of timber, wattles, and skins, such as they had seen in Britain. These were conveyed by night, each on two carts, twenty miles up the river, so as to be as far as possible out of the enemy's reach; a few soldiers crossed in them and fortified a position on the other bank. Then a bridge was begun, and finished in two days; the convoy was brought across to the right bank, Cæsar's cavalry began to scour the left bank and to cut off Afranius' foraging parties, and the tables were completely turned on the enemy, who was doubtless as much taken by surprise as was Soult when Wellington crossed the Douro almost under his very eyes. So ended, about July 13th, the second phase of this remarkable campaign.

The Pompeian generals now began to contemplate a retreat on the Ebro, and sent orders for a bridge to be built over that river to secure their passage into central Spain. They were confirmed in this plan by another device of Cæsar's. He had ditches dug, thirty feet wide, from one channel of the river to another, about a mile above Ilerda, and so reduced the volume of water in the main stream as to render it fordable at least for his cavalry, which had been compelled each day to go round by his recently constructed distant bridge.* The enemy crossed at

---

* The Segres here flows in three channels; if Stoffel is right in his conjecture, the ditches led from the main stream in the middle to the westernmost one. (Stoffel, i., 58.)

Ilerda and began his retreat before daybreak on July 25th. The left bank was of course chosen, because Cæsar could only operate on it in force with cavalry, and because supplies were still to be had there. His cavalry at once began to hang upon the retreating foe, but the infantry were detained by the depth of the ford. The men could not endure this, and clamoured to be allowed to risk the passage. Cæsar could not resist their ardour. He left all the weaker men behind, and the rest got over with trifling loss and overtook the enemy by a forced march. The armies encamped face to face that night. At earliest dawn both generals reconnoitred and found themselves but a few miles from the rocky hills which here close in from the north upon the valley of the Ebro; it was obvious that whichever army could reach the defiles first would be able to stop the progress of the other.

The Pompeians, after deliberation, determined to push for the hills next morning. Cæsar did not wait, but leaving his cavalry in the plain, turned aside, and climbing the steep hills which bounded the valley to the west, disappeared from his enemy's view. They fancied he was giving up the pursuit, and jeered at his army as it retreated; but presently they saw it turn southward along the hills, and knew that his object was to cut off their retreat. A race began for the possession of the distant defiles; Cæsar's men scrambling over rocky heights, the Pompeians hurrying along the plain. But the latter had started too late; before they could attain their goal, Cæsar had dropped from the hills into the valley in front of them. His cavalry was hanging on their rear, and their situation was a desperate one. An attempt to force a way over the mountains to the Segres only ended in the destruction of four Pompeian cohorts.

Cæsar's men wished to fall on the enemy, thus caught in a trap, but he would not hear of it. He wished for a bloodless victory, and has given such reasons for his decision as even his worst enemies must respect.* A surrender would have taken place then and there, but for the folly of Petreius, who, when the soldiers of the two armies were freely mixing together in expectation of it, called his men to arms, administered the military oath afresh, and slew all the Cæsarians who were in his reach. Not even then would Cæsar attack; he stood firm as a rock against the passion of a whole army. But the catastrophe was not long delayed. In attempting as a last resource a retreat to Ilerda, the Pompeians were once more caught and surrounded; cut off from all supplies, and from water, which in this district is extremely difficult to obtain, Afranius and Petreius at last craved humbly for quarter, and accepted the generous conditions offered them of simply disbanding their troops and leaving Spain. These terms were offered in a speech in which Cæsar has summarised for his readers his political position as well as his military policy; a speech which should be studied by everyone who would pronounce judgment on his character and conduct. The surrender took place on August 2d, and in a few days the

* B. C., i., 72.

lately victorious army was disbanded, after being supplied with corn by Cæsar, and also with such pay as was due to them from their own generals. Not a man was robbed or harmed, or even compelled to enter Cæsar's service.*

The province of Hither or eastern Spain was now in Cæsar's hands; Further Spain was still held for Pompeius by M. Terentius Varro, the famous scholar and antiquarian, who had been busy all the summer in preparing for its defence. But the news of Cæsar's victory, and the moderate use he made of it, upset all Varro's calculations, and rendered all his labour useless. The province declared unmistakably for Cæsar, though the influence of Pompeius there was supposed to be overwhelming. The chief towns closed their gates against Varro. Gades expelled its Pompeian garrison. In obedience to an edict sent beforehand by Cæsar, the chief men of every community came to Cordova to meet him; and when he reached the town himself, he had already had the satisfaction of receiving the news of the submission of Varro, who now handed over the one legion that had remained faithful to him, and came to Cordova to surrender his military chest and the public accounts of the province. At Cordova Cæsar held a general assembly, and in a set speech expressed his good-will and gratitude; remitted all burdens and political penalties imposed by Varro, and after distributing rewards to various individuals and communities, went on to Gades, where he took ship for Tarragona, and proceeded thence by land to Mas-

---
* B. C. i., 85.

silia. He arrived there about the end of September, having in three months secured the allegiance of the whole peninsula in an almost bloodless campaign.

The whole of the western half of the Empire was now in his power, with the single exception of Massilia. While Cæsar was in Spain the siege of the ancient Greek city had been carried on by the faithful Brutus with the fleet, and by Trebonius on land, and with such skill and energy that Cæsar has left as careful accounts of their methods and engineering as if he had himself been present. His record must be passed over here, for its interest is purely a military one; the only part which he took in the siege was to receive the final submission of the town, and to leave it unharmed, as a tribute " rather to its ancient renown than to any claim it had on himself." *
But the reader of these two chapters can hardly fail to be struck by two traits in Cæsar's character which have already been pointed out in the story of the Gallic War : the scientific interest which he shows in all military operations, and the generous care with which he watched and recorded the independent efforts of his lieutenants. Both these traits are also excellently illustrated in the last twenty-two chapters of this same second book of the Civil Wars, in which he has told how the province of Africa was lost to him this same summer by the rashness and inexperience of Curio.† Not a word of contempt or reproach

---

* B. C., ii., 22.

† Mommsen, R. H., iv., 393, takes a different and singular view both of Curio himself and his military ability. This view is not shared by Colonel Stoffel (vol. i., 312).

A BESIEGED CITY.

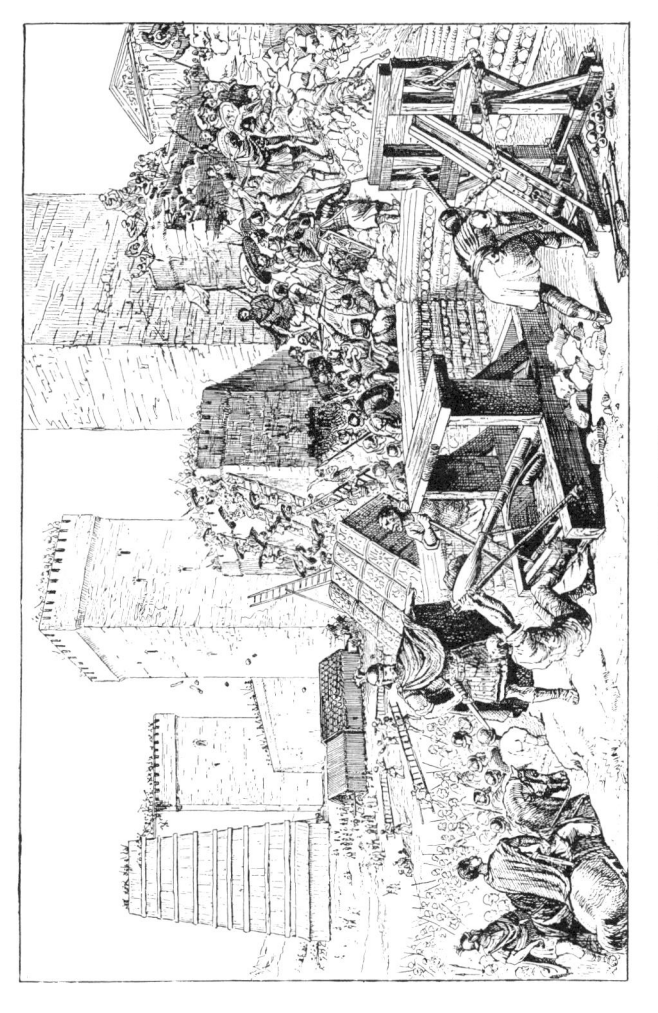

escapes him; Curio was his own choice as a general, and he doubtless felt the responsibility. But in the story he brings out clearly the faults, both of character and conduct, which brought about the disaster, as a lesson to all students of the military art. The Commentaries, let it be said once more, are not merely political pamphlets, as some critics have persuaded themselves; they are the records of the work of a great soldier and his subordinates, prompted, indeed, by a desire to have that work regarded by posterity as Cæsar himself regarded it, but chiefly by a half unconscious recognition of the space it would be entitled one day to occupy in the history of the world.

At Massilia he heard that he had been appointed dictator, with the immediate object of holding the consular elections for the next year. Lepidus, who had been left in command at Rome, could not legally preside at this election, being only a prætor. Both consuls were in Epirus, and the simplest method was to appoint a dictator, whose authority would override that of all existing magistrates. Under the circumstances it was not possible to get this done in the way which was constitutionally proper, the Senate selecting the dictator and the acting consul declaring him duly appointed; but facts are stronger than forms, and since Tiberius Gracchus the voice of the people in their assembly had been held by the democratic party to be valid without senatorial sanction. Even Sulla had acted on this principle, when taking absolute power into his hands; and Lepidus was only following this aristocratic precedent when he proposed by a law to make Cæsar dictator. The law was of course passed; but it was not yet time for Cæsar to assume such an absolutism as that of Sulla, even if he desired it. Only the western half of the Empire as yet owned his supremacy; the great struggle had still to be fought, and Cæsar was not the man to waste time in building up a new system of government before that issue was decided.

We have his own brief account of the use he made of this dictatorship.* He presided at the consular elections, and was elected himself with Servilius Isauricus. To restore credit in Italy, which had been terribly shaken by the Civil War, and to make it plain to all that he was no wild revolutionist, he passed a law of debtor and creditor, as a temporary remedy for social disquietude. He recalled, by a series of legislative enactments, a number of persons who had been exiled under the rule of Pompeius and the Senate, and might now be useful to himself. And though he does not mention it, we know from other sources that he now fulfilled an old promise, and gave by law the full citizenship to all free inhabitants of Transpadane Gaul. These, and other enactments which probably belong to the end of this year 49 B.C., will be considered in a subsequent chapter.

He held his office only eleven days. When all the necessary business had been got through, he left, apparently unwearied by a whole year of incessant toil, for Brundisium, whither the army had been sent on, and reached it before the last day of December.

---
* B. C., iii., 1.

CHAPTER XVI.

DYRRHACHIUM AND PHARSALUS.
48 B.C.

WHOEVER would understand the decisive campaign which has made the year 48 B.C. a landmark in the world's history, must first grasp the situation at its outset geographically and strategically. That done, he will be able to pursue the story sufficiently in outline, without reference to many details which must be omitted in this chapter. The third book of Cæsar's Civil Wars, if he is able to read it, will supply these omissions; and he will find no better reading in any military history, ancient or modern.

Pompeius was in unrestricted command of the whole eastern half of the Empire, with its military and naval resources. His fleets, drawn from Egypt and the Greek ports of the Levant, were cruising unopposed along the coast of western Greece and Epirus; his army, reinforced by large and useful contingents of archers and light-armed troops from the East, was being collected towards the end of 49 B.C. in Macedonia, with a view to concentration on the coast of Epirus opposite to Italy. Here the chief port was Dyrrhachium, now Durazzo; and from this point ran a great Roman road, the Via Egnatia, across the mountains of Macedonia, and along the coast of Thrace, to the Hellespont. This road was the only land-route from the Adriatic to Asia Minor and the East; and so long as Pompeius held it in its whole length, and was master of Dyrrhachium and of the seas, it was practically impossible for Cæsar to attack him. He on the other hand might easily attack or at least blockade Italy, and then proceed to use it as a base of operations for the reduction of Gaul and Spain.

Three facts will here strike the reader: first, that the strategical advantages were all on the side of Pompeius, who could strike without serious risk from an almost impregnable position; secondly, that the key of the whole military situation is the port of Dyrrhachium; thirdly, that now for the first time the eastern and western portions of the Roman Empire are seen politically separated, owning different masters, and about to engage in a deadly struggle for supremacy.

Cæsar's first object was at all risks to get possession of Dyrrhachium; but to do this, or even to hold it when seized, without command of the sea,

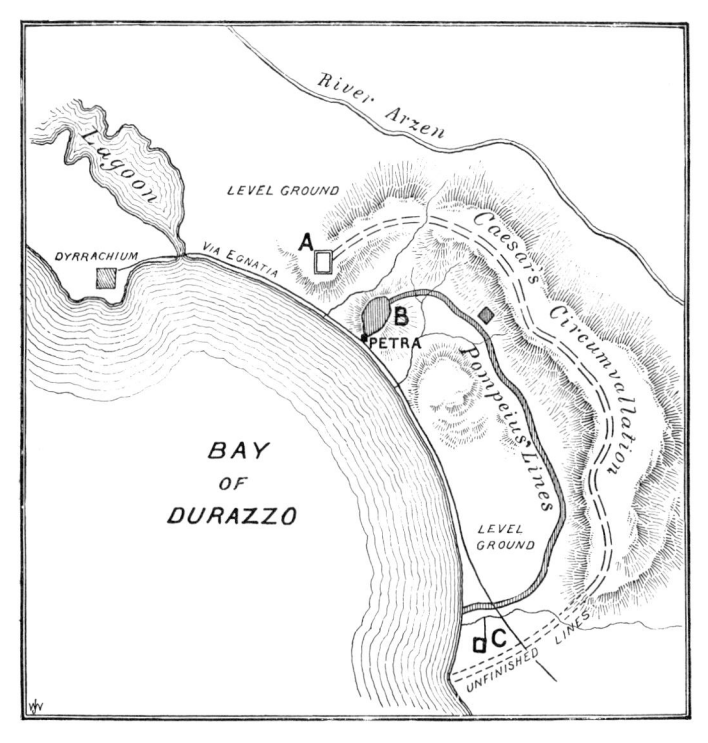

MAP OF OPERATIONS NEAR DYRRACHIUM, 48 B.C.
(AFTER STOFFEL).

A. CÆSAR'S PRINCIPAL CAMP.   B. POMPEIUS' PRINCIPAL CAMP.   C. CAMP OCCUPIED BY POMPEIUS,
THE SCENE OF HIS VICTORY AFTER BREAKING THE UNFINISHED LINES.

would be a more dangerous task than any he had ever undertaken. He might well have chosen to stay and rule in Italy and the West, and to leave Pompeius to his own devices. But there is no more signal proof of the great instincts which governed him, than the fact that he resolved to attack at all hazards. What use would there be in legislating and organising, so long as there was a power left to grow in the East, which might return at his death to destroy all his work? He never seems to have hesitated, either as to the necessity of attacking, or the way in which it should be done. The regular route from Rome to Dyrrhachium and the East was by the great road to Brundisium, whence the sea passage is less than a hundred miles; at Brundisium accordingly he had concentrated his army, with a view to a sudden descent upon the opposite coast.

His rapidity seems to have taken even his own officers by surprise; for when he arrived at Brundisium, no sufficient fleet was ready. With his usual reserve, he does not say who was to blame, but in a single sentence of eight words shows plainly his disappointment. He would not wait, but embarked with a force of not more than twenty thousand infantry and six hundred cavalry, leaving Antonius with orders to bring over the rest when the transports should return for that purpose. He set sail on January 4, 48 B.C., and landed safely next day at a little inlet in the rocky coast of Acroceraunia, some hundred miles south of Dyrrhachium, fearing to steer for any of the well-known ports on the coast, owing to the presence of the hostile fleets. The same day he started on his march towards Dyrrhachium, and the same night the fleet set sail to return to Brundisium. Cæsar himself was as usual rewarded for his swiftness, and established himself in the port of Oricum, where the Greek soldiers of Pompeius forced their commander to open the gates to him; but the fleet was too late to catch the evening breeze from the land, and thirty ships were caught by the enemy, and burnt with every soul on board. The Pompeian admiral who committed this atrocity was M. Bibulus, Cæsar's old colleague and enemy in his prætorship and consulship; he did it in a fit of rage, Cæsar says, at finding that his own negligence had allowed his foe to slip through his hands and to land unopposed.

Meanwhile Cæsar pushed on to Apollonia, an important town not more than fifty miles from Dyrrhachium. The gates were opened, as at Oricum, by the Pompeian soldiery, and the acquisition was a valuable one, because a branch road from the Via Egnatia ran down at this point to the coast. But Pompeius had before this heard of Cæsar's landing; he was returning from Macedonia along the great road to winter at Dyrrhachium, where he had collected great stores, and he now woke up to the absolute necessity of reaching that town before Cæsar. But so great was the consternation in his army on learning that Cæsar himself was at hand, that a panic and mutiny were only quelled by the vigour of Labienus, now Cæsar's deadliest enemy. He was able, however, in the nick of time to place himself between Cæsar and Dyrrhachium; as he had a greatly superior force, this was enough to keep his antagonist entirely on the defensive until the rest of his army should arrive. Cæsar fortified a camp on the southern side of the river Apsus, which flows into the sea between Dyrrhachium and Apollonia; Pompeius encamped on the opposite bank, and there the two armies remained inactive from January to May.

Inaction was to Cæsar of all things the most unbearable, but he had now to pay the penalty for his own magnificent audacity. With only half his army he had flung himself into the centre of the enemy's position, whence it was equally impossible either to retreat or to advance. Supplies were difficult to obtain; the coast was efficiently blockaded; Pompeius was only waiting for reinforcements to overwhelm him. Once his fleet·set sail from Brundisium, and was only saved by the arrival of a letter which he had sent to warn the commander that he would fall into the hands of the enemy if he attempted to cross. In these straits he tried to renew negotiation with Pompeius, but here again Labienus stood in the way, and, if we can accept Cæsar's word, by a treacherous discharge of weapons broke up an interview which had been arranged between officers on either side. It was some consolation to him that the blockading ships, being unable to land anywhere on the coast south of the Apsus, were in such distress for water and provisions that their officers also tried to negotiate, and Bibulus, their admiral, died of the privations he endured.

So the time went on, and Cæsar became more and more impatient. He sent orders to Antonius at

Brundisium that he must come at all risks, named places on the coast where he could land without great danger, and expressed himself with unusual sternness. He did not then know that Antonius had himself been attacked at Brundisium by a Pompeian fleet, and had shown great skill in baffling it and forcing it to put to sea again. A story was current in later times, which may have had some foundation in fact, that Cæsar determined at this time to cross in person to Brundisium and see for himself what caused the delay; that he hired a twelve-oared boat, rowed down the Apsus to the bar, and was only forced to relinquish his purpose by the refusal of the seamen to proceed against a strong westerly wind. So much in the story may be true, and Cæsar's habitual reserve about himself is sufficient to account for its non-appearance in his own narrative.

At last, however, the long-expected fleet was seen passing Apollonia with a strong south wind astern. From Dyrrhachium a squadron of Rhodian war-galleys at once put out to intercept it; just then the wind dropped and gave the Rhodian rowers the advantage they needed over the sailing-vessels of Antonius. Great must have been the excitement of the watchers on the shore, as the rowers gained on their prey. But once more the southern breeze began to blow, and rose till it became a gale; the Cæsarian ships flew northwards before it to the little port of Nymphæum near Lissus, while of the Rhodian force every ship was caught and destroyed by the tempest. Some few of the shipwrecked

48 B.C.] *Dyrrhachium and Pharsalus.* 287

crews fell into Cæsar's hands, who sent them all back unhurt to Dyrrhachium.

Both armies, from their camps on the Apsus, had seen the fleet sail by; but for a day or two they remained in ignorance of what had become of it. When the news arrived that Antonius had landed safely near Lissus, the camps were at last broken up; Pompeius hastened northwards to intercept him, while Cæsar sought for a ford higher up the river, and tried to effect a junction with his lieutenant by taking a circuitous route inland. The junction was safely effected, while Pompeius was lying inactive in an ambuscade, and expecting Antonius to fall into the trap; a fact which shows how greatly he was wanting in the quickness and intelligence which were so characteristic of his adversary. He brought, it seems, no power of imagination to the conduct of a campaign; that faculty which so often enabled Wellington in Spain to divine what was going on behind distant mountain ridges. He was an excellent organiser, if he had ample time and means, but his mind worked so slowly, that when in this war he was at last opposed to a man of genius, he proved utterly incompetent to turn his great advantages to account. No quick-witted general, even of the second order, would have allowed Cæsar and Antonius to join forces without a severe struggle. The result was that he was forced to fall back on Dyrrhachium, and encamped at Asparagium, a few miles south of the city. Cæsar followed, and offered battle. This was refused; and Pompeius could not of course be attacked in his fortified camp. Again the man of genius deluded his sleepy adversary; he retreated into the hills eastwards, as if bent on exploring the country for supplies, and then turning suddenly to the north, and marching day and night, he swooped down on Dyrrhachium. It was a brilliant manœuvre; the city indeed could not be taken, for it lay on a rocky peninsula, and was accessible only by a narrow neck of land between sea and marshes; but this neck was now in Cæsar's power, the great road was at this point in his hands, and Pompeius was cut off from his most valuable stores.

Surely Pompeius could be induced to fight now. "Let us have it out," Cæsar always seems to be saying in this campaign, "or make up the quarrel amicably; if we fight and you win, there will at least be a settlement, and that is what the world wants." But Pompeius would neither negotiate nor risk a battle. All along he seems to have felt some want of confidence in his own soldiers, and to have had some reason for it; Labienus, too, who knew the qualities of Cæsar's men, and their leader's tactical skill, may have advised him not to precipitate matters while his fleets were in command of the sea and could provision him without difficulty. He established himself at Petra, a conspicuous hill on the coast a short distance south of Dyrrhachium, sent orders to his fleets to collect supplies from every quarter, and sat down complacently to watch events, and, if possible, to starve out his enemy.

This led Cæsar to adopt a novel plan, for which he has been generally blamed by military critics; and until Colonel Stoffel published (in 1887) the results of his personal examination of the ground, there was apparently much to justify such censure. It was formerly believed that Cæsar attempted to perform a feat for which his forces were quite inadequate. But it appears now that the design, when first entered on, was bold but by no means hopeless, and that it was only as its execution proceeded that it became more and more exacting and dangerous for an army of hardly more than 22,000 men,* coping with an enemy of not less than double that number.

As his adversary would not fight a battle (which in ancient warfare was easily avoided by the occupation of an entrenched camp), Cæsar determined to hem him in by a line of circumvallation. The accompanying map will show that the country round Petra, where Pompeius was encamped, is hilly; it is, in fact, a tract of steep clayey hills, intersected by numerous ravines and gorges, in which ordinary military operations would be almost impracticable. But such ground might be utilised to prevent an enemy escaping through it; and this was what Cæsar now set about doing. His object, he tells us, was threefold: first, to secure his own supplies from the inroads of the strong Pompeian cavalry; secondly, to render that cavalry useless in its attempts to harass his own force; thirdly, to impress the world with the news that the great Pompeius was hemmed in, and dared not risk a battle. It is clear that he had given up all hope of a speedy issue to the campaign.

---

* Two of his legions had been detached, as will be seen later on, to prevent reinforcements reaching Pompeius.

The idea was quite worthy of Cæsar's genius, but was not destined to be successfully carried out. He had clearly intended that his line of forts should not extend over a circuit of more than eight or ten miles at the most; and in that case they would have descended to the sea at a point only two or three miles below Petra. But Pompeius saw at once that his cue was to compel Cæsar to extend his lines, and so to weaken his force at every point.* He himself had the advantage of a concentrated position, and could strike rapidly and in force at any point in Cæsar's lines; and thus, by at least one vigorous attack on his enemy's extreme left, while the work was still going on, he contrived to push back that wing and thereby to extend, by some two or three miles, the whole circuit of circumvallation, and seriously to delay its completion on this side. He also succeeded in constructing a series of defences, within Cæsar's lines, with the object of keeping his enemy at a distance, and of securing the ground he had gained on his right.

It would be tedious here to detail the operations of this blockade. It answered its purpose for some time; a vigorous attempt to break out at Dyrrhachium, backed by simultaneous attacks on other parts of the lines, was foiled with heavy loss. At last Pompeius began to feel severely the want of fodder and water for his numerous cavalry. The horses were dying in numbers, though ships were continually arriving with supplies for the men. Cæsar's army on the other hand was in excellent

* See B. C., iii., 44, 2; 45, 1.

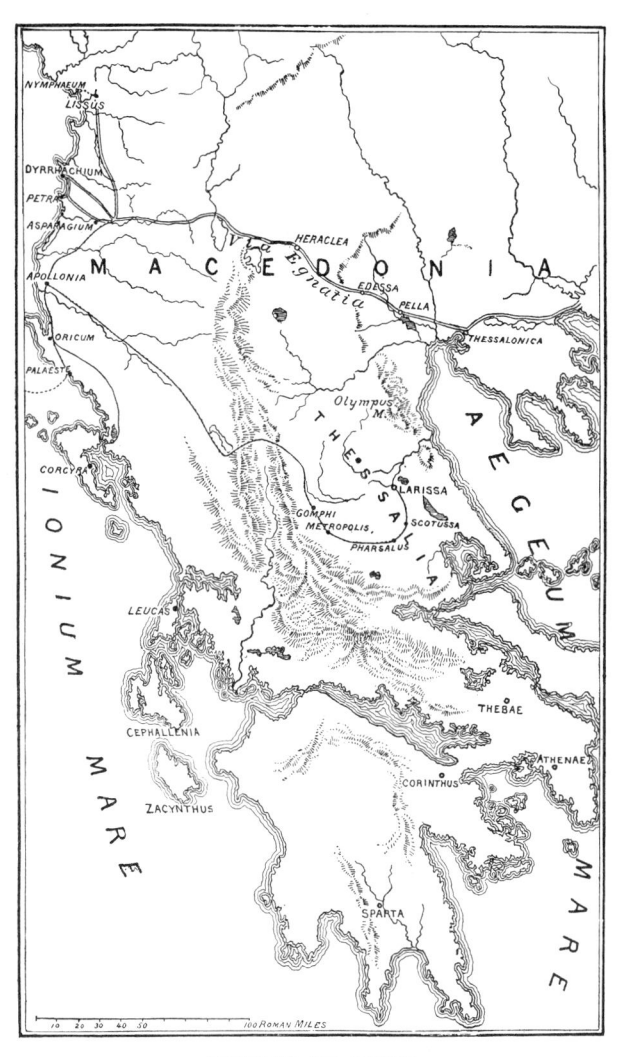

MACEDONIA AND GREECE.

48 B.C.] *Dyrrhachium and Pharsalus.* 291

health, and well supplied with water; their corn supply had been exhausted, but they had discovered a root growing on the hills, which when pounded with milk made a very palatable bread. They even declared that they would sooner eat the bark of trees than let Pompeius slip out of their grasp.

It was probably the mortality among his horses which caused Pompeius to make a last desperate attempt to break out of the net which enclosed him. His cavalry was his most useful arm, and that which, as we saw just now, Cæsar feared most. An unexpected opportunity soon occurred. Two Gauls in Cæsar's army, who had served him well and had been amply rewarded, were detected in malpractices; and though not punished by him, they thought their credit was gone, went over to Pompeius, and gave him complete information about the disposition of Cæsar's army, and the weak points in his lines. The result of this was that Pompeius determined to attack these at their southernmost point, where they came down to the sea on Cæsar's extreme left. This point was the farthest from Pompeius' camp, and he seems to have neglected it so far; Cæsar's attention, too, had been engaged elsewhere, and the works here were not as yet completed. The ditch and rampart had indeed been finished, and carried down to the shore; and another line of the same kind, facing southwards, and intended by Cæsar, as at Alesia, to check a possible attack on his rear, had also been constructed at this point.* These two

---

* This was part of a projected outer line of circumvallation, to be carried round the whole of the position.

lines were two hundred yards apart ; and as it was possible that the enemy might throw troops from the sea into the space between them, and so double up Cæsar's left wing, another cross line had been projected, to connect the two parallel ones, and so check any such attack. But this short transverse line had not been constructed ; and this was the most valuable piece of information which the two Gallic deserters brought to Pompeius.

He took advantage of it with skill. A large force of light-armed was conveyed by night in boats to the rear of Cæsar's lines, while the main body of legionaries was concentrated in front of them. All were provided with material for filling up the ditches, and also with a new form of protection for the head, consisting of osier screens fixed on the helmets. At daybreak they surprised the weak outpost of the ninth legion on duty in the lines near the sea; this was attacked first in front and rear, and then assailed in flank also by a force which landed between the two ramparts. The commander of the legion, which was in its camp not far off, came quickly to the rescue, but his troops were carried away in confusion by the flight of the outposts; and it was not till Antonius was seen descending with some thousands of men from the heights above, that the flight and pursuit were checked. When Cæsar himself arrived, summoned by the smoke of signal fires, he saw at once that the disaster to his lines was irreparable. His enemy had forced him to extend his lines, and the ground he had attempted to cover was too great for the working strength of his army. His intense dislike of renouncing any project to which he had set his hand, had led him for once into serious error. All his work was thrown away; the lines were abandoned; and a camp was constructed that same morning for the whole army near the new position of Pompeius.

In the afternoon of the same eventful day, Cæsar made an attempt to revive the spirits of his men, and to inflict loss on the enemy, by attacking a Pompeian legion which had been seen marching to occupy a deserted camp some little distance to the north of both armies. This camp had been made by Cæsar's ninth legion, and then abandoned; it was next occupied by Pompeius, who had connected it by a ditch and rampart with a stream still farther to the north, in order to secure a water-supply for its garrison. He, however, in his turn, had for some reason abandoned it; but now, as it seems to have been situated on Cæsar's right flank, he probably thought it worth re-occupying. His legion took possession of it; but Cæsar now attacked in full force, and with his left wing, which he led in person, broke down the gate and drove the defenders to the rear of the camp, where they endeavoured to rally. Meanwhile the right wing, misled by the entrenchment leading to the stream, which they strangely took for part of the camp, had followed this in search of a gate, and became separated from their comrades on the left. Finding their mistake, they made a breach in the entrenchment, and poured through, both infantry and cavalry, only to find a powerful body of the enemy pressing upon them, which Pompeius had sent to the rescue. A panic seized them, for the rampart and ditch in their rear now cut off their retreat; and the whole wing was put to rout as they tried to scale this obstacle, losing more men by the fall into the ditch than by the sword of the enemy. Panic too now seized the victorious left wing, who seeing from the camp the disaster on the right, thought they would be taken in the rear and cut off; and in a moment, by one of those strange turns of fortune which, as Cæsar here observes, decide great events, the whole army was in confusion and flight. As in the battle with the Nervii, he himself essayed to arrest the panic-stricken crowd. He seized a standard, and laid hands on its bearer, who in his wild terror (so Plutarch tells the story), actually raised his sword to strike his general, and would have killed him, had not Cæsar's shield-bearer cut off the man's arm at the shoulder.*

Cæsar does not in the least disguise the gravity of this defeat. He tells us that the whole army would have been destroyed, if the same wall which proved so fatal to his right wing, had not also served to check the enemy's pursuit. In any case, Pompeius should have followed up his victory at once; Cæsar could only account for his sluggishness by supposing that he feared an ambuscade. It was on this occasion that Cæsar is reported to have said that the enemy would have finished the campaign then and there, if they had only had a general who knew how

* Cæsar himself says that he laid hands on the standard-bearer, but omits the rest of the story. B. C., iii., 69.

48 B.C.] *Dyrrhachium and Pharsalus.* 295

to conquer.* He lost this day, by his own confession, 960 rank and file, 5 military tribunes, 32 centurions, and 32 standards. Pompeius was saluted as *Imperator* by his army, according to the old custom after a victory; but sullied his fame, if we may accept Cæsar's account, by allowing the renegade Labienus to butcher all the prisoners in cold blood, after taunting them with cowardice unworthy of Gallic veterans.

Like Wellington at Burgos in 1812, Cæsar had failed in his designs from want of a sufficient force; like Wellington, too, he could no longer venture on a battle, even if the chance were offered him. In each case the only safe course was to retreat, and in each case the retreat was conducted with admirable skill. Wellington muffled the wheels of his guncarriages, and so escaping notice for a while, got the start of his foes: Cæsar, after a short address of encouragement, sent on his wounded and baggage at night-fall under an escort, then despatched his main body, and started himself at dawn with a rearguard of two legions. Before noon he had reached his old camp from which some weeks before he had slipped away so adroitly to swoop upon Dyrrhachium; and here, on the bank of a river, he was overtaken by the Pompeian cavalry. It was beaten off, but it was necessary for Cæsar to hasten onwards; and seeing the enemy were straggling after fodder, or taking their ease in their own old camp, he started once more that afternoon, and was never again caught up. On the fourth day Pompeius gave up

* Appian, B. C., ii., 62.

the pursuit, and had to turn his attention to devising a fresh plan of campaign.

Cæsar's base of operations, so far as he had any at all, was Apollonia; and making for that town, he paid his men, deposited his wounded, and made his plans for continuing the struggle. When Antonius had joined him some weeks before, he had taken advantage of his increased numbers to despatch two legions under Domitius Calvinus along the great road * into Macedonia to check the advance of the re-inforcements which Pompeius was expecting in that direction. Domitius performed his duty well, and Scipio, Pompeius' father-in-law, had failed to get past him with the troops he was bringing. It was now Cæsar's object to re-unite with Domitius, and, by threatening to crush Scipio, to draw Pompeius away from the sea, and so to deprive him of the advantages he had so far enjoyed from the mastery of it. And if Pompeius should venture on an invasion of Italy—a course strongly urged on him by some of his many advisers,—he would have to sacrifice Scipio, and leave his enemy in entire possession of Greece and Macedonia. The lucidity of Cæsar's mind is nowhere better seen than in the short chapter in which he has explained the situation as he understood it; and probably no general ever put so much sound reasoning into words so few and so clear.†

He had hardly sent word to Domitius to join him when he found that Pompeius had himself turned

---

* This was open to him, as we saw, after his descent on Dyrrhachium, as was also the branch of it which led to Apollonia.

† B. C., iii., 78.

eastwards along the great road with a view to a junction with Scipio. Domitius was, therefore, likely to be caught between two armies; and in fact he had a very narrow escape. Some talkative Gauls in Pompeius' army, friends of the two who had betrayed Cæsar before Dyrrhachium, now did Cæsar a good turn, and in chatting with some of Domitius' foragers let them know of the danger. He escaped just in time, crossed the mountains which separate Macedonia from Thessaly, and joined Cæsar, who had meanwhile marched from Apollonia in a south-easterly direction, at Æginium in the north-western corner of the great Thessalian plain. The united armies passed southwards to Gomphi, a town of some size, and stormed it on the afternoon of their arrival. Cæsar let his soldiers plunder it as they pleased and enjoy at last abundant wine and food. Like Wellington's men in the retreat from Burgos, they are said to have here got drunk and behaved ill, as might be expected after long privation and hard work. Another town wisely opened its gates in time, and was spared the same fate; and then the army marched at leisure across the great plain, enjoying comparative plenty, and so recovering the tone and spirit which famished soldiers inevitably lose, to the neighbourhood of the city of Pharsalus, where several great roads converged.

Pompeius, too, having effected his junction with Scipio, gave up all other plans, and descended into the Thessalian plain as far as Larissa in its centre. Even now, it is said, he was still unwilling to fight a battle. He wished to wear out his subtle enemy by constant manœuvring, and to use his strong cavalry to cut off Cæsar's supplies. And there is little doubt that this was the judgment of a wise and cautious general who knew the weak points of his army. But Pompeius was no more his own master now than in the days when he had tried to govern at Rome. The same foolish clamours, the same petty competition and quarrelling, which his rival had escaped for ten years in Gaul, distracted him now, and at last induced him to fight, against his own better judgment. He marched from Larissa, and encamped on the slope of a hill facing Cæsar's position near Pharsalus. For this last of the long succession of follies, which sealed the fate of the Republic, the senators who were in his camp at the time must be held chiefly responsible.

One may well pause to take breath, like Cæsar's soldiers in the action, before entering on the description of a battle fraught with such issues as that of Pharsalus. It is not indeed so much in the numbers of the combatants, or in the intensity of the struggle, that its gravity is felt; the armed men present on the field did not much exceed half the number that fought at Waterloo, and the decisive fighting could not have lasted much more than an hour. Here, too, is lacking the interest which attaches to a battle of which the scene is known and can be visited; for the exact position of the battle-field has never as yet been placed beyond all doubt.* The interest lies rather in this, that the condition

---

* Colonel Stoffel believed he had discovered it; but in this instance he failed (as I think) to reconcile his view with Cæsar's own language.

of the Roman world and the struggle going on in it, are mirrored on this field with such astonishing fidelity. All the world's decisive battles have this interest in some degree, and the historian who neglects them loses some of his best opportunities; but in none, perhaps, have the contending forces in a world-wide revolution been so exactly focussed in two armies on a single battle-field. On one side the disunion, selfishness, and pride of the last survivors of an ancient oligarchy, speculating before the event on the wealth or office that victory was to bring them; on the other the absolute command of a single man, whose clear mental vision was entirely occupied with the facts and issues that lay before him that day. The one host was composed in great part of a motley crowd from Greece and the East, representing that spurious Hellenic civilisation that for a century had sapped the vigour of Roman life; the other was chiefly drawn from the Gallic populations of Italy and the West, fresh, vigorous, intelligent, and united in devotion and loyalty to a leader whom not even defeat could dishearten. With Pompeius was the spirit of the past, and his failure did but answer to the failure of a decaying world; with Cæsar was the spirit of the future, and his victory marks the moment when humanity could once more start hopefully upon a new line of progress.

For some days the armies remained in position; Pompeius would not advance into the plain, but drew up his army each day at the foot of the hill on which his camp was placed. Here he could not be safely attacked; and Cæsar determined to try the plan of drawing him away from his hill by a series of rapid marches. On the morning of the 9th of August the signal for marching had been given, and the camp struck, when Cæsar saw that the enemy's line of battle had been drawn out a little farther from the hill than usual; just enough to deprive Pompeius of the natural advantage of the ground. But his position was still a formidable one. His right rested securely on a stream with precipitous banks; his left extended far into the plain, and was flanked by his cavalry, 7,000 in number, and by a host of light-armed men and archers. With this left wing he meant to outflank Cæsar's right, and then to attack him in the rear; and as it appeared afterwards, he had expressed himself as absolutely confident of the result.* He had about 50,000 men on the field, exclusive of light troops.

At sight of this magnificent army Cæsar spoke to his staff, just as his own men were issuing from their camp in marching order. " We must stop the march and attack. This is what we have been looking for so long; we shall not easily find a better opportunity." He reconnoitred the enemy's formation more closely, and arranged his own to counteract it. He saw at once that his right wing was to be turned, and there of course he placed his small force of 1,000 cavalry, and the famous tenth legion, which had served him so long and so well. The rest of the army he placed in three lines, and these

---

*Cæs., B. C., iii., 86.

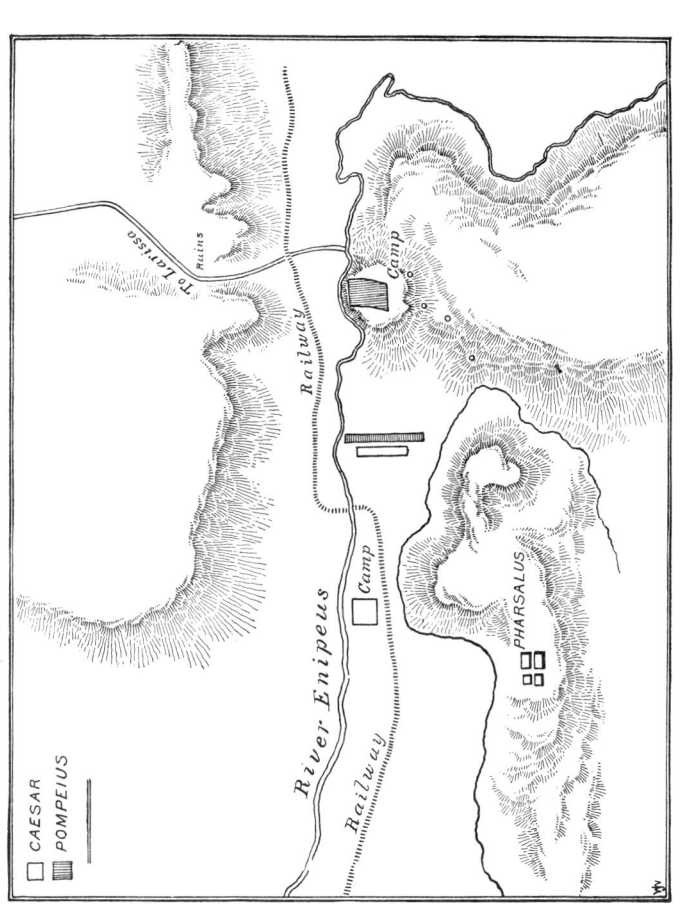

ROUGH MAP OF THE ENVIRONS OF PHARSALUS.

AFTER STOFFEL, WITH CAMPS AND ARMIES PLACED ACCORDING TO COL. STOFFEL'S CONJECTURE.

were divided into a left wing, a centre, and a right wing, commanded respectively by Antonius, Domitius, and P. Sulla, a nephew of Sulla the Dictator, who had distinguished himself at Dyrrhachium by his self-restraint, as well as his skill.* At the last moment, as it seems, he made another disposition to strengthen the threatened right wing, which, as he himself states with unusual emphasis, decided the fortune of the day. From his third line, or reserve, he drew a detachment of several cohorts, or, as we may call them, battalions, and placed them in the right rear with special orders, and a warning that victory would depend on their valour. His whole force cannot be computed at more than 30,000 strong, including light-armed troops.

When all was ready, he made the usual address, reminding the troops, as he tells us, of all his hopeless efforts to procure peace, and calling them to witness that he was forced to fight. Then he took station on the right wing and ordered the trumpet to sound for the attack. The first two lines levelled their javelins and advanced at a run; the Pompeians, in obedience to their general's order, awaited them motionless. In giving this order, says Cæsar in a couple of striking sentences, Pompeius judged wrongly; he thought the attacking line would get into disorder, but he forgot that human nature is excitable, and that in a battle such excitement must be rather encouraged than repressed. Cæsar's men, finding that the enemy did not stir, halted of their own accord at a short distance from them

---
* B. C., iii., 51.

to take breath, then moved forward again, discharged their javelins, drew swords, and charged home. The charge was bravely met, and a hard struggle ensued.

Meanwhile the whole Pompeian cavalry, covered by clouds of archers, had attacked Cæsar's right wing. His own horsemen could not resist such a force, and gradually fell back. But Cæsar was on the watch for this; he did not here commit the blunder of which he seems to have been guilty in his late defeat, of leading the attack in person and so losing touch with one half of his army. He gave the signal to the battalions he had placed in reserve. Wheeling to the right, so as to face the horsemen now descending on the right flank and rear, they ran forward at the charge, not discharging their javelins but using them as spears, and driving them against man and horse. Such tactics might seem desperate, but they answered Cæsar's expectations. The cavalry was taken aback by a method of fighting so novel; they were checked, gave way, and fled at full speed to the hills.

All this time the struggle in the front had gone on without result, but now that the enemy's cavalry was beaten Cæsar could use his third line, which had remained in position to protect the rear. It was now sent forward to support the two front lines, and this decided the battle. The whole Pompeian army fled to their camp; Pompeius gave orders to secure the gates and man the ramparts, and then retired to his tent. Cæsar, thinking that a broken army might be dislodged even from a fortified camp, appealed to his men to finish their work, though it was now mid-day and the heat was intense. The camp was stormed. Pompeius galloped out by the gate at the rear and fled towards Larissa; the troops escaped as best they could and, following the example of the cavalry, made for the summits of the neighbouring hills. They were followed the same afternoon by Cæsar, whose power of discipline could draw his men away from plundering the luxurious tents of the Pompeian officers, even after so many months of privation and discomfort. At night-fall he caught them in a position from which their water-supply could be cut off, and at the sight of his unwearied soldiers bracing themselves to this last effort with the spade, they sent to capitulate. Next morning at daybreak they descended at his orders to the plain and laid down their arms. According to his own account, he had mercy upon all, spoke a few reassuring words, and commended them to the care of his soldiers. The same day he started in pursuit of Pompeius, who had gone to Larissa with a few horsemen.

In this battle Pompeius lost some 15,000 men killed or wounded and 24,000 prisoners; a hundred and eighty standards were taken and the eagles of eight legions, besides a quantity of plate found in the camp, and much other spoil.* Cæsar, who is

---

* Including the papers of Pompeius, which Cæsar is said to have burnt without reading them. (Dio Cass., 41, 62, 63 ; who, however, says, on what authority we know not, that Cæsar put to death those of the senators and equites among his prisoners whom he had once before taken and released, as at Corfinium.)

usually truthful in such matters, even when they reflect no credit on him, puts his own loss at only two hundred, including, however, thirty centurions. Among these was one Crastinus, an old soldier of the tenth legion, who, when the trumpet sounded on the eve of the battle, had called out to his general that, whether alive or dead, he would that day deserve his thanks. He made good his word, and, if Appian's tale is true, his grateful commander had his body searched for, decorated with military honours, and buried apart from the rest.

Pompeius did not wait at Larissa. He hurried through the vale of Tempe to the coast, found a ship, and crossed the Ægean to Mytilene, where his wife Cornelia heard from his own lips the first tidings of the battle. He did not land, but took her and his younger son on board and sailed along the coast to Cilicia and then to Cyprus, in great doubt as to where to turn for help. If he had still had any vigour or decision he would have gone westwards to join the fleet from which he had so unwisely allowed himself to be dissociated; he might have carried on the struggle for years at sea, with the rich province of Africa, which was still his, as a base of operations. But of Africa he knew little or nothing, while in Syria and the East his name was known to everyone. He fell back on the scenes of his old triumphs, but found that the Oriental never worships the setting sun. At Cyprus they would not admit him, and he was told that it would be the same in Syria. There was still Egypt, which was not indeed a Roman province, but was under Roman influence,* and had in Alexandria the best and richest port in the Mediterranean. It was at this time torn by a civil war, and a boy-king, Ptolemy, had lately succeeded in expelling his sister Cleopatra, who, under their father's will, was to share the throne with himself. The boy and girl were now each with an army near the Pelusiac mouth of the Nile.

To Pelusium Pompeius sailed, and sent to the young king to ask for protection on the ground of friendship with his late father. He was invited to come ashore, embraced his wife, and embarked in a small boat which had been sent for him. As he reached the shore he was brutally murdered, unresisting, by Achillas, an officer of the King, and Septimius, an old officer of his own, now on service in Egypt. No one knew what prompted this villainous act of treachery; whether it was a desire to propitiate Cæsar, or a national feeling that Pompeius would be a dangerous guest, and might make himself master of the country.

The pathos of the story of his last days is heightened by many details in the narratives of Plutarch and others, which must be omitted here. The reader will rather wish to know what manner of man this was, who was for a quarter of a century the greatest figure in the Roman world, and who has come before us so constantly in our narrative, first as Cæsar's friend and son-in-law, then as his rival and enemy. But the fact is that of Pompeius' real

---

* There was a considerable Roman force now in Egypt, left by Gabinius after his invasion in 56 B.C., and Gabinius was an old adherent of Pompeius.

character as a man we know hardly anything. Cicero, whose letters at least might have revealed him to us, seems never to have known the man intimately, as he knew Cæsar, and the result we get from him is an uncertain and negative one. Probably Pompeius was cold and reserved, except with a very few intimates, and disliked the impulsive, pushing cleverness of his would-be friend. But if we may accept the general tradition of antiquity, he was a just and honourable man in private life, clean-handed in a corrupt age, and unwilling by nature to be cruel or treacherous. He did not shine in the fashionable or literary society of Rome, for he had no special gift of speaking or writing; he had been educated as a soldier only, and it was perhaps a consciousness of his own defects and ignorance that made him so inaccessible and reserved.

We can measure his stature better as a soldier and statesman. In the conduct of war he was prudent by nature, and experience had made him almost over-cautious. As has been already said, if he had ample time and means at his disposal, he could work out a great result; and in this way he made his three great contributions to the welfare of the Empire—the destruction of the pirates, the final overthrow of Mithridates, and the settlement of the eastern frontier on what was practically the line of the Euphrates. But the great work he did does not prove him a great man. He was wanting, so far as we can tell, not only in rapidity and resource in the field, but in that power of inspiring men with confidence in his own genius and destiny which carried

Cæsar safely through so many perils. Loyalty to the person of a great leader has a magical power in times of tumult and revolution; and loyalty could never be paid to Pompeius as it was to Cæsar. The adherents of the one were always trying to get the better of him; the friends of the other obeyed him with enthusiasm. And this was so in politics as well as in war. Men looked for leadership to Pompeius, and found him uncertain whither to lead; they looked to Cæsar, and found themselves at once in the grip of a mighty will. A man without knowledge of men, and without understanding in politics, cannot govern events when great questions have to be decided; and though we may feel tenderly towards one whose downfall was so sudden and so sad, we must allow that all his history shows him incapable of doing the work that the world was then ever more and more earnestly demanding. He came indeed within a touch of being the founder of a new monarchy, and for the three years preceding the outbreak of civil war he held a position in many points closely resembling that of the early emperors. He played a great part, and his successful rival duly honoured his memory. Yet in Pompeius there was not the material out of which great rulers are made. The recognition of the real nature of the Roman Empire, and the invention of a method of government which might solve its many problems, were not within the scope of a mind that moved with an impetus so feeble.

CHAPTER XVII.

CÆSAR'S LAST WARS.

48–45 B.C.

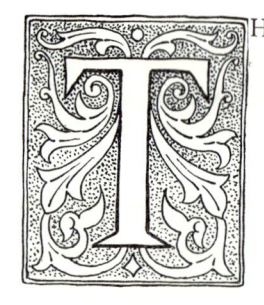

THE task to which Pompeius was unequal was, we said in the last words of the last chapter, the recognition of the true nature of the Roman Empire, and the invention of a method of government which might solve its many problems. Cæsar, as we have seen all along, understood better than any living man what this Empire was, and in what direction it was to be developed; but had he also any clear idea of a system of government which might be suited to its needs, seeing that the senatorial method was utterly worn out and discredited?

The answer to this question must be postponed to the next chapter. In the present one we must give a very brief sketch of the work that had to be done before questions of method could be grappled with.

Only let it be said at once that the work of Cæsar's life was not organisation, but the necessary preparation for it. He prepared the field, and he indicated in some degree how it should be planted, but it was left for a very different and a subtler character both to plant it and to see the crop grow. What then was this task of preparation, which was the real work of his indefatigable energy? It had been going on ever since he was consul, and appeared as the really active partner in the triumvirate; a slow but sure process, lasting through the Gallic War, through the conquest of Italy and Spain, through the campaign that ended at Pharsalus, and finding its completion in the wars now about to be summarised. It was simply the enforcement of the lesson, which the Roman world refused to learn except under compulsion of arms, that a man has arisen more deserving of loyalty than all the gathered wisdom of an old city aristocracy. Trust, loyalty, obedience, qualities which had long vanished from the Roman mind, must be created anew, even if it had to be done by the stern lessons of war, as well as by the gentler teaching of humanity and mercy. Towards this end Cæsar untiringly worked in province after province, until the whole world recognised that he was as irresistible as he was gracious, and believed in him because they could not crush him, and because they had no just cause to hate him. Though, like David, he himself for good reason could not carry out the great building that was called for, he laid great store of material for it, in teaching the world this lesson, without which all the subtle skill of his successor would assuredly have gone for nothing.

We are justified in limiting our account of Cæsar's last wars to a mere outline, not only by the compass of this volume, but because we here finally part company with Cæsar himself as an author. The three memoirs which tell of his work in Egypt, Africa, and Spain,* were written probably by eye-witnesses and officers of his army, and are no doubt fairly accurate in matters of military detail. But of military detail the reader will already have had enough, and will prefer that it should be omitted, where Cæsar is no longer telling the story himself.

The victor followed the vanquished with all speed to Egypt, only to be apprised of Pompeius' death by the ghastly spectacle of his head, brought to him by a Greek rhetorician on behalf of the assassins. He had with him a very small force, little more than three thousand legionaries; with these he landed at Alexandria, sent orders for other forces to come with speed, and began to busy himself in Egyptian affairs. It was clearly not his original intention to stay long, but northerly winds detained him until he got entangled in the meshes of Alexandrian intrigue; in other meshes too, if the stories about Cleopatra are true. He landed early in October, 48 B.C., and

---

* The " De Bello Alexandrino," is now believed by some critics to be the work of the accomplished Asinius Pollio. The authorship of the other two works is quite uncertain; that on the last Spanish war is by a very rude hand. None of the three, though modelled on Cæsar's method, can compare with his own "Commentaries" in respect of style and workmanship.

did not get out of the toils until the June following. The delay was a calamity for himself and the Empire. The secret history of these months can never be written; Asinius Pollio, or whoever wrote the book about this war, has told us nothing of it. Some writers, like Mr. Froude, have denied that there was a secret history at all, and believe that the relations of Cæsar and the bewitching Egyptian princess were merely the inventions of a later age, like so many foolish tales which we justly reject. But the delay after his arrival, and the later delay of three months after the final settlement of Egypt, taken together with the known beauty and ability of Cleopatra and the birth of a son named Cæsarion, make the inference almost irresistible. The air, the antiquity, the river of Egypt have some strange power of fascinating strangers, and when to these are added the charms of such a woman as Cæsar had not met for more than ten years, if ever in his life, we can understand the temptation and believe in the lost romance. Stories were afloat in later times that the pair projected or even carried out an expedition far up the Nile; and the myth that the conqueror of Pharsalus thought of renouncing his life's work to discover the sources of the river, may perhaps contain, like most myths, a certain grain of truth. Cæsar could not be in Egypt without discussing that ancient problem; and he could not speculate on such a matter without wishing to act.

The external history of this long sojourn we do know; it must be condensed here into a few sentences. No sooner was Cæsar in Alexandria, than he began, as Roman consul in a semi-dependent state, to regulate the succession to the throne on the basis of the last king's will. But he did not know the Alexandrians, that motley *congeries* of all the clever waifs and strays of the Mediterranean. Their pride was hurt; which perhaps would not have been the case had not Cæsar's small force been so tempting an object to molest. The young Ptolemy's army and fleet might between them destroy this man as well as Pompeius; they were under the command of a certain Achillas, the Arabi of that day, who by playing upon such national feeling as existed, roused the populace as well, and besieged Cæsar in the eastern quarter of the town, where was the palace of the Ptolemies. He had to struggle hard for very existence, for reinforcements did not arrive, water was scarce, and the enemy gradually closed him in.

So the winter passed, while Cæsar was once more clinging desperately to a hostile coast, and struggling with an enemy's fleet. The situation was not unlike that of 1882 after the bombardment and occupation of Alexandria by the English. The presence of a handful of foreign troops amid a sullen and angry population, the helplessness of the ruler of the country in their hands, the impossibility of forcing an exit out of the city, the determined character of the Egyptian military chief, and even the great conflagration, which in this case did the world irreparable damage by destroying the great library of the Ptolemies, or at least a large portion of it, all remind us of the most recent invasion of the land which has so often proved a snare to the invader.

And when at last the longed-for diversion came, it came in the same direction as in 1882, by way of the eastern Delta and Cairo.

Mithridates of Pergamum, a reputed son of the great Mithridates, had been entrusted by Cæsar with the task of bringing reinforcements by land; for access by sea was hazardous, and one legion only had been able to get into Alexandria during the winter. Why this man was chosen does not appear, but he did his work so well as fully to justify Cæsar's choice. He marched through Cilicia and Syria, collecting troops, among whom were said to be 3,000 Jews, on his way, and breaking into Egypt near what is now Port Said, stormed the town of Pelusium. Then, marching up the eastern branch of the Nile to avoid the entanglements of the Delta, he crossed the river at Memphis (Cairo). The young King, who had been released by Cæsar, and was now at the head of his own troops, tried in vain to stop him; while Cæsar, who had been apprised of his approach, joined him by shipping his force to a point west of the Delta and marching up the right bank of the western branch. The united armies entirely defeated the King, who was drowned in the Nile after the battle. No further resistance was offered, and Cæsar became master of Egypt at the end of March, 47 B.C.

Cleopatra and a younger brother were set together on the throne, and Cæsar left all his army but one legion in Egypt to secure this arrangement; for, as his historian puts it, in language singularly like that of an English cabinet minister, "he thought that the interests of the Empire demanded that if kings were set up they should be supported, and that if they rebelled, the means of coercion should be at hand." The policy is truly Roman, yet not unknown even in modern times; and, indeed, Egypt was and is quite the most dangerous corner in the Mediterranean. Whoever was master of Egypt could prevent anyone else from being master of the world. This is curiously illustrated by the fact that Cæsar left a man of no birth or prominence in command of his force there; an ambitious man might have caused him serious difficulty as well as anxiety. Cæsar's wisdom here was closely followed afterwards by Augustus.

He left Egypt in June, after the three month's delay already alluded to. There was urgent occasion for him to go at once to Italy, where Antonius, who had been left in charge, had become justly unpopular. In Spain, too, his representative Q. Cassius, had spoilt all his work by harshness and oppression, and in Africa his enemies were collecting large forces. But Cæsar's work in the East was as yet only half done, and he set about completing it with all his old rapidity. He passed through Syria, settling disputes, making friends with border kinglets and princes, visiting all the great towns, and stimulating everyone by his presence and his promises. Then, leaving a kinsman, Sextus Cæsar, as governor, he sailed to Tarsus, the capital of Cilicia, despatched all the business of that province and the neighbouring dependent states, and hurried over Mount Taurus into Cappadocia. There he received and pardoned Deiotarus, tetrarch of Galatia, who had fought against him at

Pharsalus, took with him a legion which this prince had trained in Roman fashion, and passed quickly into the province of Pontus, now in the hands of an enemy to everything Roman.

While Cæsar was in Egypt, Pharnaces, son of the great Mithridates, had taken advantage of the general confusion in the Empire to recover his father's kingdom of Pontus, which Pompeius had annexed to the Roman Empire. He had beaten Cæsar's officer, L. Domitius, in fair fight, and had become a standing danger to Roman influence in Asia Minor. He tried now to negotiate, and pretended to promise obedience, in the belief that Cæsar would have to hurry to Italy and leave him to his own devices. But Cæsar had learnt in Egypt the ways of eastern potentates, and was not to be taken in. He promptly ordered the King to evacuate Roman territory, and when he tried to play a diplomatic game, showed him at once with whom he had to deal. At Zela a battle was fought, in which Cæsar ran some risk, for he had hardly any of his veterans with him; but the result was only doubtful for a few minutes. Pharnaces fled from Pontus, and his army was entirely destroyed.* Cæsar passed on through Galatia and Bithynia to the province of Asia proper, settling affairs in every centre; and leaving the faithful Mithridates with the title of King of the Bosphorus, as a guarantee for the security of these

* This was the battle after which Cæsar is said to have written to a friend the three famous words "Veni, vidi, vici." The author of the "Bell. Alex." (77) says that he was extraordinarily delighted with the speedy issue of the campaign.

provinces, he sailed for Italy, and arrived at Tarentum before anyone was aware of his approach. If he had really wasted time or lost energy in Egypt, he was making up for it now.

On the way from Tarentum to Brundisium he met Cicero, who had been waiting for him here for nearly a year. He alighted, embraced his old friend, and walked with him some distance. The result of their talk was shown by Cicero's conduct for the rest of Cæsar's lifetime; he retired to his villas, and sought relief in literary work, encouraged doubtless by Cæsar's ardent praise. The magical effect of Cæsar's presence was felt throughout Italy; all sedition ceased, and Rome, which had been the scene of riot and bloodshed under the uncertain rule of Antonius, was quiet in an instant. The master spent three months in the city, working hard. He had been a second time appointed dictator while he was in Egypt, and probably without any limit of time, space, or power; and he acted now without scruple as an absolute monarch. Everything that had to be done he saw to himself. Money was raised, bills were passed, the Senate recruited, magistrates and provincial governors appointed. But there was no time for any attempt at permanent organisation; he must wrest Africa from his enemies before there could be any hope of a peaceful and enduring settlement. He quelled a most serious mutiny, in which even his faithful tenth legion was concerned, with all his wonderful skill and knowledge of human nature; sent on all available forces to Sicily, and arrived himself at Lilybæum in the middle of December.

He pitched his tent almost within reach of the waves, says the historian, to show the troops that he meant instant embarkation. On December 27th all was ready, and the fleet set sail with six legions and 2,000 cavalry. On the fourth day he sighted the coast of Africa, about the middle of that long stretch of coast that runs north and south from Carthage to the lesser Syrtis. But only a few ships were still with him; the others had been scattered in the transit, and when he landed at Hadrumetum he had only 3,000 infantry and 150 horsemen. For the third time since the war broke out he found himself clinging to a line of coast in the face of greatly superior forces; and these were now commanded, nominally indeed by Scipio, whose ability was small, but in reality by Labienus, the most dangerous of all his enemies. These men were desperate, for they were fighting not so much for the Republic as against Cæsar; compromise for the common good was all along abominable, and cruelty was justifiable, in their eyes.* Cato, who was at Utica in the north, was too honourable for cruel or unjust dealing; but even he was now enlisting the Mauritanian King, Juba, a fierce untrustworthy character, in the cause of what he believed to be liberty.

The first few days in this situation must have been most trying both to Cæsar and his soldiers. The author of the book on this war has given us a lifelike picture of the way in which he could overcome the anxiety of his men. One day he garrisoned the town of Ruspina with part of his little force, marched

---
* De Bell. Afr., 4, 28, 46, etc.; confirmed by Cicero.

the rest at night-fall to the port, two miles away, and there put them on board his ships, leaving the garrison in ignorance of what he was doing. The men with him were equally in the dark as to where they were going, and showed their depression too plainly; but the wonderful spirits of their general, his alacrity, his erect mien, his very look, revived them. " They settled down in peace, and trusted that by his great knowledge and judgment all things might be made easy for them." They were not deceived; next morning at dawn when he was about to weigh anchor, some vessels hove in sight with part of his missing force on board, and they found that it was to go in search of these that he had embarked. He feared that they might fall into the enemy's hands, and had taken troops with him; secrecy had been used, that the garrison in Ruspina might not know that it had been left to itself. Cæsar's character as a master of men nowhere stands out clearer than in this incident, told with enthusiasm by one who had experienced his extraordinary charm. The pity was, that there was no one living like him, and that such vast issues should hang upon a single life.

With increased forces he was able to take the field and to fight a battle near Ruspina with the enemy's innumerable cavalry and archers under Labienus. He was entirely surrounded, but by an adroit movement the exact nature of which is not clear, he quickly lengthened his line, cut the enemy's closely pressing squadrons in two, and sent them flying. But it was useless to go on with such warfare, which would soon have worn out his little force; he therefore fortified a position at Ruspina, and waited till the rest of his wandering vessels at last arrived. This was his fifth descent on a shore occupied by an enemy*; in each case his conduct was bold almost to rashness, and the peril was overcome only by his own unfailing spirits and resource.

When at length the greater part of his army was collected, he took the field and sought, as usual, for an opportunity of fighting a battle. Scipio was now in command of the enemy, and his force, together with that of the King, Juba, who had also arrived, was too formidable to be attacked except on a fair field. For more than two months Cæsar looked in vain for a favourable chance, and meanwhile he was constantly in difficulty for supplies; at one time the cavalry had even to feed their horses on seaweed. At last, in the first days of April, he determined to march southwards along the coast and invest the town of Thapsus; if he took it he would gain a good port and supplies, and might perhaps tempt Scipio to save it by a battle. The move succeeded; Scipio raced with him to Thapsus, but came too late, and Cæsar drew his lines round the town. Scipio at last, finding his enemy encamped between him and the town, determined to fight, and drew out his army for battle while his camp was being fortified in his rear. Cæsar instantly accepted the challenge. His troops were quickly arranged, as at Pharsalus, both for attack and defence. Suddenly it was seen that there was a panic or commotion of some kind among the workers at the enemy's camp. The staff

---

* Including the two invasions of Britain.

officers and some old soldiers implored Cæsar to attack at once, but he refused. On this day he hesitated, and as Plutarch tells a story that he was seized with illness and was not present himself in the fight, it is just possible that, like Napoleon at Borodino, he may have been robbed of his usual vigour at a critical moment.* But the soldiers could not and would not be held in; a trumpeter sounded the advance, the whole army rushed on the enemy, and the battle was soon over. The elephants gave some little trouble, but as usual when once put to flight, only added to the confusion. The butchery was terrible, for the soldiers had the bit between their teeth, and slaughtered even those who surrendered, under Cæsar's very eyes. They were taking their revenge for the restraint that had been so long placed on them, a restraint which had probably been one cause of their recent mutiny. Cæsar's humanity had tried their patience too hard, and he now had to learn that there was a limit to his power over them. From this time to the end of his life there must have been vexation in his heart; disappointment, like that of Cromwell, because he could not inspire others with his own ideal of just conduct; misgiving, perhaps, as well, because the greater his triumphs the more isolated he became.

Still more painful was the last and best remembered event of this grievous war. Cato had been for years the most determined enemy of Cæsar and all his

---

* The author of the "De Bello Afr.," (ch. 83) on the other hand, describes Cæsar as yielding to the men, giving the signal "Goodluck," and galloping to the front.

DEFENCES OF A CAMP.

a. VALLUM PED XII.   b. LORICULA.   c. FOSSA DUPLEX.   d. TURRES.   e. PONTES.   f. PORTA.

works, perhaps from personal reasons as well as political; yet in that age he was like Cæsar alone in this, that he had clear political convictions, and acted on them not only with consistency, but with justice and humanity. He was the only republican leader, we are told, who did not disgrace the cause in Africa by wanton cruelty. When the fugitives arrived at Utica from Thapsus in wild panic, he tried to stay their cruelty to the citizens, but in vain; and then, seeing that no resistance could be organized, he made arrangements for the embarkation of all who were ready to go, and, disdaining to fly himself, committed suicide. The story is familiar from Plutarch's narrative, and need not be told here, nor need we comment on the character of a man who had little real influence on affairs, no gifts as a leader of men, no power of seeing how good may be extracted even from apparent evil. All his fine qualities, which might have been invaluable in that age of universal corruption, were simply thrown away for want of a grain of vulgar common sense, and his death only serves to illustrate that utter want of any idea of compromise which marks the Roman revolution throughout its course. Cato had made up his mind that Cæsar was the deadly enemy of the state; but he confused the state with the constitution, and died rather than put his conviction to the test. The whole action of the Pompeian party from the outbreak of civil war is as wrong-headed, even from their own point of view, as that of the ultrarepublican fanatics under Cromwell. They forced on a military despotism, which was probably as distasteful to the despot as to themselves; they diminished by one half the available intellect of the state, because they could not endure that it should be at the service of the one man who was capable of directing it.

Cæsar left Africa in June, 46 B.C., after settling the affairs of that province, and organising a new one to the west of it, to be called New Africa, of which Sallust the historian was the first governor. He took large sums of money with him, gained by the sale of the property of King Juba and others, and by confiscations and requisitions in towns which had obstinately held out against him. He was already beginning to feel the heavy trammels of power and victory. The legions which had won the world for him must be paid all they had been promised, and the citizens of Rome, after their kind, must be made to feel his greatness. The gorgeous triumphal procession with which he entered the city, passing along that Sacred Way of which the pavement has but recently been unearthed, was long remembered, and many stories were told of it, some true, perhaps, some undoubtedly false. One fact is certain, that it was celebrated not over Roman citizens, but over Gauls and Egyptians, over Pharnaces and Juba. No captive Roman attended the car of the conqueror; but the magnificence, the lavish expenditure, the adulation, which now began to make a king and even a demi-god of Cæsar, all showed that the Romans of the city were only fit to be captives, and that their master knew how to treat them.

After the triumph, with his power confirmed by a new dictatorship and the title of Præfectus Morum, or "superintendent of manners," and with other honours, which will be mentioned in their proper place, he remained in Rome for several months, in which more permanently valuable work was done than was ever achieved in the same space of time, unless it were by Cromwell in 1653-4. Had not the headstrong pertinacity of those deadly foes alike to Cæsar and to reason, who had fled from Africa after their crushing defeat, refused to abide by the decrees of fate, and to allow a great conqueror the chance of being also a great healer, how much more might not have been done? The imperious legions, getting now ever more reckless and dangerous, might have been entirely disbanded; a Senate, no longer ruled by a narrow oligarchy, might have been gradually set to work; all that huge task of re-organisation, which had eventually to be postponed for twenty years, might at least have been got beyond a beginning. But while Cæsar was hard at work at Rome, Labienus and others were raising Spain against him. Again they made it impossible for him to use his great talents in the best way. He had no one else to whom he could entrust a fresh war, and at the end of the year he was forced to take up arms himself once more.

No war was ever more unreasonable, or more cruelly waged, than this fresh outbreak by the Pompeian party; it was a war of darkness against light. But unfortunately there was inflammable matter in Spain for which Cæsar was himself chiefly responsible. When he quitted Spain in 49 B.C. he left as governor of the further province a certain Cassius

Longinus, who was apparently the worst man he could have chosen. Cassius soon entirely ruined all Cæsar's work by misgovernment and extortion. An attempt was made to assassinate him; Corduba revolted, under one of Cassius' own quæstors, and it was only by the help of Lepidus, who was in command in Hither Spain, that quiet was restored and Cassius expelled. Cæsar appointed Trebonius, one of his tried officers, to succeed him; but this was not till after the conclusion of the Alexandrian war, and it was then too late. The mischief was done, and was irreparable. The Pompeian party had always been strong in Spain, though good government might have kept them quiet; and when the eldest son of Pompeius appeared on the scene, the fuel instantly caught fire. They could not have had a worse leader; we know from so good a witness as Cicero that he was wanting both in sense and humanity.*

This last of Cæsar's wars may be dismissed in a very few words. The events of it are both obscure and, so far as we can see, uninteresting; the temper shown on both sides was angry and cruel. The scene was the valley of the Guadalquiver about Cordova; and it seems to have consisted, like the latter part of the African war, in a long series of endeavours on Cæsar's part to get his enemy to fight a pitched battle. At last the chance came, on the 17th of March, 45 B.C.† The battle, which bears the name

---

* For his character, see Cic., Ad Fam., xv., 19.

† The calendar had by this time been reformed; this is, therefore, the true date.

of the town of Munda, was desperately contested. The Pompeians had the advantage of numbers as well as position; it is said that Cæsar himself had to lead his wavering legions a second time to the attack, and the words were put into his mouth by the story-mongers, that he had often before fought for victory, but never until now for life. The slaughter was frightful; Labienus was among the killed, and young Pompeius fled wounded only to be hunted down and murdered. With such terrible scenes Cæsar's military life came to an end. Each of these struggles, while increasing his absolutism, made it more and more impossible for him to do the work of peace.

" For what can war but endless war still breed?"

The nobler task that was awaiting his hand, still little more than begun, was not by him to be completed. He arrived at Rome early in September, after settling the affairs of Spain; and six months more of life was all that was left him. His enemies had after all done their work; in crushing them he had risen to such a height of power as the jealous Roman mind could no longer endure.

CHAPTER XVIII.

CÆSAR'S USE OF ABSOLUTE POWER.

49-44 B.C.

THE reader has by this time made a close acquaintance with the personality of the man to whom the destinies of the world were for a short space committed. In following his own account of the Gallic and Civil wars, this personality has been continually before us. Its leading features can hardly be misinterpreted by anyone who is willing to abide by what is believed to be historic truth, and to set aside the doubtful accumulations of gossip and scandal. And now that we have reached the point where Cæsar found himself at last undisputed master of the Empire, we may safely leave the man and turn to his work—or rather to that nobler part of his work which was no longer the direct result of personal struggle, self-regarding aims, or even of an unrivalled talent for the conduct of war.

Cæsar's work marks the consummation of a series of revolutionary tendencies which had been gaining strength for generations, and even for centuries. Such tendencies are from time to time perceived and interpreted by statesmen like Gaius Gracchus, whose reason and sympathy combine to qualify them as revolutionary leaders and spokesmen; but human nature is in spite of itself so intensely conservative, that it would seem to need every favourable circumstance,—the right man to lead, an overwhelming material force, a universal cry of discontent,—nay, even an almost universal lowering of the moral standard, before the world can shake itself free of old trammels, and begin again in freedom and hope. It has been one object of this book so far to show that in the world of Cæsar's time almost every ingredient was present that could lead to a revolutionary explosion: a low moral standard; a prevailing discontent which was often the result of real hopeless misery; an overwhelming material force in the shape of a well-trained professional army; and lastly, the right man both to perceive and interpret the evil, to control the forces, and to provide for the future by reconstruction.

But, to come to close quarters with this difficult subject, what were in reality these revolutionary tendencies to which Cæsar first gave clear articulate expression? We may trace three, all closely connected with each other, and forming in fact one powerful current, the direction of which had been at least discovered, if not guided, by the Roman democratic leaders from the Gracchi onwards.

First, and most obvious of the three, there was the demand for some permanent change in the character of the central government at Rome, which should take the control of affairs out of the hands of incompetent and sordid men, and deposit it with those who could be trusted to act with reason, and with goodwill towards mankind.

Secondly, and following directly on the first, there was the demand for a social change which should neutralise the enormous influence of the small body of Italian capitalists, whether used to prop up a rotten system of government at home, or to oppress the masses of population in the provinces.

Thirdly, there was the inarticulate demand, audible only to the real statesman, and arising out of complicated causes which had been at work for centuries, for a new system of political organisation, which might give new life to the numberless little communities of which the Empire was made up, and might weld them all into a compact whole, of which each might be well content to form a part.

It is easy to see at a glance that the solution of such problems as these, the task of directing such revolutionary forces to their full realisation, was utterly beyond the power of a single man or a single age. Cæsar himself could only make a beginning, and of that beginning part at least did not survive the chaos that followed his death. But in another sense he stands not as a beginner but as the finisher of a great work. In him all these forces came to a head and found expression. It was he who coerced the whole Roman world into attention, and made it hearken to the voice of reason. True, the very fact that he had to use force deprived him of the power to be a great constructor, for he spent himself in the effort, and force was rewarded by assassination. But more perhaps than any statesman in history, he was, as his very features seem to attest, a great schoolmaster of mankind. He finished the education which the Gracchi had begun; but of the use to which the new knowledge was to be applied he could make only a bare beginning.

Let us, however, try and see how, in such work of Cæsar's as we can be certain was really his, there is indicated a sense of the three great claims which the world seemed to be making on the legislator; we shall at the same time learn at least something of the way in which he purposed to deal with those claims.

I.—Reconstruction of the machinery of government.

When a constitution has been destroyed, two tasks devolve upon the destroying agent. He has, first, to carry on the work of administration *for the time*, so as to preclude anarchy; and, secondly, he has to build up a new and stable system of government, whose stability will depend on its conformity with the needs, habits, and feelings of the people to be governed. The first of these is of course far the easier of the two, and by Cæsar it was successfully carried out. The second is always difficult, as the English and French revolutions have alike taught us; in the case of the Roman Empire the difficulties were almost superhuman. Cæsar had only really begun to lay his hand to this second part of his task when it was cut short by his assassination.

We saw that in April, 49 B.C., when he entered Rome for the first time as its master, he tried to bring together a senate. This was the natural course for a man to take who had lived all his life under a constitution in which the senate controlled almost all administrative departments, and was the only permanent deliberative body. But his attempt was a failure; such senators as assembled would not do what he wished. He therefore placed Lepidus as *prætor urbanus* in charge of Rome, Antonius (in spite of the fact that he was tribune) in military command of Italy as his *legatus*, and appointed governors for certain provinces, also as his own *legati*. In other words, he assumed the supreme administrative power which had so far belonged to the Senate alone. But it is clear that he assumed it only provisionally, and still perhaps expected to be able to rebuild in some sense the old constitution. He looked forward to being consul in a regular way the next year; and his chief object in being made dictator later in the year (see p. 279) was to hold the consular elections. He was dictator for only eleven days, during which he was elected consul (himself presiding at the election) with Servilius Isauricus as colleague. During his absence, until the battle of Pharsalus, Servilius carried on the government at Rome, in conjunction apparently with a senate.

But after that battle, and the death of Pompeius, the position of affairs was changed again. All union, all compromise had been proved impossible. There had been serious disturbances in Italy; war was brewing in Africa and Spain. No permanent constitution could yet be devised. The old one could in no sense be reconstructed, while Cæsar was himself in Egypt and had before him a prospect of long and perilous warfare. Another provisional government was established as the only possible expedient. In October, 48 B.C., he again accepted the dictatorship, and as it was probably given him without definite limit of time, and was backed up by a series of prerogatives which made his personal power almost unassailable, we must consider this new provisional government as simply absolutism. Under it he could decide alone on questions of war and peace; he could appoint prætors to govern provinces; he could deal judicially with his enemies; he could control the most important elections; lastly, he could exercise the powers of the tribunate of the people, and was thus freed from the necessity of using tribunes either to initiate or to control legislation. All these prerogatives were probably based on formally regular legislative enactments; and the bestowal of them was in a sense an indemnification for his previous exercise of abnormal power. But there is nothing to show that they were meant to be permanent; even the unlimited dictatorship was probably understood as provisional only, being, like that of Sulla, a bestowal of power to build up a constitution, and in no sense part of a new constitution itself. That ancient office had always been a temporary expedient—a brief reversion to kingship,—in order to tide over a pressing difficulty. As such it was used now; for a permanent dictatorship was to a Roman a contradiction in terms.

These powers did not come into active operation until Cæsar was again in Rome in the autumn of 47 B.C. He could then only stay some two months, as the African War was pressing on him ; and he used them only to restore order, to pass some necessary laws which will be mentioned presently, to hold the elections, and to appoint provincial governors. A complete reconstruction must again be postponed. And as was shown in the last chapter, the implacable wrath of his enemies made it ever more impossible for him to harmonise conflicting interests and feelings on anything like the old constitutional lines.

It was only when he returned victorious from Africa in the summer of 46 B.C. (see p. 322), that the field seemed at last clear for the formidable task. Meanwhile fresh powers had been given him, of which we have a very imperfect knowledge. The chief was a new dictatorship for ten years, and a censorial power, which gave him complete control over the Senate as well as over the conduct of the whole citizen body. With an absolutism thus raised to the highest possible pitch, he remained in Rome for several months, working incessantly at the necessary legislation. Yet among all the laws, some of them of the greatest importance, which we know to have been passed at this time, we hear of none that went directly towards the building up of a constitution. It is true indeed that if we possessed the original texts of his laws of public violence and high treason, we might form some negative idea of what his intentions were. But all that we can with any safety guess from the work of these months, is the following. First, Cæsar did not propose to establish a *military monarchy*; he began to disband his famous legions, which of late had become fretful and headstrong, and to settle them on the soil of Italy; and before the end of his life he had even dismissed his body-guard. Secondly, he did not wish to revive the old Senate, either in respect of its composition or its prerogative. He raised its numbers to nine hundred, appointing persons who under the old *régime* could never have aspired to a seat; it is said that among these were even a few provincials, as well as men of comparatively low rank in life. He wished therefore to deprive it of its old oligarchic tone, but to retain it as a Great Council, destined perhaps in due time to represent in some degree the interests of the whole Empire. Thirdly, he thought it best that, during his life at least, one man, and one only, should guide the destinies of that Empire. He now accepted for life the title of Imperator, thus showing that he was the holder, wherever in the Empire he might be, of that united civil and military command which the Romans had always understood by the word *imperium*, the only word which could suggest in a single conception the government of Rome, Italy, and the provinces.

There is no indication as to what he wished or expected to happen after his death. He was now in his fifty-sixth year, and his health was somewhat shaken by incessant toil. He might reasonably suppose that his life would not be a long one; and in fact we know that at this very time he was several times heard to say that he had lived long enough. There was no one among his adherents who had any good chance of succeeding to his own unexampled power. Antonius, the ablest, was unprincipled and unpopular; all the rest were quiet and hard-working men of only moderate ability. To a man in Cæsar's position the outlook must have seemed almost hopeless; for a return to republican institutions was hardly to be thought of if his work was to endure. He may well have trusted to his faithful goddess Fortuna to shield his life yet awhile, until he could see some light. But it is possible that at this very time, in December, 46 B.C., when he was leaving Rome for the last time to crush the Pompeians in Spain, a solution presented itself to him.

Gaius Octavius, the son of his niece Atia, was in this year, 45 B.C., seventeen years old; old enough, that is, to see his first military service. Accordingly he now followed his great-uncle to Spain, on the old Roman footing of *contubernalis* or pupil to a general in the art of war. Of their intercourse we know nothing whatever;* but on his return Cæsar sent the lad to Apollonia to study with Greek masters, and in the will which was too soon to come into operation, he made him his principal heir and adopted him as his son. It is said also that he meant to take him with him on his projected Par-

---

* It is doubtful whether they met at all in Spain. Octavius fell ill, and according to one account was shipwrecked ; he could not well have arrived till the campaign was over. See Drumann, Röm. Gesch., iv., 252.

thian expedition, and that the reason why he sent him to Apollonia, was that he might witness the assembling and drilling of the legions that were already being concentrated there. If a successor could be found, who would inherit the name, the blood, and the wealth of Cæsar, and whose ability to govern like Cæsar were acknowledged in the Empire, the uncertain and threatening prospect might brighten up. And there was indeed great promise in this boy; he not only was fair to look on, but able, quiet, and genial. A close observer might have seen that his temperament was very different from Cæsar's; but it turned out that he possessed exactly the qualities needed for the judicious development of the main results of Cæsar's outspoken autocracy. That autocracy must always be regarded as extraordinary and provisional; but it struck the keynote by which a clever successor might tune the system to the sensitive ear of the Roman world.

We are not then surprised to find that during the last months of his life, after his return from Spain, among the innumerable honours lavished on him in flattery by an obsequious Senate and people, Cæsar accepted some which seem to mark his willingness to make his absolutism more definite, and such as might be transmitted to an heir. He entered, early in February, 44 B.C.,[*] on a final dictatorship for his life-time; a serious step, because it put an entirely new meaning on an old republican institution. He now began to allow the image of his head to be placed on the

---

[*] At some date between Jan. 25th and Feb. 15th. (Henzen in Ephemeris Epigraphica, ii., 285.)

coinage. This had no precedent in Roman history, but it had always been, in the empires of the East, the special prerogative of the monarch. He allowed his statue to be added to those of the seven kings of Rome on the Capitol. He appeared on public occasions in the purple triumphal dress; and in many other little ways, which it would be wearisome to catalogue here, allowed his person to become the centre of the pomp and ceremonial of a court. Whether in so doing he was showing signs of growing weakness,—of surrender at last to that demon of unreason which he had spent his life in conquering, is a question that can never be decided. It will be referred to again in the next chapter; all that we are concerned with now is the high probability, as resulting from these facts, that he meant the permanent constitution of the Empire to be monarchy, and that monarchy, if possible, an hereditary one. And he went far enough, in this first and purely constitutional aspect of the revolution, to leave the impress of his mind on the Roman world for the whole remainder of its history ; a result which would have been impossible, if he had not divined rightly the one method by which that world could by any possibility be held together.

II. The social change which Cæsar sought to bring about is much harder to explain. To do so effectually would entail an inquiry into the social and economic condition, not only of Rome and Italy, but of the whole Empire. We must be content with a very brief survey, and then ask in what direction Cæsar seems to have been looking for improvement.

Let us look first at the great city itself, with its vast and various population. That vivid contrast between rich and poor, which had always been the curse of the old city-state of the ancient world, had long been fatally exaggerated at Rome. The conquerors of the world had grown rich in the process of conquest, but their wealth was in the hands of a few. All Italy bore witness to this; the greater part of it was in the possession of large land-owners, whose vast estates were cultivated by slaves. The old free population had drifted to Rome, as the only place to which they could possibly migrate, and mingled there with a motley collection of waifs and strays from all parts of the world, and with a crowd of liberated slaves, all more or less idle, and destitute of any regular means of subsistence. Like the "mean whites" of the Southern States before the American Civil War, they were the dangerous product of an inhuman and exaggerated slave-system.

Efforts had been made to remedy these terrible evils; but the wealthy class was also the class that held the reins of government, the social question became a political one, and the cause of the Senate became the cause of unrighteous wealth. The two Gracchi were slain as enemies of the state they wished to save. Of all the remedies they proposed, only one was still in operation in Cæsar's day, and that was the worst—a measure in fact of relief, and not a remedy. Gaius Gracchus had begun the practice of feeding the Roman unemployed by the distribution of cheap corn; Sulla had wisely abolished it. But the senatorial party had revived it for their own purposes in 73 B.C.; and Clodius in 58 had taken advantage of this to do away even with the small sum that the recipients of the dole were expected to pay. All the rest of the Gracchan projects—land distribution in Italy, colonisation, and custom duties, had practically come to nothing. Italy was more than ever depopulated, Rome was poorer and more congested than ever; rich men had amassed wealth amounting even to millions of pounds, and they were for the most part wrapped in the slumber of an utterly selfish indifference, or at least content to enjoy the pleasures of a literary luxury without casting even a glance at the awful abyss on the brink of which they stood. Among them were some honourable and right-minded men; but history must judge of them as a whole, and can pronounce but one verdict on a class which only woke up to activity when its own private interests were threatened.

And this is not the whole of the indictment. If we ask whence the wealth of these great capitalists was derived, the answer is that it came in great measure from the provinces which they were called on to govern, or to help in governing. That is, the governor and his retinue, and the whole *posse* of tax-gatherers and money-lenders who flourished under his protection, carried back to Rome enormous profits, as legitimate spoil; and this was drawn ultimately from the labouring classes in the provinces, who thus spent their strength for the benefit of a small and idle section of their masters. If we could imagine the England of to-day governed by Indian nabobs, and the India of to-day regarded only as a fair field for the enrichment of that governing class; and if by a further effort we could substitute for the English working classes a population composed chiefly of slaves; we should then have some idea of the picture presented by the Roman world during the greater part of the last century of the republican government. On the one hand a compact oligarchy, without any sense of duty or trusteeship, maintaining its hold on the government by wealth wrung from its best subjects; on the other, a proletariate, idle at Rome, dying out in Italy, and impoverished in the provinces. And below all, a vast slave-population, which had already been proved to be in itself a serious danger to the state, as well as indirectly a chief cause of other perils. As Mommsen has most truly said, none of the evils for which the capitalists of our day can be called to account, are to be compared for a moment to the hideous ruin which the Roman oligarch had wrought in a couple of centuries on the fair shores of the Mediterranean.

It will be obvious at once that there could be no panacea for such a social and economical condition, reacting with such deadly force upon the body politic. The best that could be done was, while applying some temporary remedies, to induce a healthier tone in the patient, and so to make it possible for nature eventually to work an improvement. And no statesman had any chance of effecting even this, without qualifications which have rarely if ever been united in a single man. He must understand the nature of the disease in its entirety, and not only in part; he must be acquainted with the condition of the Empire, not of Rome or Italy only. He must have a nature to claim, and a power to exact, that feeling of loyalty and trust, without which no physician can work to any good purpose. And he must be patient enough to put aside all quack remedies, and to expect no more than a gradual amelioration, of which he might not himself live to see more than the beginning.

All these conditions were realised in Cæsar, and this fact, far more than his military exploits, forms his chief claim to be considered one of the world's greatest men. It is true that his own hands were not altogether clean; he was reckoned among the capitalists; he had drawn great sums from his provinces, and had spent them in securing his political position. He had lived in fact like his fellows, and had been carried down the polluted stream. But his wealth, his knowledge, his power, and his patience, were not used in these last years of his life only to serve his own purposes, but for the good of the state in its whole length and breadth. Let us try to show that this was so, even from our imperfect knowledge of his own necessarily imperfect work.

Of temporary remedies, the first to notice is a law issued during the few days which Cæsar spent in Rome in November, 49 B.C., before leaving Italy for Epirus (see p. 280). Its object was to restore credit in Italy, and to neutralise the natural effect of civil war in producing unmerited bankruptcy on the one hand, and exaggerated capitalist tyranny on the other.

The revolutionists of the day would no doubt have gladly seen him wiping out all debts at one stroke, and abolishing house-rent and interest; such proposals had always been in the programme of the " extreme left " since Catiline's conspiracy, and were the natural result of an utterly unhealthy economic condition. Cicero, writing wildly to Atticus at this critical time (49 B.C.), expresses his conviction that Cæsar will actually go these lengths, forgetting, curiously enough, that Cæsar was a creditor on a vast scale, and that he himself was among his debtors. Only a year later Cicero had to learn that violent attacks on property were more likely to come from his own foolish friends than from statesmen like Cæsar; for it was his old pupil Cælius, a clever butterfly of the day, and later his son-in-law, Dolabella, and his old friend Milo, who actually tried the tempting game of appealing to popular greed, and so outbidding the master. Cæsar, on the other hand, looked as usual to the interest of all classes, not of one only, knowing well that Nemesis awaits the man who deals unjustly even with unjust doers.

What he did was this, as he tells it himself.* He enacted, first, that debtors should be allowed to make over their property to their creditors in payment of debt, and secondly, that such property should be estimated by arbitrators at the value it *would have borne, had no civil war broken out.* The first of these regulations practically constituted a new law of bankruptcy, and was followed in due time, probably under Augustus, by a more complete

---

* Bell. Civ., iii., 1.

and permanent enactment on the same lines. It relieved the borrower from the liability to personal bondage, which had been hitherto always recognised by statute, and we may see in it the germ of our modern laws of bankruptcy. The second regulation was a temporary expedient in the interest of the debtor, wild enough according to our ideas of economic science, but characteristic of antiquity; a strong remedy applied to a serious disease. If creditors everywhere called in their debts, while all values were lowered by the Civil War, innumerable debtors would be utterly ruined, and capitalism would gain instead of losing by a war of which it was itself one main cause. Cæsar is also said to have ordered, like Solon, that all interest already paid should be deducted from the capital sum; and Suetonius reckons the loss to the capitalist on this score as on an average one fourth of the sum lent. We hear also of a law directed against hoarding, and of another which compelled the capitalist to invest part of his capital in land, for the benefit of Italian agriculture, and to discourage the usurer's business; these were probably passed two years later, and meant as permanent enactments.

All this had been skilfully framed in the interest of the poor debtor, without doing more injury to the rich than was necessary and deserved. But the idle poor of the great city, the curse of the last few generations, were not encouraged to look for special indulgence. We may even now read some of the rules laid down by Cæsar for the proper management of those doles of corn which had so long been making Rome a refuge for all the lazy paupers of Italy.* The effect of them was simply to change a flagrant abuse into a well regulated system of relief. The number of recipients was reduced from 320,000 to 150,000, and that this latter number was to be rigidly adhered to is proved by the fact that the magistrate who should give a dole to anyone whose claim had not been publicly sanctioned, was liable to a fine of not less than £400. And Cæsar was not content with putting this unlucky institution of Gaius Gracchus on a rational basis; he also set to work at the great design which Gracchus had projected, to act as a remedy destined eventually to supersede all necessity of relief. Rome and Italy were now to pour their unemployed into the various provinces, where they were to be settled in colonies after the old Roman fashion, with allotments of land and the prospect of gaining a healthy livelihood. But it was with Cæsar as with Gracchus; the great design had but just begun to take effect when its author fell a victim to the blindness of republican "patriots." We only know for certain of a few colonies which were actually founded, chiefly in southern Gaul and in Spain.†

The veteran soldiers of the famous legions which had borne Cæsar to power were not allowed, when their service was over, to recruit the pauperism of

* Lex Julia Municipalis, first six sections.

† He did not live to see Corinth and Carthage colonised, but it is certain that these foundations date from the year of his death. The two great commercial cities of former times were to rise from the ruins in which the Republic had laid them and to flourish afresh under the Empire.

the capital, like those of Marius, nor to become a standing menace to the peace of Italy, as had long been the case with Sulla's old warriors. They were either settled in the above-mentioned colonies, or were distributed over Italy, after the African campaign, in such a way as to prevent them from concentrating their strength again. The difficult task of providing them with land was carried out without injustice or violence, for it was the master's object and interest to leave no cause for irritation in any class of the population. These veterans were splendid men, used to labour of all kinds, and if they could be localised apart and take root in their new homes, might be a help rather than a hindrance to the regeneration of Italy. They were not entirely without the means of starting a small farm; each legionary had received from Cæsar after his triumph a sum equal to more than £150 of our money, and the centurions much more. And here it is worth noting that the vast sums which passed into Cæsar's hands, from confiscation of the property of vanquished enemies or in other ways, were not used by him as personal property, but as held in trust for the whole state, and were allowed to filter thus through his hands as it were into the soil of Italy, or were converted into state treasure, or destined in his will to be distributed in very small sums over the whole body of Roman citizens.

That Cæsar was not working merely by instinct in all this, but consciously endeavouring to reduce the evil effects of ill-used capital, is shown by one or two other measures which we can do no more than mention. How far they were or could be carried out is indeed doubtful, but their meaning is plain. Every great holder of a cattle-run in Italy was to have not less than a third of his labourers free men and not slaves, a rule which would compel payment of wages and decrease the opportunities of enormous profits. Idle luxury he sought to check by direct sumptuary laws, no doubt in vain; more effectively, perhaps, by the re-imposition of customs-duties on foreign goods landed at Italian ports. By this last measure, in which he once again followed the steps of G. Gracchus, he at once encouraged Italian production and made the rich pay something to the state for the luxurious privileges of wealth. Lastly, to stimulate a healthier tone of mind in this same effeminate class, he forbade any son of a senator to leave Italy save in the course of a military education, or in the retinue of a provincial governor. And no citizen of any rank was to be more than three years continuously abroad between the age of twenty and forty—that is, they were not to settle in the provinces except as permanent colonists, or to range over the Empire, as the equestrian class had so long been doing, in order to glut themselves on the weakness of pauperised provincials.

" *Quid leges sine moribus vanæ proficiunt?* " So wrote Horace, under Cæsar's successor, seeing as yet no moral regeneration at work in the Roman mind. And there is indeed no greater mistake than to conceive of Cæsar as a teacher of morality. The idea of a new righteousness to leaven the world was not to come, and could not come, from Italy; not from the humane instincts of the man of action, nor yet from the second-hand philosophy so exquisitely Latinised by Cicero. But in public life at least, Cæsar showed a recognition of the law that justice must form the basis of all social well-being ; and if we turn for a moment from Italy to the provinces, we shall see that he included in that idea of justice all the inhabitants of the Empire.

Two leading motives seem to have governed his dealings with the provinces. First, there was the instinct of self-preservation, which led him to appoint the governors directly himself, or to leave but a nominal power of selection to his Senate. If the Empire were to hold together any longer, it was essential that these satraps should be really dependent on, and responsible to, a master who was strong enough to punish disloyalty or injustice. His own rise to power was now a warning to him. It was he who introduced as a definite system the practice of nominating his own *legati* to governorships ; men, that is, who were in the position of subordinates to his own *imperium*, delegates bound to obey his orders, and punishable by himself alone. This was one example of that " tyranny," which so astonished and horrified the official mind at Rome ; in reality it was only the substitution of a real for a sham system of responsibility. It was continued by Augustus, and though it was applied by him and his successors only to a certain number of the governorships, the existence of an autocratic centre of power rapidly affected the whole system, and secured for the provinces on the whole a far better chance of development than they had enjoyed under the real tyranny of irresponsible republican rulers. Though not theoretically perfect, and depending for its efficacy on the industry and vigilance of a single man, it was the only possible alternative to disruption and misgovernment in that age. We still note with admiration, in the correspondence between Pliny and Trajan a century and a half later, the paternal care with which a hard-working autocrat could interest himself in the administrative details of a distant province, and the affectionate loyalty of a trusted representative of his power.

By such methods it became possible to do at least something towards staying that continual drain of provincial wealth to Rome and Italy, which, as we saw, was at the bottom of the whole social corruption of the time; and this, if we interpret Cæsar rightly, was the second great motive in his mind in dealing with the provinces. He wished, in fact, to correlate his reforms at home with the necessary reform in provincial government. He had in his first consulship thoroughly revised the law against extortion in the provinces, and he now put it in force with vigour, ejecting (says Suetonius) from the Senate all who were convicted under it. The proper administration of this law, of the law of high treason,* and of that against bribery at elections, would go far towards stopping the accumulation, as well as the misuse of ill-gotten wealth. And if the govern-

---

* This was also fully revised by Cæsar, and the result was approved even by Cicero (Phil., i.,9). We unfortunately are in the dark as to the additions or improvements which he made in it.

ors themselves ceased to be sharks, it would naturally follow that a healthier tone might be anticipated among the members of their retinue and the Roman men of business in each province. Lastly, the state itself was no longer to be the great destroyer of provincial wellbeing; for little as we know of Cæsar's financial intentions, we can at least be sure that what he did was in the right direction. The tithe-system of direct taxation, which had ruined the rich province of Asia since G. Gracchus, was either abolished entirely, or at least the collection of the tithes was placed in the hands of the provincials themselves. The new province of Gaul was taxed in a lump sum, and not a heavy one. The project of a general census, though Cæsar did not live to carry it out, made it plain that he wished to lay the foundation of all righteous financial dealing, by ascertaining and registering the tax-paying capacity of all property in the Empire.

Thus, wherever we turn, we see indications of an attempt to remedy the most crying social and economical evils of the day. The power of vast capital to do infinite material and moral harm, was checked both by measures of immediate application, and by the more far-sighted method of shutting up the sources of illegitimate accumulation. And it must be allowed, that in spite of all the evils incidental to a system of absolutism, we can trace in the era of the early Empire a steady progress in the material well-being of the masses, and some tendency towards a better public morality in the region of government; and we must refer the origin of this to the width of view and the right instincts, not only of Augustus, but of the man who was his master and, in some respects at least, his model.

III. We have now seen something of the new form of central government which Cæsar initiated, and also something of the attempts he made to remedy the social demoralisation of the age. There remains the question whether he conceived, or tried to put into effect, any scheme for the political re-organisation of the Empire. The reader who is not conversant with the histories of Greece and Rome, may be at a loss to understand what is here meant; yet it must be understood, if Cæsar's position in the world's history is to be adequately recognised. Let us begin by explaining very briefly what need of re-organisation there was.

If a traveller had passed through the Empire at this time, inquiring how the business of government was carried on in the different parts of it, he must have come to the conclusion that there was no unity of system, either in matters of law, finance, or general administration. In Italy he would find the Roman law everywhere applied, because all the inhabitants were now citizens of Rome; but in any town he visited he would probably be told that its local authorities were in a very uncertain position, that their relations to the Roman magistrates were ill-defined or not defined at all, and that in many cases the local magistracies and councils were filled by persons quite unfitted to serve, whether from inexperience, low birth, or bad character. In Cisalpine Gaul he would probably find a better moral tone, but a far more anomalous legal position. This rich district was a *province*, and governed like other provinces by a proconsul or proprætor; yet all the inhabitants south of the Po had long been Roman citizens, and in 49 B.C., as we saw, Cæsar gave the full citizenship also to the district between the Po and the Alps. After that date, all the free inhabitants of the peninsula were qualified to vote in the elective and legislative assemblies at Rome—that is, to elect the magistrates who were to govern them, and to vote on the laws they were to obey; yet they could seldom or never be present on such occasions, the laws were passed and the magistrates elected by the people of the great city only, and the rest were left to manage their own affairs as best they could, with little sense of the privileges they nominally possessed. An intelligent Italian might well have told our traveller that he was living in a state of political chaos. "Long ago," he might have said, "most of us belonged to free communities, and after we fell under the Roman power, we were at least nominally independent, though bound to serve in Roman armies. Now that we have become Roman citizens, we seem to be neither governors nor governed; our local affairs are going to pieces, and we cannot influence the affairs of the Empire."

Let us now imagine that our traveller has crossed from Brundisium to Epirus, and is making a tour through the cities of Greece, Macedonia, and Asia Minor. Here he would find a state of things doubtless more intelligible, but far less promising. Most of these cities had had a history, and in many cases an inspiring one. The old Greek idea of the free and self-sufficient city-state still lingered on among them, and some few were even now called free cities, or boasted an "alliance" with Rome. But even these last were really at the mercy of the Roman provincial governor; and all the less privileged cities only retained their local institutions at his will and pleasure. Everywhere the traveller would find that the law itself and its administration, the security of person and property, the operation of wills and covenants, even the rate of interest, depended on the temper and industry of the provincial governor and his suite, and might be at any time altered on the arrival of a new one. Under a good governor, and in time of peace, these cities might enjoy the phantom of a local autonomy, and elect their own magistrates and council, as of old; but the Roman *imperium* cast its grim shadow everywhere, chilling men and disheartening them, like a London fog of to-day. The Greeks, not only in the East, but wherever they had settled, must have felt that at best they were only allowed to play at governing themselves, and that such amusement was hardly better than the most abject state of servitude.

In the far West, in Spain as well as in Africa, and in the vast newly acquired territory of Gaul, there had been no memory of a time when every city was free and self-governing, as in Greece. In Spain there were not as yet many towns, though the Romans had everywhere recognised the value of them; in Gaul there were hardly any. The inhabitants lived in villages, and were gathered into tribal groups, such as the Ædui or the Carnutes. There was here, then, no question of even a nominal independence, except where the Romans had bestowed it on some ancient Greek colony like Massilia, or allowed a Gallic tribe to call themselves the friends of the Roman people. Here the provincial governor was checked by fewer ancient traditions or usages, and the Romanisation of the people was an easier task. No real civilisation had preceded the Roman in the West.

Supposing our traveller to have made his tour of inquiry in the year 50 B.C., just before the Civil War broke out, he might well have asked what possible bond of union could be discovered, capable of holding together such a chaos of races, languages, religions, traditions, interests, and forms of local government, as the so-called Roman Empire then contained. At one time the great council of the city of Rome had really held this empire together by virtue of the immense prestige won for it by its indomitable firmness alike in victory and defeat. But now the task itself was a far larger and more complicated one, and the Senate had utterly discredited itself. The two great sources of decay which had everywhere disintegrated the ancient form of city-state, had done their work effectually at Rome ; conquest had corrupted both the conquered and the conqueror, and the quarrels of rich and poor had demoralised both parties within the state itself. There was in fact no single city-state of the true old type, free and self-sufficing, now left in the whole civilised world.

Rome herself had grown out of all limits, and all the other cities had lost their freedom, and depended for their very existence on the will of Rome and her magistrates. If the Greek political philosophers had re-entered the world in this year, they would have found their analysis of political life and duty no longer applicable; the old idea of the state was gone, and what was there to take its place? A year or two later, even the existing semblance of union threatened to disappear; the East was arrayed against the West in the plains of Thessaly, and Italy, helpless and impoverished, seemed likely to be crushed between them.

Yet we have but to look forward half a century, to find the whole Roman dominion once more firmly knit together and at peace; content and prosperity beginning to reign both in East and West, Italy well-governed, and the great cosmopolitan city quiet and enjoying its life. And still more astonishing is it to find that this unity, in spite of severe shocks, survives for several centuries; that an entirely new era of political life has begun, and impressed itself so indelibly on men's minds, that when it finally passes away in the hurricanes of barbarian invasion, the memory and the worship of it remain, and become a solid basis on which new structures can be raised. It is true enough that this unity was never real in the sense in which the France of to-day is united; the East and West always differed, and were eventually separated. But in the sense of belonging to a great whole; in the realisation of a unity of power, competent to protect; in the possession of something to which to be loyal—a clear, visible impersonation of the majesty of the Roman government,—in all these ways there came to be a unity of the Empire, which bridges over the gulf between the ancient and the modern state. And this was the result in the main of two great political conceptions : 1. The idea of a central unit, not now a city, but a person, to whom all other units in the system should look up as the ultimate and universal referee ; 2. The idea of a form of local government, applicable throughout the whole system, with modifications suited to pre-existing institutions and the character of the various populations.

Both these conceptions, afterwards so inseparable from one another and so closely interwoven, had been in men's minds before Cæsar fought his way to absolutism ; but the notion of creating a new political entity out of them had probably been fully realised by no one. In any practical problem, it is less hard to discover what conditions are present, than to see how to utilise them to advantage. We are justified in believing that it was Cæsar who first fully grasped the conditions of the problem before the Roman statesman, and at the same time discovered the right solution. If this be so, he may indeed be called the founder of the Roman Empire ; for though the outward form and show of government which Augustus devised was not that which Julius had adopted, yet if we look a little closer, we shall find that the two chief factors in the imperial system were henceforward those to which the first Cæsar had pointed, as the only possible life-giving principles in a huge collection of decaying matter.

Let us try to show that these two principles were really in Cæsar's mind. That he conceived of personal government as a permanency, we have already seen. He became legally absolute himself, he prepared the way for a successor, he depressed the capitalist class which supplied the material for the dispossessed oligarchy. But he did more than this. He left no rival in the Empire, as Sulla had done; and there was no part of the Empire that had not felt his presence. He was not a name only in distant provinces. His person was familiar to the leading men of Gaul, Spain, and Africa; he had settled the affairs of Syria and Egypt, and of the three provinces of Asia Minor. It was known everywhere that the governors of all the provinces were now his men. He knit together the Roman world with a strength it had never known before, and the centre of the system was beginning to be felt to be his mind, and not the city of Rome.

The second idea, that of a limited local self-government, so far as it was Cæsar's, is in part plainly visible to us, in part beyond our reach. So far as the communities of Roman citizens were concerned, whether in Italy or beyond it, we know that he organised their civic life, and endeavoured to purify and elevate it. The Museum at Naples even now contains a great part of the famous municipal law by which this object was to be achieved. And as this same law contains ordinances for the good government of the city of Rome, and even for the regulation of traffic in her streets and of the corn-dole for her poor inhabitants, we may fairly guess with

Mommsen that Rome herself was to be henceforward in the eye of the law only a municipal town, the first of all in dignity, but not in power. She was to resign her place as mistress, and to be no more than a convenient centre for the conduct of the business of the Empire. She was to be the type, and like her, all other cities which possessed Roman rights were to have their council and their magistrates on the model of her own, and to manage their own affairs within certain limits *; but no one city was henceforth to dominate the rest. The task of supervising the whole was to be the duty of one man ; but he was to be helped in each individual community by the free action of the communal authorities. This, as briefly stated as is possible, was the idea we believe to have been in Cæsar's mind, and it foreshadows the actual future of the Empire, and ushers in a new era of political life. It would be too much to assert that he contemplated the application of it to the provinces also, *i.e.*, to all the innumerable cities and cantons which had no share in the Roman citizenship. But there is something to be said in favour even of such an hypothesis as this. For in two ways, henceforward, the course of local government in the provinces was left free and unimpeded as compared with what it had been ; first, the governor was kept more closely in check, and could no longer safely trample on such liberties as were possessed by the cities which he governed ; secondly, the Roman citizenship already spread over Italy, was now beginning to

* We still possess a fragment of a law (Lex Rubria), passed at Cæsar's instigation, which regulated these limits for Cisalpine Gaul.

creep into the provinces. Cæsar was the first to bestow it entire upon a foreign community, when he enfranchised all the inhabitants of the free city of Gades, the native place of the faithful Balbus. Colonies of Roman citizens, as we have seen, according to the plan of G. Gracchus, were now beginning to be freely planted in the provinces. The Latin "right," a diminished form of the full citizenship, was conceded to all Sicily and perhaps to a considerable part of the old Transalpine province of Gaul.* And wherever such rights were bestowed, the municipal organisation came into force, and the provincial governor was no longer able to exercise his caprice. From such facts we may quite reasonably infer that Cæsar foresaw with approval the gradual extension of Roman citizenship over the whole Empire, and the consequent security and uniformity of municipal life. And with this too would go the gradually increasing sphere of Roman law, that wonderful systematisation of the rights and duties of civilised men, under the influence of which the legal ideas of modern Europe are to a great extent still unconsciously moulded.

This most imperfect account of Cæsar's work and projects, long as it has been, cannot be closed without an allusion to one other point in which his deeds reflected the light of a mind more luminous than that of any great ruler since Pericles. We have seen how he tempered strong government with justice and humanity; but these virtues were not unknown to

---

*Cic., Ad Att., 14, 12, 1, does not make the point certain as regards all Sicily: but at least there was an intention of the kind.

Roman civilisation, though for nearly a century they had been crushed out by party hatred. What is really new in Cæsar is this:—that now for the first time in Roman history, what we should call *scientific intelligence* was brought to bear on the problems of government.* His turn of mind, as has been already pointed out, was not rhetorical but scientific; it was not words or ideals that attracted him, but facts and knowledge. In other words, he did not follow the pseudo-Hellenic culture of the day, but asserted the truly Roman character of his understanding without reverting to the older Roman model of stubborn ignorance. This is visible in all his writings that have come down to us, which are the expression in the fewest possible words of an invaluable series of military, geographical, and ethnical observations. It was doubtless also to be found in his other writings, such as those two books on grammar which were composed, as it is said, in one of his long journeys from north Italy to join his army in Gaul. And lastly it may be traced in the whole of his political work; not only in his steady refusal to deal with ideals and fancies such as delighted and misled Cicero, but in the actual application of scientific knowledge and order to matters of public concern. To him we are still under obligation for the boon of a scientifically ordered calendar. It was he who first projected the codification of the several elements of Roman law,—a plan in harmony with that more comprehensive one for the unification of the whole Empire. He too first proposed a general census on scientific prin-

* This is indeed to some extent true also of G. Gracchus and Sulla, but in a far less degree.

ciples, with a practical and humane object. The collection of a vast library of Greek and Latin works was another of his aims; and as Suetonius tells us, his former enemy, the learned Varro, was commissioned to set about the work. Everywhere he sought out men of knowledge and men of letters, pressed them into his service, and if they were without it, gave them the Roman citizenship.

When we add this last consideration to all we have learnt of his military genius, his acquisition and use of power, his social legislation, and his plans for the creation of a new type of political organism, we must allow that we have here a man whose equal as a ruler of men has probably never been seen since. Never, we may at least conclude with confidence, have problems on such a vast scale been met by genius of such a kind. As a human being he was doubtless far from perfect, though capable of loving and being loved like humbler men; but if we think of his work only, we can allow to no other statesman an equal meed for the lasting value of his labour. We feel the truth of that presentation of him by our own greatest genius, where it is not the bodily presence of the hero that is the protagonist of the play, but the spirit of Cæsar that lives after him. Brutus and Cassius and Antony are the human characters in the drama, each with their strong and weak points, but over them all towers the spirit of the slain Cæsar, destined for centuries to claim immortality and worship, while their weak and disunited efforts to control the destinies of the world became no more than material for the biographer and the poet.

CHAPTER XIX.

THE END.

44. B.C.

WE left Cæsar returning to Rome after the bloody struggle in Spain in the spring of 45 B.C. There are some facts which seem to suggest that the savage nature of the resistance offered him, and the growing brutality of his own men, had worked their natural effect even on his mild temper. It is said too that he suffered severely in Spain from the seizures to which he was constitutionally liable, and to this we must add the vexation which every man of high aims must feel when he is continually thwarted by irreconcilable enemies and forced again and again to postpone the work of peace. The rude historian of the Spanish war has preserved for us a broken outline of the speech he delivered at Hispalis before leaving the province, which clearly shows the indignation he felt towards the people of Further Spain for taking sides with his enemies. They had always been his peculiar care ever since he served his quæstorship among them, and they had requited him with rebellion at a time when it was to him most vexatious and damaging.

His return had been most anxiously awaited at Rome. Cicero, deep in literary work, was eagerly inquiring of Balbus when he might be expected. Antonius and Trebonius set off to meet him at Massilia, perhaps in some doubt as to their reception, or with an evil design in their hearts; Marcus Brutus, whom Cæsar loved as his own son, is also said to have gone there in some expectation of a new turn of mind in the conqueror.* It seems indeed possible that the more sanguine republicans half believed that the master would now lay down his abnormal power and allow the old constitution to get into its familiar lumbering motion once more. Cicero, writing to an exiled friend at this time, tells him that when the wars are at last over, the moment must come which will decide whether the Republic is to perish utterly or gain a new lease of life.† And Cicero too had been meditating, and had partly written, an address to Cæsar on the condition of the state, which, in spite of the flattery with which he deemed it necessary to spice it, must have contained suggestions of this kind. But he was sick at heart, and could not finish it.

---

* Cic., Ad Att., 13, 40. Brutus sent word home that Cæsar was coming round to the views of the "honest men." "Where are they?" says Cicero.

† Fam., vi., 2.

There was indeed much to make honest men, of the older and narrower political faith, as restless and hopeless as Cicero. Their feelings can only be realised by those who can peruse the mass of correspondence between Cicero and his friends during the last fifteen months of Cæsar's life. The reader of these will mark three alternating characteristics which tell a true story of the painful situation of these men. Submission to the new master, with a tendency to flatter him, yet occasionally to think of him even now as a man and a friend; intense repugnance to the dulness, or more truly the non-existence, of political life in the capital—the appalling contrast to that life of excitement and agitation on which Cicero's sensitive soul had fed, even while it pained him; and lastly, an utter absence of any interest in Cæsar's great projects for the good of the whole Empire, showing, better than anything else can show us, how great was the gulf which separated the man whose eyes were ever on the past from the man who stood at the helm and looked far into unknown seas.

When Cæsar at last arrived in September, all such fanciful hopes were rudely dispelled. He made no sign of restoring the Republic. On the contrary, he seems from this time to have exercised his power with greater confidence, greater audacity, and with less consideration either for the feelings of others or for the safety of his own life. He made his will on September 13th, at his estate of Lavicum, before reaching Rome; a step which turned out to be of the utmost importance for the future of his great

MARCUS BRUTUS.
FROM THE BUST IN THE MUSEUM OF THE CAPITOL IN ROME (*Visconti*).
(*Baumeister.*)

projects. He then entered the city, possibly for the " Roman games" on September 15th, and soon afterwards celebrated a fresh triumph with great pomp. It would have been better to have dispensed with this, for the victory was over Roman citizens; yet not only did Cæsar triumph himself, but he allowed two of his *legati* the same honour on separate occasions, though they had shown, as it was said, no special merit. At the games which followed this triumph, there was a singular illustration of the completeness of the new despotism. A famous playwright, sixty years of age, named Laberius, was invited by Cæsar to take part in the performance of one of his own plays. It is hard to believe that Cæsar meant this as a deliberate insult to a man of talent who was a Roman knight; but it is certain that the poet took the invitation as a command, for we still have the verses in which he deplored his own obedience.* We cannot explain the story, or extenuate the injury, except by reference to Laberius' well-known bitterness of speech; we can only be sure that it was unlike anything we have yet learnt of Cæsar's courteous and considerate nature.†

Another act of absolutism, which hurt tender consciences, was the sudden election of consuls and prætors for the rest of the year. Cæsar had himself been sole consul this year; the city had been governed by Lepidus his " master of the horse," and by " prefects" nominated by him, instead of by the

---

* Macrob., Sat., ii., 7.

† On this very occasion the poet made a bitter jest to Cicero, which will be found in Macrob., Sat., ii., 3, 10.

usual magistrates. He now laid down the consulship, and relieved the prefects of their office. But in the eyes of Cicero and his friends, downright despotism was better than a sham republic. These new consuls and prætors were really nominees of the master*; they were not independent magistrates, each going his own way in that delightful confusion dear to lovers of the old *régime;* they were "functionaries," as M. Boissier happily calls them,—*i. e.*, they had business to perform, and performed it under the supervision of a higher authority. That such authorities should be controlled, and feel themselves only as wheels in a machine, was intolerable to Roman feeling; yet Cæsar did not seem to care to disguise the truth. His nature was to face facts, not to conceal them, and he hazarded his life by his frankness. For Augustus the task was easier, and the man's nature was better suited to reconcile the sensitiveness of the city with the needs of the Empire. For Cæsar there was now no compromise possible between republic and monarchy. For him monarchy meant the liberation of the Empire; for the republicans it meant the oppression of the city. For him the republic meant confusion and scandal; for them it meant freedom and lawful gain. His idea of government was that every authority should work in due subordination to the rest and to the centre; to them it appeared as the free irresponsible action of every magistrate during his term of

---

* On the last day of this year Cæsar showed his contempt for the consulship by having a man elected to fill for a few hours the place of one of the consuls who died that day.

office. How could such a constitution perform the task of government which the world required of Rome? To restore the republican constitution would have been to destroy all his work, to be false to all his aims; and he seems to have now resolved to make the monarchy a more living and obvious reality.

There was no lack of opportunity. Personal privileges and distinctions were heaped upon him in a continuous stream during these last months of his life; the reader of Dio Cassius and Appian wearies of them, and is not surprised to find him only too ready to escape from this weary round of adulation, in another frontier war. Some he accepted, others rejected; but the golden chair in the Senate, the triumphal robe on all state occasions, the head stamped on the new coinage, the statue added to those of the seven kings, were quite enough to proclaim the new monarchy, even before the question of the title of Rex had been raised. If ever there was a king, Cæsar was one, though, like the greatest of our English kings, he never bore the title.

But up to the end of this year, 45 B.C., it does not seem that the adulation reached its highest point. Cæsar had his hands full; he was busy, so far as we can discern, with the reconstruction of the Senate, which must have taken much time and thought; with the settling of his veterans on their newly acquired land; with the completion of his vast buildings in the city, which had lately given employment to the poor, and were making old Rome into a new and splendid city; with his new gold coinage; with the creation of new patrician houses, a plan, as it would seem, for reviving the old nobility of birth, in place of that worn-out nobility of state service, which had come to an end with the extinction of its functions under his own sway. Other far-reaching projects belong perhaps to these months, such as the draining of the malarious Pomptine marshes, and the construction of a new harbour at the mouth of the Tiber; works which would have given useful employment to the idle proletariate of the great city. It is said also that he wished to cut through the Isthmus of Corinth, and thus secure a direct route by sea, connecting Italy with the East. These plans mean nothing more than that one who had never yet found difficulties insurmountable in war, was now employing his engineers in devising such works of peace as might serve to knit the Empire more strongly together, and make trade and travel quicker and more easy. They surely do not mark the overweening ambition of a tyrant, as some thought then and afterwards; what they show us is indeed an extraordinary and restless activity, which the slow-going conservative Roman could neither appreciate nor forgive. Here was indeed a kingly mind, though one perhaps now beginning to show some faint signs of feverishness.

In December, however, he took what had long been for him an impossibility and a dream—a brief holiday in the country. It was really December, for the new calendar had come into force at the beginning of this year; and Cæsar moved southwards in state, with the military guard he had not yet abandoned, to that mild and beautiful sea-coast of Campania which the Romans loved so dearly. For a moment the mist is lifted that enshrouds the persons of the great men of antiquity, and on the 19th of December we catch a glimpse of Cæsar as he really was. He had spent a night near Puteoli, at the villa of a connexion of his own, Q. Marcius Philippus, who had been consul in the critical year 56 B.C. Cicero, too, had a villa in the neighbourhood, and happened to be staying there. The Dictator proposed a visit, and Cicero, in an ever memorable letter, describes to Atticus what happened. Cæsar remained at Philippus' house till twelve or one o'clock, and admitted no one but Balbus, with whom (as Cicero guesses) he was going over accounts. Then he took a walk on the shore, and in the afternoon came to Cicero's villa. There he bathed, and was anointed, and after taking some kind of stomachic medicine, as was apparently his habit, sat down to dinner. The suite was accommodated also, though Cicero had been much put about for ways and means; the escort of soldiers was encamped in the park. Cæsar ate and drank and talked with much freedom and enjoyment, but the conversation was entirely literary. Cicero, too, evidently enjoyed the visit, though he tells Atticus that his guest was not one to whom you would readily say, Come again, my dear friend, on the first opportunity. It is sad to think that a few weeks later Cicero was exulting over the cruel death of the man on whom he had lavished his hospitality. At the end of his letter Cicero adds that as the Dictator passed the villa of Dolabella, whom he had reason to distrust, his guards, who always rode at a little distance, for once closed round his horse; and so he disappears from our view.*

Dolabella had been promised the consulship for 44 B.C.; but Cæsar now assumed it himself with Antonius, promising it to Dolabella when he should have started for the East. He was now beginning to be fully occupied with the preparations for his expedition against the Parthians, on which he was to set out in March. This was a project of long standing; it was the inevitable result of the actions of his former confederates. Pompeius had made Syria into a province, and brought the Roman Empire into touch with the Parthian, which extended from central Asia to the Euphrates. Crassus had been utterly defeated in invading Parthia, and ever since his disaster, the Parthians had been menacing the frontier, and had frequently broken through it. At this very time they were in Syria, and in active support of the last of the Pompeian commanders, Cæcilius Bassus, who had worsted the Cæsarian generals, and was practically in possession of part of the province. There was no time to be lost; this cloud might grow into a serious storm in the East, and the lately won unity of the Empire might once more be threatened.

Expecting to be away for some time, he made all necessary arrangements for at least two years to come. Two steady and trusty friends, Hirtius and Pansa, were to be consuls in 43 B.C., and were actually

* Cic., Ad. Att., xiii., 52.

elected; two others, D. Brutus and Munatius Plancus, were selected for 42 B.C. The well-beloved Marcus Brutus was to be *prætor urbanus* for this year, and then to govern Macedonia; C. Cassius, a much older man, and a skilful soldier, this year *prætor peregrinus*, was after his office to proceed to Syria, where he had already served with distinction, and would be useful to Cæsar. These two, among others, had fought against Cæsar till the battle of Pharsalus, but now seemed to be readily responding to the claim of his generous policy of trust and reconciliation. But Decimus Brutus was to govern Cisalpine Gaul, the strategical key to Italy; it was thus in the safe-keeping of one of Cæsar's oldest and most trusted soldiers, whom we have seen long ago beating the maritime tribes of western Gaul on their own element. All the provinces were provided with governors, and many other arrangements were completed, for which no place can be found here; but the very fact that all these appointments could be made, that they were accepted, and that Cæsar could venture to absent himself again for a long period from the capital, shows that he felt himself now entirely secure, and justified both in displaying his confidence, and in assuming, more distinctly than ever, the outward semblance of a monarch.

For he now dismissed all his guards, and was often seen in the city quite unprotected.* At the same time he restored the statues of Sulla and of

---

* Hirtius and Pansa are said to have remonstrated with him on this point; he answered that it was better to die once than to be always in fear of death. Velleius, ii., 57

Pompeius, which had been thrown down by the mob after the battle of Pharsalus. Now burst out afresh the flood of adulation; Cæsar was to be a god as well as a king. A new *collegium* of Luperci, the priests of an ancient and unknown deity, was instituted and called by his name. A temple was to be erected to Jupiter Julius and Clementia; the month Quinctilis was to be called after his gentile name, which it still bears; a score at least of other such offerings were made at the shrine of his greatness, in that strange oriental spirit of mingled cringing and irony which seized on a weak generation and was handed down to its successors. For some at least of these Antonius the consul was responsible, for he now became the head of the Julian Luperci, and priest of Jupiter Julius [*]; the man who had long been Cæsar's evil genius, and was even now luring him to his destruction.

Repeated attempts were also made to get him to assume the title, as well as the reality, of monarchy. But the word *rex* was ever hated at Rome, and this was but too plainly a stratagem to bring him into general odium. He seems steadily to have refused all such appeals, whether suggested in private, or on such public occasions as the Lupercalia (February 15th), when the famous scene seems really to have occurred which Shakespeare has embodied from Plutarch in his play. "I am no king, but Cæsar," he said on another occasion. Again, a story is told, which wears the appearance of truth,[†] that one day, when

---

[*] Cic., Phil., ii., sec. 110.

[†] It is told in various forms, of which I adopt that given by Nicolaus Damascenus (Vita Cæs. Oct., ch. 22).

he was busied with the building of his new forum, talking to his architects, and apportioning the work, the Senate came to him in procession, with the consuls and all the other magistrates at their head, to offer him a new list of these regal and divine honours. Cæsar remained sitting, talking and consulting his papers, and with difficulty could be persuaded to relinquish useful work, and to turn and face folly. Much more to his purpose than all these vanities, was the fact, which we now know, that before February 15th he had accepted the dictatorship for his life. (See p. 335.)

But he was now oh a far higher pinnacle of personal power than any one man can safely hold, who has won it by force of arms and in a state corrupt and diseased. It was not his work that was recognised and lauded, but his power. For his absolutism men like Cicero could dread and hate him, while they laughed at his reform of the calendar, or wept over his neglect of some ancient maxim of city-law. Whatever he did was sure to hurt the feelings of someone. Placards were put up, urging men to abstain from showing his new senators the way to the Senate-house. The distribution of offices brought him many enemies, just as it brings enemies to every new President of the United States. The men who flattered him hated him because he was above flattery, and doubtless those who abstained from flattery hated him because he was its object. At the very time when all seemed most ready to do his will, and better satisfied (as Cassius had expressed it some months before *) to have a wise and gentle absolutism

---
* Cic. Fam., xv., 19.

than such an one as Cæsar's enemies would have exercised if victorious, the clouds of ill-will were gathering and threatening him on every side. Only a few trusted personal friends were really left him, such as the acute and ready Balbus, the gentle Oppius, who had for years acted with Balbus as his confidential secretary and agent, and whose pen was afterwards used in his master's honour; and the quiet and retiring Matius, a true friend, whose touching letter to Cicero, after the Dictator's death, is most fortunately preserved for us in Cicero's correspondence. To these we may add Hirtius, and Pansa, and Lepidus, among his old divisional generals, with Asinius Pollio, afterwards the historian of his deeds, and a few others, who, like Pollio, were now absent from Rome; but the ablest living Roman apart from Cæsar himself, Antonius, the unprincipled and self-seeking, had been too often a trouble to his master to be reckoned among the really intimate and faithful.

When all this discontent drew to a head, and who it was who first kindled the inflammable material, we can never know. The idea of assassination was familiar to the old-fashioned republicans, who believed, for example, that the murder of the two Gracchi was justifiable and necessary; and beyond doubt Cæsar's life had long been a perilous one. Cicero afterwards accused C. Cassius, Trebonius, and Antonius, of having on two occasions planned the murder of the Dictator;* and the accusation may have been true in regard to Cassius if not the others.

---

* Phil., ii., sec. 26 and 34.

But Cicero himself, though assuredly not the prime mover in the actual conspiracy, is not free from suspicion; a letter he wrote to Atticus some months before, shows plainly that he contemplated the possibility of such a deed.* A consistent tradition represented Marcus Brutus as only drawn into the plot with difficulty, and Decimus Brutus, as one of Cæsar's oldest and most trusted friends, can hardly have been the real instigator. The evidence points on the whole to Cassius, a "lean and hungry" man, of a bitter and jealous spirit. He had sufficient cause to hate Cæsar personally; he had served under Crassus and Pompeius, and had surrendered a superior fleet to him after Pharsalus, when as it is said, he might easily have destroyed him. He had suffered the ignominy of being liberated and pardoned. He had tried to kill Cæsar in Asia Minor, if what Cicero wrote is true; and recently he had been placed below Brutus, though he was much his senior, in the list of prætors for the year just beginning. The truth may be, that Cassius, or some lesser man of the same type, such as Casca or Ligarius, was the first to suggest the idea of murder, when Cæsar gave up his guard, and became at once more kingly and more confident; and that the cause was not so much republican enthusiasm as personal malice and vindictiveness.†

Whoever may have been the original leader, and

---

* Cp. Ad Att. xiii., 40, with Phil., ii., sec. 26. The coincidence of the language in the two passages is striking.

† Plutarch, Brutus, ch. 9, who however here follows an authority evidently prejudiced against Cassius.

whatever his motive, there were plenty ready to follow him for political reasons, whether among former friends of Cæsar or among outwardly reconciled enemies. Sixty are said to have joined in the plot, and with such numbers it would certainly have been discovered, but for Cæsar's own pre-occupation and confidence, and his comparative inexperience of the intrigues and meannesses of life in the capital.* It is this frank carelessness of his that gives such pathos and irony to the tragedy which follows—a pathos which is deepened by the fact that the victim's worst foes were his chosen and trusted friends. Of the most famous of these, the Marcus Brutus on whom his own folly and Shakespeare's genius have bestowed an unmerited immortality, only a word can be said here. He was perhaps one of those weak men, students of life chiefly in books, who are apt to attach themselves to stronger characters, but cannot guard themselves alone against outbreaks of folly or even of cruelty. Brutus had long ago been associated with Cato, whose daughter he had lately married; after Pharsalus, where he fought against Cæsar, and was joyfully received by him immediately after the battle, he devoted himself to the new master, whose affection for him led some to fancy that he was the great man's illegitimate son. Since Cæsar's return from Spain, his devotion seems again to have cooled, perhaps under the influence of his wife and of Cicero. Such men are apt to love, to speak, and sometimes to act, with a force that astonishes; it was of Brutus that Cæsar said, "What-

* Nic. Dam., 20.

ever he desires, he desires with all his might. These qualities make a man the object of a certain tenderness in his friends; they feel that he has instincts for righteousness, they pardon his vehemence, and respect his enthusiasm. But the type of mind is a narrow and feeble one, and in times of hot political feeling, where a cool judgment is necessary, and the power to recognise facts as they are, it is as likely to go wrong as to go right. Brutus was not born to be an independent man of action.

Every effort was now made to fan the lukewarm feelings of this student into a glow of hatred against the monarchy. He was reminded, by papers left in his prætor's seat, of his alleged descent from Brutus the tyrannicide. Stories were told that his wife urged him to action by showing that she could wound herself with a dagger unmoved, and that Cassius by subtle speech persuaded him that liberty could only be gained by murder. We cannot test the truth of such tales; all we can be sure of is that Brutus was hard to gain, but that once persuaded, he went into the plot with all the enthusiasm of weakness. But he insisted that Cæsar should be the only victim; he struck, he said, not at the monarch, but at the monarchy, and would have no unnecessary bloodshed. Thus Antonius and Lepidus owed their lives to him; and events showed with a sad irony that in his wrong-headedness he had done exactly the opposite of what he intended. The monarch was murdered, and the monarchy left untouched.

There was no time to lose. Cæsar was to leave Rome on March 18th, and after that date his person would be secure from attack. At any time the plot might be betrayed, or at least his suspicions might be roused. More than one scheme for the murder was proposed and given up; at last it was resolved that the deed should be done on the Ides (15th) of March, for which day a meeting of the Senate had been summoned, when Cæsar was to resign the consulship, and announce Dolabella as his successor. Cæsar remained heedless of all rumours, and true to his maxim that "it is better to die once than to be always in fear of death." On the evening of the 14th he dined with Lepidus, and brought Decimus Brutus with him. Busy as ever, he was despatching letters while conversation went on. He was listening, however; his power of attending to many things at once was not the least of his many wonderful gifts. The guests began to talk of death, and the question was raised, what kind of death is the best? Cæsar looked up from his papers, and said, "That which is least expected."

This story has some claim to acceptance; but the myths that gathered round the events of that night and the next day must be passed over in silence. In the morning Cæsar was late in coming to the Senate, and Decimus Brutus went to fetch him. When conspiracy is in the air, some dim consciousness of what is impending may invade solicitous minds; and Cæsar's wife Calpurnia is said to have been unwilling to let him leave her. It is strange that the Roman writers who believed Cæsar to be the enemy of other men's wives, should have so eagerly commemorated the tradition of this tenderness in his own.

The End.

The traitor succeeded in his mission, and Cæsar came in a litter from his house under the Palatine, across the forum, beneath the northern end of the Capitol, to the theatre of Pompeius. Attempts were even now made, it was afterwards said, to warn him in time, but in vain. He entered the building, the Senate rising to receive him, and took his seat on his golden chair of state. Tillius Cimber, one of the conspirators, urged on him a memorial praying for his brother's restoration from exile; the rest crowded round him; Trebonius held the dangerous Antonius in conversation at the door. Cæsar refused the petition. Cimber took him entreatingly by the hands while Casca crept behind him. Then Cimber seized his toga and tried to render his hands useless. Cæsar rose and called aloud, and then Casca struck him with an ill-aimed dagger. It was the signal for a shower of blows, against which the victim struggled for a few moments, wounding one man with the metal *stilus* he carried; then he covered his head with his toga, and reeling a few steps, propped up only by the multitude of his butchers, he fell dead at the feet of Pompeius' statue.

It is the most brutal and the most pathetic scene that profane history has to record; it was, as Goethe has said, the most senseless deed that ever was done. It was wholly useless, for it did not and could not save Rome from monarchy. It was cowardly and treacherous in all its details; and it was utterly wrong-headed, for it showed that the men who were guilty of it knew neither what liberty nor government meant. It plunged the Empire into another long period of civil war, in which whole provinces were devastated, the East divided against the West, and all fair hopes shattered of unity and honest government. All this ruin could be caused by a handful of men, who, pursuing a phantom liberty and following the lead of a personal hatred, slew the one man who saw the truth of things.

Three slaves carried the body home, bleeding from twenty-three wounds, while the people looked on aghast. Two or three days later it was burnt in the forum by the mob and the soldiers, in a scene of the wildest excitement, while the " liberators of their country " were hidden away in terror. Cæsar's will was read beforehand, and it was found that his principal heir was the young Octavius, who was also adopted as his son. He had left his gardens beyond the Tiber to the use of the city, and a sum of money to every resident citizen of Rome. But what most moves us, as it moved those who listened in the forum that day, is that Decimus Brutus, the man who led him into the fatal snare, occupied the second place in the destined succession to his property.

ROMAN SWORDS.

EPILOGUE.

HE who pursues his reading from Cæsar's death into the period of the Empire, cannot fail to be struck by a change which becomes more and more decided as he goes onwards. It is not so much the history of Rome that he is studying, as the history of the civilised world; the history, that is, of the various dependencies of Rome, and of their relations to the central authority. Even when following the lead of a conservative historian like Tacitus, whose political horizon was not much wider than that of Cicero, we feel this change in some degree. But it is only fully realised when we pass beyond Tacitus to the reigns of Hadrian and the Antonines, and when we have learned to appreciate the immense value of the fresh material that the collection of inscriptions has of recent years placed within our reach, enabling us to recognise in the life and institutions of the provinces the really essential facts in the history of the Empire.

It is when we have learnt this lesson that we begin to understand the full force of Cæsar's work, and his place in the history of the world. We seem to have passed out of the close atmosphere of a great town, where our view was on every side shut in, and where the chatter of cliques and pedants was continually misleading us, into a wide and open country, and a freer and fresher air. We feel the bracing effect, just as we believe Cæsar to have felt it during those nine years of strengthening discipline in Gaul. Whether we study the government of the Empire, or its law, its religion, its society, its army, we feel that a great change has taken place, and that even if it be a change which in some ways, as for example in art and literature, has lowered the level of human effort, it is yet one which has raised the mass of mankind in material well-being, and has made them the constituent body of a great protective political union. And more than this, it has even brought within their reach a simple and universal doctrine of right and wrong; a rule of conduct based on beliefs and hopes, for which the older world, which knew no such union, could not, so far as we can guess, have ever found a place. Under the Empire art and literature slowly decay, with the decay of that civic or national life in which they seem best to flourish; but in the imperial unity room is found for other influences more suited to the needs of the age and of more universal efficacy.

Epilogue.

Let us take an illustration of this change from the history of religion, which has not as yet been touched on in these pages. The religious ideas of the old Greeks and Italians had been, like their politics, strictly *local* in character. Just as every little community was ideally independent of every other, so also each had its own peculiar worships, in which god and priest, temple and ritual, were conceived as belonging to that locality only. To transfer a worship from one city to another was a matter of extreme difficulty—nay, it was even impossible, unless the god himself signified in some way his readiness to move. No doubt certain worships, like certain states, gained a wider renown and a more universal influence; but the great mass of Greeks and Italians were wholly without any idea of a religion binding upon all men, just as they could at most but dimly perceive that man has any duties outside his own political community.

The conquest of the world by Rome took off the keen edge of all these narrow ideas and prejudices. Local politics lost their interest, and local religions their prestige. Rome may be said to have cast a great shadow over the peoples of the Mediterranean, and the details and the brightness of all their civic life and religion were obscured as the light lessened. By Cæsar's time the obscurity was great, and was probably telling on the public and private morality of the world. What power for good there had been in the old worships had been irretrievably weakened, and there was no sign of anything to take its place. The age of local religions was past, and no universal belief or practice seemed likely to knit the peoples together. As in politics, so in religion, the Græco-Roman world was, in the last century B.C., in a state of chaos.

But after Cæsar's death we at once begin to find that the world is open to a universal cult. The form which it took is to us strange enough, and at first sight inexplicable. But we do not need here even to touch on the questions which lie around the curious phenomenon of the worship of the Cæsars; what we have to notice is simply the fact that it rapidly spread over the whole Empire, mingling with, or superseding, the older religious forms, and that it became a most powerful instrument in holding together the whole political system. Cæsar was not indeed himself the man intentionally to start on its course an idea so hollow; but it was he who, by turning the eyes of all men on his own unique personality, made it possible for something like a universal worship to take the place of the dying local religions. This worship lasted for a while as a reality, and lingered some time longer as a survival; but it could not long satisfy the wants of mankind, for it laid down no rule of conduct, and raised neither hope nor fear for the future. But it showed that the world was open to a new and real religion; it put the finishing touch to the destruction of the old local worships; it established a connection between the government of the world and its religion; it was in a certain sense the foreshadowing of the acknowledgment of Christianity as the religion of the Roman Empire. And it is but a single illustra-

Epilogue.

tion of the difference between the world before Cæsar and after him, and of the extraordinary force which his work and his personality exercised on the minds of men. He stood, as we said at the outset, at the end of a long series of revolutionary tendencies, and sums them up; he also laid the foundation-stone of a new era of the world's life.

It cannot then be said of Cæsar, as it has been said of Pericles,* that in destroying an ancient constitution which had in its time done good work, he did but initiate a period of degeneracy. Among the Romans themselves the seeds of degeneracy had long been sown; they had passed through their period of freedom and glory, and what they were still to contribute to the world was not to be the fruit of their own peculiar genius. For the world which Rome had conquered, it was not a period of degeneracy which Cæsar initiated, but one of hope and development; the interests of the rulers were now no longer in antagonism with those of the ruled. For the selfish rule of a city-aristocracy had been substituted the autocracy of a single hard-working man; and henceforward the governed knew that they might expect to be protected from enemies within and without the limits of the Empire, and that they might hope to rise eventually to the political status of their rulers.

At first, indeed, when Cæsar's murder had left the world again without a master, all was once more chaos. It was only after thirteen years of division and discord that the man whom Cæsar had probably

---

* See the preface to Mr. Abbott's "Pericles," in this series.

destined to be his successor, found himself at last in the position which his uncle had occupied. Then came the period of organisation—an organisation based in the main on Cæsar's foundation, leaving it only where for the time there was need of a more skilful adaptation to the wants and feelings of weary humanity. A long life, an incomparable tact, and a deep dislike of war, enabled Augustus to complete this organisation, and to hand it over to a successor of no mean ability. But of necessity there were weak points in it, and in the reigns of Tiberius and his successors these came to light, and all but wrecked it. A better season set in, when in 69 A.D. Vespasian took the helm into strong hands, and from that time to the death of the last of the Antonines, the whole vast region which had known Cæsar's footsteps, from Britain to the Euphrates, and from the Rhine to the African deserts, enjoyed, on the whole, peace, plenty, and prosperity. And for many centuries afterwards, when the world was once more torn asunder by internal division and barbarian invasion, men still found a hope of salvation in the two inseparable ideas of the great Empire and its monarch, each of them now illuminated by the Christianity for which Cæsar's work had made space in the world.

AUGUSTUS AND IMPERIAL ROME.

FROM A REPRODUCTION IN WIESELER'S "DENKMÄLER DER ALTEN KÜNST" OF THE CAMEO IN VIENNA.

INDEX.

A

Achillas, Egyptian leader, 48 B.C., 305, 312
Acta Senatus, publication of, 105, 106
Aduatuca, 209 *ff.*, 215
Ædileship, 69
Ædui, 137 *ff.*, 141, 147, 148 *ff.*, 163, 214, 219, 224
Afranius, 270 *ff.*
Agrarian bill, 72
Alauda (the legion), 240
Alesia, siege and battle of, 229 *ff.*
Alexandria, 305, 312 *ff.*
Allobroges, 81, 136, 140, 147
Ambiani, 167
Ambiorix, 209 *ff.*
Amiens, 167, 169, 209, 212
Antonius, Marcus, acts for Cæsar as tribune, Jan., 49 B.C., 255, 267; joins Cæsar at Dyrrhachium, 286 *ff.*; at Pharsalus, 301; commands in Italy, 314 *ff.*, 330; meets Cæsar at Massilia, 45 B.C., 361; consul 44 B.C., 368; character, 372; present at Cæsar's murder, 377
Apollonia, 284, 286, 296
Appian, history of, 105
Apsus, river, 285 *ff.*
Aquileia, 144
Ariminum, 260

Ariovistus, King of Suebi, 137, 142, 149 *ff.*
Arverni, 136, 148 *ff.*, 163, 220, 223
Asinius Pollio, historian, etc., 260, 310, 311, 372
Augustus, 10, 97, 205, 268; in Spain with Cæsar, 334; his system of government, 354, 364; Cæsar's heir, 388
Aurelia, 11 *ff.*, 92
Avaricum (Bourges), 221

B

Balbus (L. Cornelius), Cæsar's secretary, etc., 96, 97, 101, 263, 367, 372
Bankruptcy, Cæsar's law of, 341 *ff.*
Belfort, 154
Belgæ, 163 *ff.*, 205, 240
Besançon, 152, 160, 164
Bibracte, 146, 228
Bibrax, 166
Bibulus (M. Calpurnius, consul 59 B.C.), 98, 105, 111, 246, 284; death of, 285
Boii, 147
Boissier, Gustave, 364
Bona Dea (rites of), 92
Britain, invasion of, 194 *ff.*; place of landing in, 196

Index.

Brundisium, 89, 264, 280
Brutus (Decimus), 184, 220, 270, 369; betrays Cæsar, 376; mentioned in Cæsar's will, 378
Brutus (M. Junius), 361 and note; conspires against Cæsar, 373 ff.

C

Cælius (M. Rufus), 251, 341
Cæsar, personal appearance and physical powers, 19; boyhood, earliest political experiences, 20 ff.; quæstor, 57; ædile, 68; prætor, 91; consul, 104; in Gaul, 126; commentaries, 128 ff.; campaign in Gaul, 129, ff.; campaign in Germany, 148 ff.; in Brittany, 176 ff.; invades Germany and Britain, 187 ff.; returns from Britain, 207; represses Gallic rebellion, 209 ff.; campaign in Spain, 266 ff.; final campaign against Pompey, 281 ff.; his last wars, 308 ff.; his use of power, 326 ff.; his death, 360 ff.; his life's work, 380 ff.
Calendar, reform of, 358, 371
Cantii, the, 205
Capitalism, evils of, 337 ff.
Capua, 113, 261
Carthage, 4; colonised by Cæsar, 343
Cassius, C. Longinus, conspires against Cæsar, 371 ff.
Cassius, Q. Longinus, governs Spain for Cæsar, 324
Cassivellaunus, 203
Catilina, L. Sergius, 68, 79 ff., 87
Cato, M. Porcius, speech in Senate, Dec. 5, 63 B.C., 85, 89; defeats Cicero's policy, 99; opposes Cæsar's land bill, 109; proposes to surrender Cæsar to the Germans, 191; evacuates Sicily, 265; at Utica, 317; death and character, 320
Catulus (Lutatius), 78, 79, 88
Catuvellani, the, 203
Charleroi, 174, 211 ff.
Cicero, M. Tullius, early connection with Cæsar, 14; his oratorical studies, 36, 38; his consulship, 73 ff.; defeats Catiline's conspiracy, 80 ff.; relations with Pompeius, 88 ff.; declines to join the triumvirate, 101 ff.; exiled by Clodius, 123; policy after return, 178 ff.; meets Cæsar at Ravenna, 251; at Formiæ, 266; at Brundisium, 316; his relation to the conspiracy against Cæsar, 361 ff.
Cicero (Quintus), 84, 178, 181, 209, 211 ff.
Cinna (L. Cornelius), 27, 28, 105
Civil war, outbreak of, 238 ff.
Claudius (the Emperor), 205
Cleopatra, 310, 311, 313
Clodius, P., 12, 92, 93, 123, 124, 178; death of, 246
Coinage, Cæsar's, 9, 365
Colonisation, 113, 343
Commentaries of Cæsar, 18, 127 ff.
Commius, 195
Corfinium, 262 ff.
Corinth, colonised by Cæsar, 343, note; isthmus of, 366
Corn, distribution of, controlled by Cæsar, 337 ff.
Crassus, M. Licinius, commands in slave war, 48; consul 70 B.C., 50 ff.; relation to conspiracy of, 65, B.C., 68; to that of 63 B.C., 79 ff.; lends money to Cæsar, 94; coalition with Cæsar, 101; relation to publicani, 115; meets Cæsar at Lucca, 181; death in Parthia, 244
Crassus, P. Licinius (the younger), 158, 165, 174, 177, 184

Index.

Crastinus, 304
Cromwell, 86, 91, 107, 120, 208, 320, 323, 365
Curio, 255, 256, 265

D

Dictatorships, Cæsar's, 279, 330 *ff.*, 335, 371
Dio Cassius, history of, 94
Divitiacus, 165, 168
Dolabella(P. Cornelius), 36 *ff.* 308
Domitius Calvinus, 296, 301
Dumnorix (the Æduan), 141, 200
Dyrrhachium, 282 *ff.*

E

Education at Rome, 15 *ff.*
Egypt, 70, 71, 179, 305, 311 *ff.*
Empire, unity of, due to Cæsar, 353, 379 *ff.*
Equites, the, 74, 99, 118, 180

G

Gabinius, 61
Gades, 95, 277, 357
Gallic rebellions, 207 *ff.*
Gaul (Cisalpine), 120 *ff.*, 143, 175; political condition of, 350
Gaul (Transalpine), 122, 132 *ff.*, 240, 350
Geneva, 134, 139 *ff.*
Gergovia, 223 *ff.*
Germans defeated, 156 *ff.*
Gnipho, Cæsar's tutor, 13, 14
Goethe, opinion of, on Cæsar's murder, 377
Government, organisation of, 350 *ff.*
Gracchus (Gaius), 7, 19, 22, 58, 76, 105, 119, 250, 327, 337, 343
Gracchus (Tiberius), 6, 26, 110

H

Helvetii, 138 *ff.*
Hildebrand, 2

Hirtius A. (consul 43 B.C.), 128, 239, 258, 368, 372

I

Ilerda, 270 *ff.*
Illyria, 121, 176
Imperator, title of, 333
Isauricus, Servilius, 280
Italians, political status of 22 26

J

Juba, King of Mauretania, 317, 319
Judices, 46, 93
Julia (Cæsar's aunt), 7, 9, 57
Julia (Cæsar's daughter), 115, 178, 208; death of, 245
Julia gens, 9 *ff.*
Julian calendar, the, 366

L

Laberius, compelled by Cæsar to act in his own play, 363
Labienus, T. Atius, prosecutes Rabirius, 75 *ff.*; proposes bill for election of pontifex maximus, 79; Cæsar's legatus in Gaul, 143, 163 *ff.*, 184, 202, 209, 227, 234; deserts to Pompeius, 258 *ff.*; at Dyrrhachium, 284 *ff.*; at Pharsalus, 295; in Africa, 317; death at battle of Munda, 325
Larissa, 297 *ff.*
Legatio libera, 123
Lepidus (M. Æmilius), 268, 279, 330, 363, 376
Lex agraria (of Rullus), 72; (of Cæsar), 108
Lex Julia Municipalis, 343, 355
Lex repetundarum (of extortion), 116 *ff.*
Lex Rubria, for Cisalpine Gaul, 356, note
Lex Vatinia, 121, 176
Lucca (conference at), 181

Luceria, 262
Lucullus, M. Licinius, 44, 53, 54, 60, 61, 66, 114
Lupercalia, scene at, 370
Luperci, Julii, 370

M

Marcellus, consul, 254
Marius C., 7, 9, 20, 21, 24, 27, 57, 70, 104, 107
Massilia, 95, 133, 134, 136, 269, 278
Memphis, 314
Menapii, the, 186
Metellus Nepos (tribune 62 B.C.), 26, 88, 89
Metellus Scipio, 247
Milo, T. Annius, 246, 341
Mithridates, 21, 33, 39, 41, 66
Mithridates of Pergamum succours Cæsar in Egypt, 313
Molo, 37 ff.
Mommsen (Th.), 183, 278, note, 339, 356
Monarchy, Cæsar's intentions with a view to, 336
Morini, the, 186, 194, 199
Mühlhausen, 154
Munda, battle of, 325

N

Narbo, 134, 136
Nervii, 169 ff.
Noviodunum, 167

O

Oppius, C., 259, 263, 372

P

Parthians, Cæsar's projected expedition against the, 368
Patrician families, 10; new ones created, 365
Pericles, 383
Petreius, 276

Pharnaces, son of the great Mithridates, 315
Pharsalus (battle of), 297 ff.
Philippus, Q. Marcius, 367
Piracy, 8, 61
Pliny, correspondence of, 347
Pompeia (Cæsar's wife), 12, 92, 93
Pompeius, Cn. Magnus, under Sulla, 29; commands against Sertorius, 44; consul 70 B.C., 48; campaigns against the pirates and Mithridates, 60 ff.; conquests in the East, 66, 71, 114; returns to Italy, 87 ff.; renounces power, 90; coalition with Cæsar, 100 ff.; his veterans, 109; marries Julia, 114; at Lucca, 181, 243; sole consul 52 B.C., 219, 244 ff.; allies with Senate against Cæsar, 248 ff.; negotiations with Cæsar, 254, 256, 261, 264; his campaign in Epirus and Thessaly, 281 ff.; death and character, 306–308
Pompeius (Cnæus), son of P. Magnus, 324; death of, 325
Pomptine marshes, Cæsar's plan for draining, 366
Pontifex maximus, 77 ff., 92
Portus Itius, the, 196, 200
Prætorship, the, 88, 91
Ptolemy Auletes, 71, 179
Publicani, the, 99, 115
Puteoli, Cicero entertains Cæsar at, 367

Q

Quæstorate, 55, 56 ff.
Quinctilis, month of, changed to July, 370

R

Rabirius, C., 75, 76, 77
Religion, local character of, before Cæsar, 381 ff.

Remi, 164 ff. ; 214
Rhine, the, 159, 162, 175 ; (bridge over the), 193, 217
Rome, the beginnings of, 4
Romney marsh, 196
Roscius, 260
Rubicon (the river), 59, 260, 269
Ruspina, battle at, 318

S

Sabinus (Titurius), 165, 184, 210 ff.
Sabis (Sambre), battle of the, 169
Sallust (the historian), 83, 85 ; Governor of New Africa, 322
Samarobriva, 209
Senate, functions and power of, 5, 63, 65 ; attempts to repress civil war, 266
Sequani, 137 ff., 148 ff., 160, 163
Sertorius, 48, 57, 58, 65, 71, 91, 135, 162
Servilius Rullus, 72
Sestius, P., 180
Shakespeare, his conception of Cæsar, 359
Silanus (consul 62 B.C.), 81, 82, 85
Slaves, 8, 16, 42, 48, 339
Spain (provinces of), 56, 91, 94, 243 ; political condition of, 352, 360
Spartacus, 40
Stoffel, Colonel, 260, note, 272, 274, note, 288, 298
Suebi, 137, 187 ff., 214
Suessiones, 165, 167
Suetonius, history of, 254
Sugambri, the, 192
Sulla, L. Cornelius, the Dictator, 27, 29 ff., 33, 35, 44 ff., 55, 59, 88, 279, 337
Sulla, P. Cornelius, 301
Supplicatio, 175
Syria, Pompeius in, 67, 304 ; Cæsar in, 315

T

Tax-farmers, 115
Tencteri, 189 ff.
Tenth Legion, 143 ff.
Thapsus, battle of, 319
Tiberius Nero, 82, 85
Tigranes, 39
Tigurini, 145
Tolosa, 135
Traján, correspondence with Pliny, 348
Transpadani, 59, 60, 80
Trebellius, 63
Tribunate of plebs, 11, 35, 45, 47, 56, 64
Trinobantes, the, 203 ff.
Triumph, 98 ; Cæsar's first, 322 ; second, 363
Triumvirate, formation of, 100 ff.

U

Ubii, the, 188 ff., 214
Usipetes, the, 189 ff.
Uxellodunum, 239

V

Varro, M. Terentius, the scholar, 129, 277, 359
Veneti, 177, 184
Vercingetorix, 217 ff. ; surrender of, to Cæsar, 236
Vesontio, 152
Vespasian, 384
Veteran soldiers (allotments to), 108, 344
Vienne, 219
Volusenus, 194

W

Wellington, Duke of, 274, 287, 295, 297
Wissant (portus Itius), 196, 200, 202, 204

Z

Zela, battle of, 315